THE ECONOMIC DEVELOPMENT OF INDIA

THE ECONOMIC DEVELOPMENT OF INDIA

A Marxist Analysis

Brian Davey

SPOKESMAN BOOKS
1975

Published by The Bertrand Russell Peace Foundation Ltd.
Bertrand Russell House
Gamble Street, Nottingham
for *Spokesman Books*

Printed in Great Britain by
Bristol Typesetting Co., Ltd.
Barton Manor
Bristol

ISBN 0 85124108

To my parents

Preface

This book was originally written as a thesis for the degree of M.Phil. at Nottingham University and was finished in October 1973. In its present version the only substantial change from the thesis is in the last chapter where I have added a section on questions of revolutionary strategy. The rest of the text has been left unchanged—though, of course, it has been slightly dated by emergence of the international oil and energy crisis and the seriously deteriorating situation in the world capitalist economy. Although he will not agree with this work—and especially my new ending—my thanks are especially due to Professor J. R. Parkinson who gave me the opportunity to write this book. Also to Dr. S. Ghatak, my acting supervisor, to Audrey Beecham for putting me up in Oxford on several occasions, to Tariq Ali for looking over my new ending, to Michael Barratt Brown, my typists Joan Young, Sue Kerr, and Angela Fullerton and many others who gave help and encouragement. Finally I would like to thank Comrades of the International Marxist Group for their help and encouragement and the publishers, Spokesman Books.

November 1974

Contents

CHAPTER I

Introduction

To understand so-called 'underdevelopment' we must first understand development itself for in human history it is rapid economic growth, industrialisation and rapid social change that is abnormal. Understanding economic development means something more than simply documenting its symptons—a higher rate of savings, more rapid technological change, a growth of industrial employment and so on. Though these are necessary to the analysis it has to be explained WHY people save more, WHY people devote themselves to a greater extent to scientific and technological enquiry. These are the more crucial questions and their answer lies in the analysis of the development of social relations between men.

Men and women satisfy their needs by social labour in which they enter into interactions with others. The development of the productive forces, by which we mean the existing state of rationality, science and productive technique, the mode of organisation of production and the degree of development of man himself, brings with it changes in the patterns of social relations—more strictly the relations of production. By relations of production we mean the way in which the products of human labour are appropriated, the social conditions under which labour takes place, as well as the principles of distribution, the modes of thought and ideology and so on. Among these relations of production those associated with the ownership of the means of production (i.e. property relations) occupy a crucial place in that they determine the forms in which the social surplus product—the surplus over the consumption needs of the producers and the need for replacement of the means of production—is utilised.

Corresponding to different levels of development of the

productive forces we observe different patterns of relations of production; and an integrated complex of social relations and forces of production is called a *mode of production.* Within such modes of production we can distinguish certain classes on the basis of their role in the production, circulation and appropriation of the social product. In real life we do not find modes of production in their pure form but it is necessary to identify them in the analysis because 'In the analysis of economic forms, neither microscopes nor chemical reagents are of use. The force of abstraction must replace both.'[1] Every given socio-economic formation will consist of mixtures, amalgams and so on of modes of production having a variety of 'impure forms'—this follows in particular from the uneven and combined nature of the historical process which does not evolve uniformly on a world scale but in certain areas more rapidly than others. The interaction between the advanced and backward countries then enables the backward to skip 'historical stages', combining advanced social forms with the remnants of their more outdated socio-economic relations.

The relationship between the productive forces and the relations of production is not simply of the former determining the latter. Rather it is a contradictory relationship in which a particular pattern of production relations may advance or hold back the productive forces. The development of a mode of production will be a period in which the relations of production —in particular the property relations affecting the disposal and utilisation of the social surplus—will advance the development of the productive forces. The decay of the mode of production will correspond to that period in which the pattern of relations of production block the adequate development of productive forces and possibly turn them into destructive forces. From this standpoint Marxists see the colossal and sudden economic advance of the last 200 years as having its origins in the development of the capitalist mode of production in which the relations of production have encouraged the rapid development of the productive forces. The crises and catastrophies of the twentieth century—the world wars, the depressions, the threatening ecological imbalances are seen as evidence that capitalist relations have outlived their historical usefulness in developing the productive forces. The theme of this thesis will be in showing how, despite its successes in the 'advanced' capitalist countries of today, capitalism failed to develop the productive forces in 'Third World' countries like India. This was historically a product of the uneven and combined development of capitalism on a world scale and the relations of subordination between the 'advanced' and 'backward' capitalist countries (imperialism). The weakness of capitalism is manifested in the weakness of its representative —the capitalist class or bourgeoisie. In our preliminary remarks, therefore, we shall dwell on what it is in capitalist relations of production that has so stimulated the productive forces in the past and why the bourgeoisie in more backward countries who adopt capitalism as part of a combined process of development are far less vigorous in developing the producutive forces than the bourgeoisie in the pioneering capitalist countries.

In the words of Marx and Engels the bourgeoisie 'cannot exist without constantly revolutionising the instruments of production and thereby the relations of production and with them the whole relations of society. Conservation of the old mode of production in unaltered form was, on the contrary, the first condition for the existence for all earlier industrial classes. Constant revolutionising of production, uninterrupted disturbance of all social conditions, everlasting uncertainty and agitation distinguish the bourgeois epoch from all earlier ones.'[2]

In consequence of this :

'The bourgeoisie during its rule of scarce one hundred years, has created more massive and colossal productive forces than have all preceding generations together.'[3]

In *Capital* Marx explains the reasons for this extraordinary dynamism which he draws from the various implications of producing the wealth of society in the form of commodities. The very starting sentence of *Capital* is a comment to the effect that social wealth in capitalist societies consists of an 'immense accumulation of commodities.'[4] Moreover both human labour power and the means of production are also commodities which can be bought and sold on the market. This is the key aspect of capitalist relations of production which so enormously stimulate the productive forces. In such a society, where social relations are mediated through exchange relations and social wealth takes the form of commodities it is not the use values (utility) that concerns their producers but their exchange values. The capitalist, as purchaser of the means of production and human labour power, is concerned to make money because money provides the key to power over the world of things and men. Money is the 'universal equivalent'—all commodities can be converted into it and it, in turn, can be converted into all commodities.

'But money itself is a commodity, an external object, capable of becoming the private property of an individual. Thus social power becomes the private property of private persons. The ancients therefore denounced money as subversive of the economic and moral order of things . . .'[5]

But in modern society the damage has been done. Moreover the capitalist must accumulate exchange values because in a society where uncontrolled market forces hold sway for finished products, as well as for labour power and means of production, uncontrolled competition exists between commodity producers. Stability and safety lies only in a permanent drive to make more money which must be ploughed back into new techniques, new equipment, new products, reserves to buy up competitors and money to bribe politicians.

With the development of capitalism it therefore becomes 'not only profitable but indispensable to reinvest money in expanding production' and we get an 'economic compulsion for a social class to productive accumulation of the social surplus product.'[6] In other respects too, the relations of production stimulate the productive forces. The rise of capitalist society is, for example, accompanied by a general rise in rationality which breaks the grip of traditional thought described by Sombart as follows: 'In deciding on some undertaking or activity, a man does not look in front of him, to his goal, he does not exclusively consider the purpose of his decision, but looks back to examples and experiences of the past.'[7] Now, however, a multiplicity of human goals are replaced by one—that of making money. A more analytical approach can be used in this context of evaluating the usefulness of any activity. The development of science and technology and the unprecedented growth of the productive forces are the result.

It is, therefore, the development of the capitalist mode of production which has accounted for the extraordinary break in the history of mankind. But the development of capitalism does not take place everywhere on the globe simultaneously. Rather it develops in an uneven and combined way—and it is in the study of this uneven and combined process evolving on a world scale that we can understand so-called 'underdevelopment'. It is not simply that some societies develop capitalism ahead of other societies—i.e. that the development of capitalism is uneven—but there is also an interaction between the 'advanced' and the 'backward' societies in a way which permanently affects the development of the latter. This interaction manifests itself in many ways. But principally the backward societies may adopt certain aspects of the productive technologies developed in the advanced countries together with capitalist relations of production—these existing side by side with pre-capitalist production technologies and pre-capitalist relations of production. Thus the development of the backward countries takes a peculiar 'combined' form within which a capitalist mode of production co-exists and interacts with a pre-capitalist mode of production in a specific socio-economic formation. This is not all, however, as combined development may take place within the pre-capitalist mode of production—for example, the commercialisation characteristic of capitalism may develop side by side with the maintenance of parasitical forms of property relations within the pre-capitalist sector. Again the accumulated scientific and medical developments from the advanced countries are adopted at one go bringing down the death rate radically in the pre-capitalist mode of production and thus leading to a population growth which has important effects upon the society in which it takes place. Because of this process of combined development within the pre-capitalist mode of production we shall adopt the practice at a certain point of referring to it as a non-capitalist mode of production—for the changes within it are related to the development of capitalism on a world scale.

This is why the term 'underdevelopment' is inappropriate to a country like India. For 'underdevelopment' implies that poor nations are rather like the advanced nations—though at an earlier stage of their historical development and that, with help, they will develop in a similar way. The term, then, emphasises only the uneven aspect of the development of capitalism. As we shall see the truth is more complex. To be sure poverty in India is partly an inheritance from the past—remnants of a pre-capitalist mode of production do still hold back the development of the productive forces—but poverty in India is also partly a created condition. India's evolution cannot be similar to that experienced by today's advanced capitalist countries.

The privilege of historical backwardness is of being able to skip historical stages—but this privilege is accompanied by very profound disadvantages. Above all in the combined social formation that inevitably arises in backward countries the bourgeoisie emerges as a weaker social class and not as undisputed leader of the nation. The way it develops in combined socio-economic formations leaves it with a reactionary tinge to its character—this is a product of the bourgeoisie's historical function in the pre-capitalist mode of production and the fact that it co-exists with pre-capitalist ruling classes corresponding to the remnants of the pre-capitalist mode of production. In the pioneering capitalist country, Britain, capitalism emerges after, and as the product of, a long process of disintegration and decomposition of the pre-capitalist mode of production. The petty production of independent peasants and artisans undergoes a long period of differentiation and the society that gave birth to the first Industrial Revolution was thoroughly permeated with market relations.[8] In North America similarly, capitalism developed substantially unhindered by the reactionary influence of pre-capitalist ruling classes and so in a relative 'pure' form involving little combined development.

But in countries like Germany, Japan and Russia that are latecomers to industrialisation and 'modernisation' the process is very different. In such cases it is actually the pre-capitalist ruling classes—or a 'progressive' section of them—that take the initiative to transform the existing social order and foster industrial, and to a lesser extent, agricultural, capitalism. In such cases of belated development we thus find that capitalism is created by transformations and manoeuvres at the top of society rather than as the logical end product of the process of the disintegration of the pre-capitalist mode of production. The old ruling classes are forced to this course of action to protect their positions given the dynamic development of capitalism elsewhere in the world and as Trotsky observes

'The solution of the problems of one class by another is one of those combined methods natural to backward countries.'[9]

So in Germany the barriers to growth are removed by the Stein Hardenberg edicts of the early nineteenth century which abolish serfdom and introduce capitalism into Prussian agriculture. Agrarian change takes place as a process controlled from above in which the landlords or Junkers become the capitalist farmers employing the erstwhile serfs as wage labourers. The agrarian aristocracy organised within the Prussian military regime leads the struggle for the unification of Germany thereby creating the basis for the industrialisation process. The barriers of growth are removed by the aristocracy due to 'the influence of pressure exerted within Germany by the changes that were taking place in other countries.'[10]

At the same time the preservation of the power of the agrarian/military ruling class and of their dynastic state meant that the full process of capitalist development was slowed down. Protection of the agricultural sector against the competition of New World foodstuffs kept food and raw material prices high and slowed the process of contraction of the agrarian sector. A substantial section of the peasantry survived together with many craftsmen and artisans of the old type and the small entrepreneurs and traders linked to them. The bourgeoisie would have gained by a more rapid process of transformation of the older order, by cheaper foodstuffs for example, but they were afraid that they had much more to lose if they put up a fight against the aristocracy.[11]

'The German bourgeoisie had developed so slothfully, cravenly and slowly that at the moment that it menacingly faced feudalism and absolutism it saw itself menacingly faced by the proletariat and all factions of the burghers whose interests and ideas were alien to those of the proletariat. And it saw inimically arrayed not only a class behind it but all of Europe before it. The Prussian bourgeoisie was not, as the French in 1789 had been, the representatives of the whole of modern society vis-a-vis the representative of the old society, the monarchy and the nobility.

It sunk to the level of a sort of social estate, as distinctly opposed to the crown as to the people, eager to be in opposition to both, irresolute against each of its opponents, taken severally because it itself already belonged to the old society, representing not the interests of a new society against an old but renewed interest in a superannuated society.'[12]

So the German bourgeoisie was content as long as its unified market was created—it did not mind how, or under whose auspices, so long as it could depend on stable and orderly government at home and backing for its enterprises abroad.

In Japan we find a similar pattern. A transformation of society from the top protected existing modes of exploitation and of social relations and so, while laying the basis for industrialisation, did so in a constrained context of protection for much of the old order. As in the German case it is the outside threat which catalysed development—leading to the Meiji Restoration and everything that flowed from that. Since the Revolution was controlled from the top of society 'there was no capitalist transformation of agriculture, because of the survival of the feudal relations of production in the countryside and the preponderance of the jinushian landownership. In the economic evolution of Japan there was no agrarian revolution, nor any differentiation of the peasantry between capital and free salaried workers. Thus cottage industries persisted among the small peasants—controlled by the merchant industrialists. So workers would remain attached to their patch of ground and stayed in the country.'[13] As in Germany we have a bourgeoisie of a 'slothful and craven' character—a haute bourgeoisie of merchants and financiers (zaibatsu) whose interests are already adapted to and partly merged with the pre-capitalist regime . . .' The industrial revolution proceeded under the domination of the haute bourgeoisie of privileged, great, merchant-industrialists; thus Japanese capitalism right from its origin, had an oligarchic and monopolistic character. It did not have any trait of economic liberalism nor the constant improvement in the organic composition of capital through the free competition of individual capitals.'[14]

Russian development displayed similar features and trends. In his analysis of the evolution of agrarian relations in Russia Lenin described how in many areas capitalism was developing by a painful process in which the landlords themselves were being turned into capitalist farmers. This was a slow process in which Czarism and the feudal interests were careful not to destabilise the social order and prejudice their own position.[15] Trotsky was another perceptive analysis of this pattern of evolution 'under pressure from the European bourgeois development, the progressive nobility attempted to take the place of the lacking Third Estate . . . In 1861 the noble bureaucracy relying upon the liberal landlords carried out its peasant reform.' A reform directed from the top of society like this was inevitably 'niggardly and thieving.'[16] While a thoroughgoing solution to the agrarian question was necessary to develop the productive forces in agriculture and to develop the home market for capitalist industry the bourgeoisie was too weak to fight for such an agrarian revolution. In 1861 it could do little more than play 'the role of humble chorus.'[17] With further capitalist development the bourgeoisie became no socially stronger—if anything it became weaker. Evolving late by a process of combined development Russian industry skipped over the handicraft system and was at once created in a factory system. In the factory system the proletariat was concentrated in large masses that showed their independence and hostility to the bourgeoisie in the class struggle. In the Revolution of 1905 the workers threw their own organs of power—Soviets. The liberal bourgeoisie was not interested in leading a rebellion that would put its whole existence in question.

Besides the Russian bourgeoisie was actually half foreign. The foreign interests 'did not desire to become a component part of the bourgeois opposition within Russia.' It was guided in its sympathies and antipathies by the principles formulated by the Dutch bankers Hoppe and Co., in the conditions for the loan to Tsar Paul in 1798: 'interest must be paid irrespective of political circumstances'. The European Stock Exchange was even directly interested in the maintenance of absolutism, for no other government could guarantee such usurious interest! So the Russian bourgeoisie remained impotent between the concentrated proletarian masses and the autocracy 'very small in numbers, isolated from the "people", half-foreign, without historical traditions, and inspired only by greed for gain.'[18]

What conclusions emerge from this analysis? It would seem that the bourgeoisie of historically backward countries are not always able to show the same degree of dynamism that Marx and Engels described 'continually revolutionising the means of production and with them all the relations of society.' The Bourgeoisie has already adapted to the pre-capitalist order, it has reason to fear revolutionary change and its desire for social transformation is in any case grudgingly met by the existing ruling classes. This is, of course, a matter of degree and in the analysis of any particular case the 'privilege of backwardness' also has to be taken into account. Thus Germany by the end of the nineteenth century was overtaking Britain as an industrial power and so also Japan at a late period. In the United States the 'privilege of backwardness' is not offset by any pre-capitalist ruling class seeking to preserve its own privileges and position, and capitalism could develop unconstrained by feudal burdens of one kind or another. Thus did Lenin choose to contrast the Prussian path of the capitalist development of agriculture with the American path. 'The United States is unequalled in rapidity of development of capitalism at the end of the nineteenth and beginning of the twentieth century, in the high level of development already attained, in the vastness of its territory—on which is employed the most up-to-date technical equipment suitable for the remarkable variety of natural and historical conditions—and in the degree of political freedom and the cultural level of the masses of the people. Indeed this country is in many respects the model and ideal of our bourgeois civilisation.'[19]

At the other extreme in the countries we have examined stands Russia where the bourgeoisie is weak and impotent. In our study of India we shall find that the conditions prevailing there are much more similar to pre-revolutionary Russia than to America or even Germany or Japan.

When turning to the analysis of a country like India the patterns which we have discovered in these latecomers are reproduced again. However, the weaknesses of bourgeois development in India are more manifest than with a country like Germany. At the risk of oversimplification there are two reasons for this. Firstly India was in a sense 'more backward' at the time of the beginning of its relationship with developing British capitalism. Secondly, as a result, its relationship with Britain was one of subordination to imperialism. Countries like Germany and Japan were able to respond to the challenge of more advanced and developing neighbours and their response enabled them to retain their independence. This was possible because of the internal articulation and level of development of these societies which were sufficiently advanced to be able to respond. There were powerful social forces that were willing to make or to allow the effort towards development. The same cannot be said for India and it became colonised as a result. While many of Marx's writings on India can now be seen to have been based on inadequate knowledge, we can agree the following assessment:

'How came it that English supremacy was established in India? The paramount power of the Great Mogul was broken by the Mogul Viceroys. The power of the Viceroys was broken by the Mahrattas. The power of the Mahrattas was broken by the Afghans, and while all were struggling against all, the Briton rushed in and was enable to subdue them all. A country not only divided between Mohammedan and Hindu, but between tribe and tribe, between caste and caste, a society whose general framework was based on a sort of equilibrium, resulting from a general repulsion and constitutional exclusiveness between all its members. Such a country and such a society, were they not the predestined prey of conquest?'[20]

Indian society then, was more 'backward' than Germany and Japan at the time of its conquest. Whether it would have subsequently developed of its own momentum is a purely speculative question that cannot be argued for certain. Marx himself considered that Indian society was too static and unchanging to be able to develop without the impact of British rule. In this sense he thought that the British impact laid the pre-requisites for development—but that

'The Indians will not reap the fruits of the new elements of society scattered among them by the British bourgeoisie, till in Great Britain itself the now ruling classes shall have been supplanted by the industrial proletariat or till the Hindus themselves have grown strong enough to throw off the English yoke altogether.'[21]

According to Marx, therefore, Britain destroyed certain of

the bases of the old society without which development was not possible—but it retarded the development of a healthy and independent industrial bourgeoisie.

This thesis is written in this spirit. It is not a worthwhile project to attempt to establish that the subordination of India to the advanced capitalist countries—in particular Britain—'caused' undevelopment. This could only be proved by showing that India would have developed of its own momentum and that British imperialism blocked the process. Any discussion on this question could only be speculative and could never be finally proved. It is far more fruitful, on the other hand, to analyse how India *did* develop and to show the basis of its present pattern of social and economic relations. On this basis we can ask the by no means irrelevant question 'Can India develop while it still remains in subordination to the advanced capitalist countries?' 'Will the weakness of the Indian bourgeoisie prevent it from developing the productive forces along capitalist lines in a manner that is adequate to meet the needs of the vast majority of the Indian population?'

NOTES

1 Karl Marx, Preface to the First Edition of *Capital*, p. 12 of the Kerr Edition, Chicago 1919.

2 'Manifesto of the Communist Party', in Marx and Engels' *Selected Works Vol. 1*, Progress Publishers, Moscow 1962, p. 37.

3 *Ibid* p. 38.

4 Karl Marx, *Capital Volume 1*, p. 41.

5 *Ibid* pp. 148–149.

6 Ernest Mandel, *The Inconsistencies of State Capitalism*, IMG Publications, p. 3.

7 Quoted in H. Rothman, *Murderous Providence: A Study of Pollution in Industrial Societies*, London 1972.

8 M. Dobb, 'Transition from Feudalism to Capitalism' in *Papers on Capitalism, Development and Planning*, London 1967. Also the paper by H. K. Takahashi in *The Transition from Feudalism to Capitalism. A Symposium*, Science and Society (undated).

9 Leon Trotsky, *History of the Russian Revolution*, London, Gollancz 1934, p. 30.

10 Tom Kemp, *Industrialisation in Nineteenth Century Europe*, Longmans 1969, p. 95.
11 *Ibid* 106–113.
12 Karl Marx, 'The Bourgeoisie and the Counter Revolution', in Marx Engels *Selected Works Vol. 1*, pp. 68–69.
13 H. K. Takahashi, 'Quelques Remarques Sur La Formation des Classes Ouvrières Industrielles au Japon' in *Third International Conference of Economic History 1963*, Paris 1968, p. 217.
14 *Ibid* p. 216.
15 V. I. Lenin, 'The Agrarian Programme of Social Democracy in the First Russian Revolution' in *Collected Works Volume 13*. Moscow 1962 pp. 238–242.
16 Trotsky, *op. cit*, p. 30.
17 Leon Trotsky, *Results and Prospects*, New York 1970, p. 50.
18 *Ibid* p. 51.
19 V. I. Lenin 'Capitalism and Agriculture in the United States of America'. *Collected Works Volume 22*, p. 17.
20 Karl Marx in *Karl Marx on Colonialism and Modernisation*, (Ed.), Shlomo Avineri, Anchor Books, Garden City, New York 1969 p. 132.
21 *Ibid* p. 137.

CHAPTER II

The Pre-Capitalist Mode of Production

The study of Indian socio-economic relations prior to the British conquest which follows is not written out of abstract historical interest but rather to illuminate the subsequent evolution of India's society and economy. In particular it is necessary to explain the reasons for the inability of Indian society to respond to the challenge from British imperialism with an autonomous thrust for its own development. By studying the inability of Indian society in this period to develop we can also more fully understand what are the essential features of development—in particular capitalist development. As has already been discussed the process of development for latecomers is a combined one—in which aspects of the old and new go together in a unique structure. For this reason by a study of the old we can analyse more clearly various elements of the Indian social structure that are still criticised today for inhibiting development—such as caste and the joint family.

This discussion will be based upon the use of the Marxist method of social analysis if not to a great extent upon Marx's own writings upon Indian society. While containing some important insights it would appear that Marx's own sources for his analysis of Indian society were inadequate and sometimes incorrect. The concept of an Asiatic mode of production elaborated by some writers, whatever its value for other Oriental societies, is evidently not adequate for a comprehension of India prior to the British conquest. In his late life when Marx read some of the writings of Kovalevsky on developments in India property relations, it would seem that he dropped his references to the Asiatic mode. He did not, however, elaborate any alternative conceptions.[1]

The key to understanding any society—in its patterns of

development and its social and political forms—is in the analysis of that society's mode of appropriation of the social surplus product.

'Upon this is founded the entire formation of the economic community which grows up out of the conditions of production itself, and this also determines its specific political shape. It is always the direct relation of the owners of the conditions of production to the direct producers, which reveals the innermost secret, the hidden foundation of the entire social construction . . .[2]

In capitalist societies the direct producers (wage labourers) have to work for the propertied class because they do not own the means of production to employ themselves. The capitalist class are able to appropriate the social surplus product because their ownership of the means of production enables them to purchase human labour-power for less than the value of total production in society. To make this point in another way, we can imagine a hypothetical society in which the direct producers owned their own means of production as private property. In such a society each producer would appropriate his income undifferentiated into 'profits' and 'wages'. 'Profit therefore emerges from the social relations of production in which the direct producer has been separated from his means of production and, as Marx stresses:

'. . . capital is not a thing. It is a definite interrelation of social production belonging to a definite historical formation of society . . . Capital is not the sum of the material and produced means of production . . . Capital signifies the means of production monopolised by a certain part of society, the products and material requirements of labour made independent of labour power in living human beings and antagonistic to them . . .'[3]

With pre-capitalist societies, such as Mughal India, the mode of appropriation is different since the direct producers do 'possess' the means of production. They are not, therefore, under any *economic* coercion arising out of the nature of society to part with their surplus product. In such societies social relations are those of dependence because it is evident that:

'. . . In all forms, in which the direct labourer remains the "possessor" of the means of production and labour conditions of his own means of subsistence, the property relation must at the same time assert itself as a direct relation between rulers and servants, so that the direct producer is not free. This is a lack of freedom which may be modified from serfdom with forced labour to the point of a more tributory relation.'[4]

In this form of society the direct producer organises and undertakes the process of production but is deprived of the wherewithal and the incentive to develop the productive forces. The mode of appropriation tends to be parasitical as a result. We can contrast it with capitalist production in which, as we have said, the social surplus accrues to the capitalist class which organises production and which is compelled to plough back at least a substantial proportion of the social surplus.

Capitalist production comes only with the separation of the direct producer from his means of production. In pre-capitalist societies where this is not the case capital nevertheless exists in the form of usurers capital and mercantile/financial capital wherever commodity production and monetisation are sufficiently advanced. Users and merchants' capital must also get its profits from the direct producers because the mere process of lending and repaying money, of buying and selling does not create wealth. The profits of the usurers and the merchants are also imposed upon the process of production from outside, are parasitical in form, and are based on the dependence of the direct producer. This dependence may derive from the ties of debt, or from the inability of the small artisans or peasants to get access to distant markets and sources of raw materials except through the merchant class.

Pre-British Indian society displayed all these features and in certain respects still displays them today (though alongside and interrelated with developed capitalist features in a combined social formation). We find that social relations are based upon dependence and that both the ruling class and existing forms of capital extract the social surplus in a parasitical fashion from the direct producers.

The most important and indispensable pre-condition of labour in Mughal society was, of course, the land. No one person can be said to have 'owned' the land in the sense of having private property rights as understood in the modern sense.[5] Rather, the relations of dependence between direct producers and surplus receivers were defined in terms of the rights and duties which each person possessed in relationships embracing every aspect of social, religious and cultural life. In this respect caste played a key role in cementing the whole set up—particularly at the village level.

Within the village itself relations of dependence, mediated through the caste division of society, defined the relations between the cultivating peasant castes and the artisans and those untouchables who performed menial and unclean tasks for the village as a whole (demiurgic system) or for certain leading families in the village community (jajmani system). The untouchables were at the bottom of the ladder in a society in which successive rights and power were established by conquest and subordination over centuries.

While Hindu religion and ritual as well as social status served to confirm and ideologically justify these social and productive divisions the whole structure was, in the last analysis, based on force and was always potentially subject to redefinition by the force of arms. In capitalist society the property owner protects his capital by continually expanding it—ploughing back the social surplus, partly at least into the expansion of production at a greater level of efficiency. In Mughal society access to the social surplus was protected by the maintenance of a military establishment of armed retainers by every would-be chieftain or lord. Thus the zamindars—or local chiefs having a claim to a portion of the land revenue from particular areas—maintained nearly 4.3 million infantrymen and 0.3 million horsemen in the Mughal Empire (Northern India) according to the official census of 1595.[6] The main military force, however, was that maintained by the Mughal Emperor himself and it was to the Mughal State and its members that the bulk of the social surplus was creamed off in the form of land revenue. Perhaps $\frac{1}{3}$rd to $\frac{1}{2}$ of the total agricultural production was taken as land revenue. This was monetised in form—the cash nexus being highly developed at least as far as the social surplus was concerned[7].

The land revenue was collected from the peasant in the name of the Mughal Emperor. It went either directly to the royal treasury from the Khalisa land or was assigned by the Emperor as jagirs to his mansabdars (officers or nobles) in lieu of their pay for the maintenance of the imperial military contingents. In particular the mansabdars were responsible for the maintenance of cavalry contingent with horses of standard breed which was the secret of the military strength of the Mughals.[8]

Among the top 445 mansabdars the maintenance of the cavalry expected of them by the Emperor took 77.2 per cent of their total pay. Habib estimates that expenditure on the army took possibly ⅔ of the nobilities' total income and comments that 'Such a large diversion of resources to the maintenance of armed men is to be expected in a system where exploitation was . . . superimposed . . . on the productive system and so requiring for its enforcement constant use of the menace of armed power.'[9]

The jagirdari system allowed for a centralisation of power in the hands of the Emperor whose nobles remained completely dependent upon his will. To prevent the establishment of local power bases, which might have been created with permanently sited jagirs, jagirs were rarely held for more than two or three years. After this they were reassigned.[10] The dependence of the mansabdars upon the Emperor was confirmed by the fact that they were thus divorced from any rights to the land—jagirs essentially being an assignment of revenue assessed and expressed in cash. This, in turn, 'could only have been possible in a society where the cash nexus was well established . . . (and) agrarian trade well developed.' Both these conditions were present in Mughal India.[11]

The nature of the assignment system was the very opposite of what was necessary for the development of the productive forces. Since the jagirdar had no long term interest in the territory assigned to him he unhesitatingly fleeced the peasant.[12] Given his unstable position the optimum situation for the jagirdar was to die in debt to the state.[13] The situation in the Khalisa was probably somewhat better in this respect because of the State's long term interest in agricultural prosperity. However, when the royal treasury was under financial pressure the distinction might wear thin. For this reason the actual condition of the agriculturist would be determined in the main by 'the manner in which administrative and political power were distributed and deployed.'[14] The impoverishment of the peasantry which resulted from the increase in the number of jagirs over time and the very nature of the jagirdari system seems to have been the main factor which brought down the Mughal Empire. The peasantry followed or were drawn into various revolts behind ambitious chiefs and warlords and the Empire split up.[15] The eighteenth century then witnessed a free for all to grab the right to extract the social surplus from the hapless peasants. When the dust had settled, as one British observer of the early nineteenth century described the situation in South India, 'It is wonderful how much, in times such as the last century, the robber, the raja and the zamindar run into one another'.[16]

As has been indicated the system of revenue extraction under the Mughals was fairly centralised. The land revenue accrued to the monarch and he in turn assigned it to his officials. Local claims to surplus—by the zamindars were only a relatively subordinate share of the land revenue—not more than 10 per cent in Northern Indian and 25 per cent in Gujarat.[17] Moreover, the imperial administration was always trying to convert the zamindars into functionaries of the State. However, in the eighteenth century the grabbing of rights at the local level and the establishment of various warring principalities broke up the relative homogeneity. There is evidence that the big jagirs were broken up and a class emerged with a hereditary right to collect revenue over part of the erstwhile big jagirs.[18] In addition it would seen that the zamindars, always a thorn in the side of the Empire in so far as they represented a local claim to the surplus and an independent political and military force, were able to go on to the offensive against the Empire and played a leading role in revolts like those of the Marathas and the Jats.[19]

The peasantry from which the surplus was extracted seemed mostly to have held land on an individual basis[20] though nineteenth century village officials do describe common ownership patterns and systems of periodic redistribution. While such communal systems may have been partly something that emerged in the period of political and administrative anarchy[21] it would seem that it also partly represented a much longer term survival. Thus in the Tamil areas of South India the mirasi, communal system of landholding survived into the nineteenth century in a variety of forms.[22] But in general peasant cultivation was organised on an individualistic basis. While the peasant family had a generally recognised right to permanent and hereditary occupancy of the land it tilled, the peasant was also tied to the land and had to cultivate it.[23]

Given individualistic patterns of cultivation and quite a high degree of commodity production any great equalitarianism in the village community was ruled out. The villages contained their wealthy and influential sections, the small peasants who would probably constitute the vast majority and, finally, at the bottom of the economic and caste hierarchy various outcastes performing menial and degrading tasks. No uniform pattern probably existed but the wealthy and influential section would possibly include the local zamindar, merchants and money lenders—as well as various officials such as the village headman (muqaddam) who might use his position to thrive up to the position of zamindar—if the village was not utterly ruined by the revenue demand. Since land was the main source of wealth those caste peasants having possession of the land would come next in the caste hierarchy and below them various caste groups deriving their share of the produce of the village by virtue of a ritual and economic relationship with the cultivating groups in which they provided various services for these groups. At the bottom of the hierarchy would be the 'untouchables' who undertook work considered abhorrent by the caste peasants such as tanning, scavenging and so on. Such outcastes were also, to a considerable extent, agricultural labourers working under various conditions of agrestic servitude to the particular communities of caste peasants or zamindars that had established dominion over them after generations of conquest and struggle.[24] Despite this stratification, as should be already evident, certain communal institutions did exist which arose out of the indispensability of collective action in the face of hardship and oppression and which provided a certain security for their members. The joint family, caste and village community all, in one form or another, filled certain roles in this respect. The joint family was based upon the collective labour of its members and the necessity for the family to provide for the educational, cultural, recreational, health and other needs of its members that in more developed societies are provided by specialised institutions outside of the family unit. The necessary interdependence of its members welds them 'into a homogenous, compact, egoistic unit, strengthens emotions of solidarity and co-operation among them and fills them with family pride. They develop more collectivist family consciousness and less individualistic traits.'[25]

Caste also played an important role in protecting its members. If caste status determined the individual's rights and disabilities in the hierarchical structure of dependence it also served to protect those rights which caste members did possess and to guard against the worst aspects of despotism. An eighteenth century observer Abbé Dubois commented how:

'Sometimes one may see the traders through a whole canton shutting up their shops, the farmers abandoning their labours in the fields, the different workmen and artisans quitting their booths, by an order from the cast, in consequence of some deep insult which it had suffered from a governor or some person in office. The labours of society continue at a standstill until the dignity is repaired or the injustice atoned for, or at least till the offended cast has come to an accommodation with the person in power.'[26]

Even the untouchables had their combinations and despite the various positions of agrestic servitude in which such groups might find themselves, strike action was not uncommon to protect such rights and positions as they had. Dhama Kumar writes of how the 'slave castes' of Tamil Nad 'had the practice of striking work, complaining of various grievances and threatening desertion. On this occasion the agricultural labourers had to be given promises of better treatment and small presents by the masters.'[27]

The physiogomy of the village community was determined by similar necessities—for self sufficiency and defence in periods of war and alien domination and for the security provided by the collectivity in the face of human oppression and the vagaries of the monsoon.[28] While land was held on an individual basis (with the exceptions noted) the village as a whole would frequently combine to face the state. The available evidence suggests that in the Mughal period the peasants paid into a collective financial pool from which the village representatives satisfied the revenue demand.[29] Within this context villages might withhold part of their revenue but not quite enough for the government to send in the nearest armed force.[30] In extreme cases of oppression migration would also demand collective action by the village community. The relationship between the village and the ruling classes was by no means one of reciprocity—a fact reflecting the parasitical mode of appropriation of the social surplus. Very little of the land revenue pumped out of the villages came back in any form and the central state certainly did little in the way of large scale productive works such as irrigation as Marx erroneously supposed.[31] Maddison suggests that the irrigated land in the Mughal Empire was not more than 5 per cent of the cultivated area and state works were a very small proportion of this.[32] To the extent that the state did promote production at the village level its aid was largely fiscal—in the form of revenue concessions on the cultivation of new lands or lands that had gone out of cultivation or in the form of taquavi loans to the peasants.[33]

By and large then the village had to provide for their own needs and had to look to a high degree of self sufficiency. This took a form that Marx characterised as the 'domestic union of agriculture and handicrafts' with a service relationship of the village artisans and servants to the village as a whole or to certain families within it. On the evidence, at least of 18 Maharashtian villages[34] it would seem that most of the village servants were employed by the village as a whole. They would receive remuneration in the form of a prefixed share of the product of each peasant, as well as various perquisites. In return they would offer their services to individual peasants and villagers belonging to the territorial community. The system was flexible and such servants might hold their position by virtue of a watan (inherited right, patrimony) or they might operate as upari (newcomer, stranger) on a more tenuous basis. As far as the Brahmin priests were concerned, however, the very nature of their occupation limited the availability of their 'services' to certain caste families within the village community. The Brahmins were not cultivators and would frequently be supported by the untouchables that cultivated lands under the possession of the Brahmins.[35]

The inner articulation of the village community and the service relationship of the artisans to their 'customers' rendered the development of productive techniques relatively impervious to external stimuli and change. However, at least there was a fair degree of efficiency in which the raw materials were usually ready at hand, there was no transportation charge for finished products or middleman's profit. Moreover, centuries of acquired skill and tradition produced fairly reliable results in providing for the relatively simple needs of the peasants such as for plough and yoke. Since customer and labourer were in an immediate inter-dependent relationship there was no tendency to skimp the work or use poor materials as may be the case where production is for sale.[36]

The Capitalist Class

The discussion of the nature of pre-British Indian society so far has not revealed any striking dynamic element which might have led to the development of the productive forces and the development of capitalist production. Indeed, so far we have seen that Indian socio-economic relations profoundly militated against the development of the productive forces and the parasitic and unstable nature of the Mughal system of land revenue extraction had created an agrarian crisis by the beginning of the eighteenth century which was converted into a political crisis with peasant uprisings and rebellions throughout the Empire. If we now turn to examine the nature of the Indian capitalist class in this period the picture is not much more favourable to development. As has been said capital may exist in pre-capitalist societies where the direct producers still have rights of possession over the means of production—so long as commodity production and monetisation have developed to a certain degree (c.f. Marx 'The existence of usurer's capital requires merely that at least a portion of the products should be converted into commodities, and that money with its various functions should have developed along with trade in commodities'.[37]) However, such capital, taking the form of usurers' and merchants' capital, also tends to be parasitical. It leaves the organisation of production to those in possession of the means of production and merely extracts social surplus from such producers, rendering them more poverty stricken.

In India, as has been said, there was a relatively high degree of monetisation of the social surplus under the Mughals and in consequence we do find evidence of capital imposing itself in the non-reciprocal relations between the urban and rural areas —in the extensive agricultural trade which the land revenue must have entailed and in moneylending to the village community and its members. A contemporary traveller Tavemier remarks how 'in India a village must be very small indeed, if it has not a money changer called a shroff, who acts as a banker to make remittances of money and issues letters of exchange.'[38] Such moneylenders and rural merchants would take advantage of the urgent need of the peasant for cash to meet the revenue demand which forced the peasant to sell after the harvest while the price was still low—and would subsequently sell again when prices had risen. Merchants' capital in all pre-capitalist societies makes its profits by buying cheap and selling dear—this it can best do by imposing itself between the producer and his markets as the only possible buyer. Though officially prohibited in Mughal India the scourge of monopolisation seems to have been widespread with the peasant being forced to sell to one buyer or one group of buyers 'local monopolisation seems to have been a common phenomenon.'[39]

In the main the relationship between the urban centres and the rural areas was a one way, non-reciprocal one reflecting the wider pattern of social relations and surplus extraction that has already been described. 'The relationship of mutual exchange between town and country which developed in Europe in the late Middle Ages and its consequences in terms of specialisation and division of labour are absent from the Indian scene.'[40] Thus the towns were primarily concerned with 'services'—more precisely they were the centres for the imperial administration and aristocracy, together with their military contingents and the apologists and propagandists of the existing order (men of learning, religious devotees etc.).

Thus material production within the towns mainly took the form of supplying for the military and luxury needs of the aristocracy[41] and apart from mediating in the process of surplus extraction in the countryside Indian capital at this stage would also serve to facilitate the flow of these goods to the ruling class consumers.

Even at its height Indian capital's relation to production was primarily parasitical and did not serve to develop the productive forces. As has been said the village society was largely self-sufficient and there was, therefore, no mass market for developed capitalist production. The means of production remained in the hands of the direct producers who were sucked dry by the merchants. In 1665, for instance, a profit rate as high as 12 per cent in dealings with the artisans was common for the broker compared with 6 per cent for coastal and inland trade and 1 to 3 per cent in brokerage. This left the artisans often with little more than a mere pittance and no margin to improve their techniques.[42]

Apart from engaging in local and regional trade and financial operations a certain section of the Indian capitalist class was also actively engaged in long distance trade. In the seventeenth century certain cities and ports and the hinterlands with which they were integrated developed under the influence of the rise of Western trade. This was true of areas like Gujarat, Malabar, Coromandel and Bengal—of which Gujarat witnessed the earliest and most serious penetration of its economy by western commercial interests. Surat was the key port town in Gujarat and dominated the foreign trade of India for over a century[43] but the impact of this commercial revolution spread inland. Thus a town like Ahmedabad with probably about a million inhabitants and situated inland was deeply affected in its economic growth by foreign investment and the rise of the indigo trade.

'This international impact on the economy of Ahmedabad located inland rather than on the coast as was Surat, was a fact of great economic significance in seventeenth century India. It demonstrated the penetration of international (especially European) economic influences deep into the interior of the country and making it part of the economic revolution proceeding at that time in the far flung parts of the world. The local Banian class was deeply involved in this revolution and as its dependence on the international market and the European companies increased, its identification with them also became inevitable as was witnessed by the movement of Ahmedabad merchants to Bombay after 1675.'[44]

The fatal weakness of the Indian capitalist class thus clearly emerges. Instead of being rooted in production and having an independent basis (i.e. being based on wage labour with the capitalists owning the means of production) it either existed 'within the pores' of Mughal society and was dependent on that society (mediating in the process of land revenue extraction and supplying the ruling classes) or became dependent upon the foreign merchant companies in so far as these merchant companies dominated long distance trade. Thus in the subsequent crisis of the Mughal system the indigenous basis for Indian capital disappeared altogether and the Indian capitalists could only continue in subordination to the European—in particular British companies.

In short, Indian capital was dependent for its prosperity on the very existence of the Mughal pre-capitalist mode of appropriation and on the foreign merchant companies. As such it had no economic and therefore no political independence, despite the vast accumulation of wealth that its members acquired.

Tapan Raychaudhuri argues that the growth of regions in the subcontinent under the impact of overseas and Western trade created conditions that might possibly have enabled industrialisation. He puts forward tentatively that 'the conditions in these regions were favourable rather than unfavourable to industrialisation and a different set of historical factors—e.g. the failure of the East India Company to occupy these territories and a decision of the local powers to modernise the army in order to resist Western aggression, might have led to a different pattern of economic change.'[45]

As an important part of such an argument he suggests that Indian merchant capital—e.g. of Surat—was influential over Mughal commercial policy and 'the same merchants of Surat also gave evidence of their ability for successful combined action against the imperial bureaucracy.'[46] However, the evidence he gives for such an assertion does not back him up. He cites an event documented in W. Foster's 'English Factories in India' 1668–69 as evidence for 'successful combined action.' (on p. 190–192). This concerns the persecution of the merchants of Surat by the local Kāzi which put a stop to trade in the port. A letter by a local agent of the East India Company describes how 'the general body of the Bannians began to groan under their affliction and to take up resolves of flying the country.' The merchants pleaded with the East India Company's agent Gerald Angier 'imploring his assistance and protection on your island Bombay', but were turned down. Instead they went to Ahmedbad to plead with the King to reduce their burdens. The height of the 'combined action against the imperial bureaucracy' [*sic*] is described as follows:

'The Cozzy to affright them, threatens to pull downe all their remaining churches and to circumcize the most principall of them, if they doe not returne. But the Bannians, growne hardy by often sufferings, defy him, telling him they goe to the King for justice.'

This proves not the strength, but the weakness of the merchants and testifies for all those who argue like Gokhale that the attitude of the Mughal government was often anti-capitalistic and had a real effect in retarding the process of capital accumulation. The Bannian were 'easy meat' for the Mughals and the Marathas and 'it was not surprising, therefore, that he sought safety and security with the European powers when they demonstrated that they had the ability to withstand pressures from both. With the development of the port cities of Bombay, Madras and Calcutta much of the capital from the interior of the country tended to flee to the English controlled cities where it played a subsidiary role to the activities of the European financiers.'[47] No wonder contemporary observers described how the Hindu brokers lived, not in stately homes but in shacks so as not to excite the cupidity of local rulers.[48]

Serious decline set in in the eighteenth century with the break up of Mughal power which, as has been said, provided the basis for the prosperity of Indian merchant capital. The first serious breakdowns in the heartlands of the Empire in the first two decades of the century seriously affected the security of transport in the region of Agra and Oudh and Gujarat was cut off from the centres of production in North and Central India. As the Mughals lost control of the rural areas and hence of the land revenue to the Marathas, they were forced to maintain larger bodies of troops that could only be maintained by the barely concealed plunder of the merchants of Surat, Ahmedabad, Cambay and Broach. In 1732 the merchants were even recruited troops, fought pitched battles on the streets of the town and defeated the governor but such was their position that this only brought a temporary respite to their problems.[49]

Similar problems hit the merchants in Malabar, in Coromandel and probably also Bengal where contemporary Dutch observers accounted for the decline in trade as being due to the oppressions of local officials.

By the mid eighteenth century Indian merchant capital only existed in areas under European protection and in trade connected with the European companies. European capital had itself taken the opportunity of hitting at their independent competitors among the Indians—as in 1734 when the East India Company blockaded Surat and took advantage of the problems of the merchants there. The only protection they were prepared to give was to collaborators, not to potential competitors. Habib summarises the essential features of the demise of Indian merchant capital:

'In so far as capital confined practically to the sphere of commerce, had failed to develop any independent basis for itself, its fortunes would lie with the Mughal ruling class, and, after its collapse with such other classes as imitated the methods and institutions of that class. Denied during the eighteenth century the large market that it had been provided with by the Mughal Empire, merchant capital had no choice but to atrophy. With this also receded into the background those prominent economic landmarks that in the better days of the Mughal Empire might have been mistaken for capitalistic features.'[50]

Conclusion

In pre-capitalist society the low level of development of the productive forces is expressed as the low level of development of the division of labour—in other words productive techniques are based on small units—the individual, the household, the village. To the extent to which there is specialisation this is largely confined within these basic units of a mainly rural society. Only a few essentials and the luxury and military needs of the ruling classes are catered for through specialisation and its concomitant—exchange. For the bulk of the population of South Asia in pre-British times social and economic intercourse stopped at the boundaries of the village community. The reciprocal relations between the cultivating peasants and various specialised village servants and artisans provided for all essential needs.

In a society where productive techniques are individual—the direct producer must himself take the decisions concerning production and, in consequence, the means of production (the land and other instruments of labour) must remain in the possession of the direct producer himself. In turn this means that the relations of exploitation between the producers and the ruling class take a form different from that which prevails in capitalist society where the producers are compelled for economic reasons to go to work for the employing class. This is because the means of production are under the ownership and possession of the employing class. In the pre-capitalist mode of production where the direct producers possess the means of production the compulsion to produce surplus for the ruling class is not at all economic —it is imposed and maintained by military force and conquest, codified in various rights and duties regulating the relations between the various layers of masters and lords and sanctified by religious and ideological means in notions of status, caste and so on. This exploitation imposed from above on the mode of production, kept the producer in a state of servility, removed the incentive and the resources that would allow him to develop production and rendered more stagnant still a society whose self-sufficiency already made it impervious to outside stimulus and change.

Such was Indian society prior to the British conquest—the basic units of production being the peasant and artisan household and the village community. Imposed on these were various local lords (zamindars) and officials and on top of this layer an urban war lord aristocracy extracting perhaps $\frac{1}{3}$rd of the produce of the village to maintain their military cohorts and to cater to their luxury needs.

At the very top of the entire structure the Mughal Emperor held ultimate power—to keep it and to prevent his lieutenants acquiring established rights and building up local bases of independent military power he periodically moved his main nobles from one area to another. Thus the military officers of the Emperor—the top layer of the aristocracy were assigned the right to collect land revenue from the peasantry but their rights of assignment were insecure and not based on particular localities. The jagirdars, having no interest in developing estates from which they would shortly be moved, unhesitatingly fleeced the peasantry. This situation was instrumental in the creation of an Agrarian crisis which was reflected in a political crisis. The desperate peasantry rose in revolt following local ambitious warlords. The Mughal Empire began to collapse.

Indigenous capital which had mediated in the process of surplus extraction through moneylending and trade went down with the Empire except where it got protection as the junior partner of European merchants capital.

NOTES

1 See Irfin Habib, Problems of Marxist Historical Analysis, pp. 52–67. *Enquiry N. S.*, Vol III, No. 2, Monsoon 1968.
2 Marx, *Capital Volume III*, Kerr Edition 1909, p. 919.
3 *Ibid* pp. 947–948.
4 *Ibid* p. 918.
5 Walter C. Neale *Economic Changes in Rural India—Land Tenure and Reform in Uttar Pradesh 1800–1955*; Yale U. P., 1962, pp. 19–25.
6 Irfin Habib 'Potentialities of Capitalistic Development in the Economy of Mughal India', *Journal of Economic History* Vol. XXIX March 1969 No. 1, pp. 53–54.
7 Tapan Raychaudhuri, 'The Agrarian System of Mughal India', *Enquiry N. S.*, Vol. II, No. 1, Spring 1965, p. 118.
8 Irfin Habib, *The Agrarian System of Mughal India 1556–1707*, Asia Publishing House, Bombay 1963, Chapters VI, VII, VIII, and IX.
9 Habib 'Potentialities . . .' pp. 55–56.
10 Morris D. Morris, 'Trends and Tendencies in Indian Economic History', Indian Economic and Social Hist. Review, Vol. V, No. 4, December 1968, pp. 356–357.
11 Habib, *Agrarian System* . . ., p. 319.
12 Morris, *op. cit.* p. 357, Habib 'Agrarian System' Chapt. IX.
13 Angus Maddison, 'Historical Origins of Indian Poverty', Banca Nazionale Del Lavaro, *Quarterly Review*, March 1970, p. 39.
14 Raychaudhuri, *op. cit.*, p. 112.
15 Habib, *op. cit.*, Chapter IX.

16 In Dharma Kumar, 'Land and Caste in South India', *Cambridge University Press,* 1965, p. 10.
17 Habib 'Potentialities . . .', p. 38.
18 Raychaudhuri, *op. cit.*, p. 103.
19 Habib, *Agrarian System . . .*, pp. 334–338.
20 *Ibid* Chapter IV.
21 Raychaudhuri, *op. cit.*, pp. 98–99.
22 Kumar, *op. cit.*, pp. 15–17.
23 Habib, *op. cit.*, Chapter IV.
24 Kumar estimates agricultural labouring castes in varying degrees of agrestic servitude at 10–15 per cent of the total population of the Madras presidency at the beginning of the nineteenth century. See Kumar, *op. cit.*, Chapter IV.
25 A. R. Desai, 'Rural Sociology in India', 4th Edition, Bombay 1969, p. 33.
26 In H. R. C. Wright *The East India Company and the Native Economy in India: The Madras Investment 1795–1800,* International Conference of Economic History Paris 1965, pp. 763–764.
27 Kumar, *op. cit.*, p. 48.
28 Habib, *op. cit.*, pp. 123–129. Angus Maddison *Class, Structure and Economic Growth: India and Pakistan Since the Moghuls,* London 1971, p. 29.
29 Habib, *op. cit.*, p. 125.
30 Wright, *op. cit.*, p. 764.
31 Habib, *op. cit.*, p. 256.
32 Maddison, *op. cit.*, pp. 23–24.
33 Habib, *op. cit.*, pp. 249–253.
34 Hiroshi Fukazawa, 'Rural Servants in the Eighteenth Century Maharashtian Village—Demiurgic or Jajmani System?' *Hitotsubashi Journal of Economics,* Vol. 12, No. 2, February 1972, pp. 14–40.
35 Kumar, *op. cit.*, pp. 30–31.
36 D. H. Buchanan *The Development of Capitalistic Enterprise in India,* New York 1934, p. 103.
37 *Capital Vol III*, p. 696.
38 In B. B. Misra *The Indian Middle Classes—Their Growth in Modern Times,* 1960, p. 25.
39 Habib, *op. cit.*, p. 79.
40 Raychaudhuri, *op. cit.*, p. 119.
41 Habib, 'Potentialities . . .' pp. 57–61.
42 B. G. Gokhale, 'Capital Accumulation in XVII Century Western India', *Journal of Asiatic Society of Bombay,* Vols. 39/40 1964/65, pp. 54–55.
43 *Ibid* p. 51.
44 B. G. Gokhale 'Ahmadabad in the 17th Century', *Journal of the Economic and Social History of the Orient,* Vol. XII Part II, April 1969, p. 190.
45 Tapan Raychaudhuri 'A Re-interpretation of Nineteenth Century Economic History' *Indian Economic and Social History Review,* Vol. V, 1968, p. 87.
46 *Ibid* p. 87.
47 Gokhale 'Capital Accumulation in XVII Century Western India', p. 57.

49 A. Das Gupta, 'Trade and Politics in Eighteenth Century India', in D. S. Richards (Ed.), *Islam and the Trade of Asia—a Colloquium*', Oxford 1970, pp. 181–214.

50 Habib, 'Potentialities . . .', p. 78.

CHAPTER III

Changes in the Pre-Capitalist Mode of Production

We may summarise the essentials of the pre-capitalist mode of production in India as follows. Production is primarily based upon the individual or household. In other words it is petty production as compared with capitalist production which is based upon socialised labour processes and co-operation—these facilitating the introduction of machinery and rising labour productivity. For the bulk of the population production is organised within the relatively self sufficient village community which, apart from a monetised portion of the surplus product extracted as tribute by the exploiting classes, was outside of the commodity economy. Individual village artisans and peasant producers existed in a service relationship one to another. The direct producers retained possession of the means of production and were thus responsible for the organisation of production. The extraction of social surplus is thus based upon relations of dependence established by force and thus maintained by a military establishment rather than productive reinvestment. The hierarchical pattern of rights and responsibilities is sanctified by religion and confined within the caste division of society. The relationship of the towns to the countryside reflects the parasitical nature of the extraction of the social surplus—the towns returning little to the countryside and production within them being orientated to the luxury and military needs of the aristocracy. Indigenous Indian capitals existed 'in the pores' of this society mediating in the process of surplus extraction. By and large Indian capital was not rooted in production and was itself a parasite upon production.

Effects of the Development of Capitalism on Pre-Capitalist Modes of Production

The development of capitalism in the metropolitan capitalist countries had a disintegrative effect on the pre-capitalist modes of production on a world scale but the regenerative role of capital remained geographically concentrated in the metropolitan countries. This disintegrative effect was felt in the pre-capitalist economies in a variety of stages which capitalism evolves through in the metropolitan imperialist countries. To fully understand these processes it is necessary to clarify the process of capital accumulation itself.

As has already been explained capital is not a thing but a social relationship and capitalist production arises when two kinds of commodity possessors come face to face with each other and enter into a mutual relation. 'On the one hand, there must be the owners of money, of the means of production, and of the means of subsistence, who desire by the purchase of others labour power, to increase the sum of values they own. On the other hand there must be free workers, the sellers of their own labour power, and therefore the sellers of labour.'[1] The 'free workers' must be 'free' in the sense that they are not tied by relations of dependence like serfs or slaves to the means of production nor must they own the means of production as their private property. Thus the capitalist system pre-supposes a divorce between the workers and the ownership of property in the means of production and 'the process which clears the way for the capitalist system, therefore, can be nothing else than the process whereby the worker is divorced from ownership of the means of labour, a process which, on the one hand, transforms the social means of subsistence and the social means of production into capital: and on the other, transforms the actual producers into wage workers.'[2]

In this process of primary accumulation the operations of European merchants' capital exploitation of its colonies is not unimportant. The expropriated wealth flowed from the colonies into Britain providing resources to enable the emerging industrial bourgeoisie to invest in the new means of production or into luxury consumption that stimulated various manufacturing industries.

Once capitalist production is able to stand on its own feet 'it does not merely receive (the) divorce between labourer and the means of labour as a legacy from the past, but reproduces it upon a continually increasing scale.'[3] In other words the capital accumulation process involves a continual process of expropriation and appropriation in which there is a progressive dissolution of remnants of pre-capitalist production in the advanced capitalist countries themselves and the undermining of pre-capitalist societies on a world scale. The principal instrument of this process at this stage is competition in so far as petty producers cannot compete with the lower prices of capitalist enterprise that are operating at a higher level of productivity. Unable to compete they are themselves thrown on to the labour power market. But if the development of capitalism necessarily thereby undermines pre-capitalist production there is no logical reason why the process of capitalist accumulation will be everywhere sufficiently rapid to absorb the free labour thus thrown on to the labour-power market and to redynamise the stagnation and decay of the pre-capitalist economy. What will be crucial here will be the pace of capital accumulation and this in turn will depend upon the existence of markets and adequate resources (surplus value) to stimulate and facilitate accumulation. An unemployed surplus population would be produced that would constantly increase were the size of existing markets to remain constant and all growth to take the form of a simple replacement of the capitalist mode of production at a higher level of labour productivity for the pre-capitalist mode at a lower level of productivity.

But for any individual country or region it is clearly not the case that the size of the market will never grow sufficiently to offset the effects of rising productivity on the unemployed surplus labour population. For one thing any given country can appropriate markets in other countries. Additionally, capitalist production requires machinery, new means of production and other imports. Sectors will grow to provide these. In addition innovations and state expenditure will provide new outlets for production. So in any given country the rate of capital accumulation may be either sufficient or insufficient to offset the effects of the decay of the pre-capitalist mode of production (manifested principally in the appearance of a surplus labour population).[4]

History shows that while the effects of rising productivity and the undermining of pre-capitalist production was experienced on a world scale as capitalism opened up a world wide market for its products the process of capital accumulation—and hence of reabsorption of the pauperised petty producers (surplus population) did not take place on a world scale but was geographically concentrated in the metropolitan capitalist countries. The exploitation of the Third World by European merchants' capital in part provided the resources for an initially high level of capital accumulation (resources also came from the heavy exploitation of the young proletariat). The markets to sustain such a high level of capital accumulation are in part provided by the conquest of external markets (including, as crucial to the argument, pre-capitalist markets in the 'Third World') and in part these are provided by the increased demand for means of production to sustain industrialisation via backward linkages to the producer goods industries. Thus 'L'absorption d'emploi realisee grace au proces de l'accumulation du capital tendait a plus que compenser la repulsion d'emploi, operee par l'amelioration de la productivite du travail. Pendant toute la phase de conquete due mode de production capitaliste le taux de croissance de l'accumulation depassant le taux de croissance de la productivite du travail . . . . permettant ainsi une elevation de l'emploi productif superieur a la destruction de l'emploi operee dans les secteurs precapitalistes'.[5]

Once established in the imperialist countries capital accumulation tended to remain geographically concentrated there due to existence of external economies (using the term in the widest sense). On the side of production capital accumulation in a given region leads to the creation of skills, social and economic overheads which reduces costs of production in those areas. In addition to this the cumulative process of growth creates the largest markets within the advanced countries themselves and 'despite the crucial qualitative role of pre-capitalist or "exogenous markets" quantitatively "endogenous" factors become more important, i.e. a large part of growing capitalist production is marketed within the mode itself' and 'capital tends to flow near where the market is' while the backward countries become comparatively more marginal.[6]

The situation in the colonial countries is the obverse of that in the imperialist countries. Contact with the developing capitalist countries (particularly Britain) brings a decomposition in the old mode of production but capital accumulation takes place only marginally in non-competing spheres of production like the plantations where a market can be carved out. The ties of dependence between the metropolitan countries and the colonial and semi-colonial economies are weakened after World War One and some capital accumulation in competitive spheres does take place. But this is still limited due to the remaining ties with the metropolis. Moreover the techniques of production adopted are those developed in the imperialist countries in conditions of more expensive labour power—hence these techniques of production are at a high labour productivity (i.e. output per man hour). The internal development of capitalist industry, where it does take place, is thus unable to reabsorb the labour power that it sets free in the pre-capitalist production mode.

Two qualifications to the argument made above have to be made. Firstly, the processes sketched out should not necessarily be seen as one in which there is an *absolute* decline in the numbers employed where contact with the developing capitalism has a destructive effect. This may be true in some instances but more generally it is only necessary to analyse the processes relatively to what happened in the imperialist countries. In other words *relatively speaking* the rate of capital accumulation was higher in the imperialist countries thus offsetting the effects of rising labour productivity and the destructive effects of capitalist development. This was in part *because* the rate of capital accumulation was lower in the colonial countries. So these latter countries felt the effects of rising productivity without experiencing *to the same degree* the rejuvenating effects of capital accumulation. Secondly it is necessary to take into account the effects of rising population in the colonial countries like India—contact with the metropolitan countries bringing a higher population growth for reasons which will be explained later. Higher population growth also tended to create a surplus population which because capital accumulation was insufficiently rapid, had to reorientate itself within what remained of the pre-capitalist section and carve out a living as best it could.

A few words are necessary about agricultural production in the pre-capitalist production mode. The agrarian economy while being affected by the excesses of merchant capital's get-rich-quick activities is not undermined directly by the competition from the capitalist sector (as are the artisans). A large portion of the peasantry's produce remains outside the sphere of commodity production altogether and those commodities that are traded are non-competing with goods in the capitalist sector—whether this sector be in the metropolis or, as later in the twentieth century, inside the colony itself. Thus agriculture is not affected in the same way by developing capitalism. Indeed as far as the capitalists are concerned the peasantry are not competitors but customers and suppliers of raw materials and other inputs, and the capitalists are thus even prepared to allow the colonial state to spend some money on developing agricultural production—like in the state irrigation works in India—provided such money secures a respectable return. In a variety of ways the peasant economy is dragged into the expanding capitalist world market. The products of the peasantry to a greater extent than previously are turned into commodities—a greater portion of agrarian surplus is required in cash, the peasants begin to acquire manufactures from abroad or from indigenous industrial centres instead of from local artisans, sending their produce in exchange via the expanded transportation network. At the same time the effects of greater commercialisation and the efforts of the capitalists to bring change to agriculture lead to changes in the old pattern of production relations and property rights within agriculture—land is turned into a commodity that can be bought and sold and alienated from its immediate possessors—the peasants themselves.

So contact with expanding capitalism also brings changes in the peasant economy. However, as already mentioned it is not directly undermined in the same way as are the artisan producers and all the changes do not add up to the development of capitalism in agriculture. On the contrary, the agrarian economy remains characterised by a parasitical structure of property relations. Moreover the growing pressure of population on the land which is the result of the lack of capital accumulation and its failure to absorb the unemployed surplus population puts the landowners and receivers of surplus in the rural areas in an even stronger position. They are able to draw off the agrarian surplus without any necessity for productive reinvestment because the competition for land and jobs keeps rents high and wages low.

What develops in colonial economies like India is, therefore, combined social structures in which a weak capitalist mode of production evolves side by side and interlocked with a non-capitalist mode of production in agriculture. The non-capitalist mode of production consists of the remnants of the pre-capitalist mode of production. In this chapter we shall trace out in more detail the fate of the pre-capitalist mode of production in India analysing the transformations through which it has passed. In the subsequent chapter we shall analyse the development of capitalist production in India—its nature and its limitations.

The Expropriation of the Pre-Capitalist Ruling Class

There is a certain logic in the process of growth of the territorial power of the East India Company that led to its subordination of the Indian sub-continent. The Company was, of course, in India to make a profit and this inevitably meant conflict—not just with other European trading companies but also with indigenous Indian classes that were already in receipt of the social surplus product. In this conflict none of the participants were secure while the others retained political and economic power. The resolution of this clash of interest could only lie finally in the dominance of one power. By the end of the eighteenth century it was clear that this would be the English East India Co.—though the English did not fully complete the process of subordination till after the Sepoy Rebellion of 1857 which was the last major attempt of the pre-British ruling class to assert its independence. Thereafter struggles against British imperialism were carried on, but sporadically by a leaderless peasantry until socio-economic developments provided other leaderships for the independence movement in the twentieth century.

Merchants' capital makes its profits by buying cheap and selling dear. In the initial stages of the trade with India contacts were very irregular and the fact that the merchants only did business when their ships were in port put them in an unsatisfactory bargaining position vis-a-vis Indian purchasers and suppliers. Such Indian merchants knew that within a few days the ships cargo would have to be sold and another bought and were able to get favourable terms accordingly. For this reason 'factories' were established and regular trading and warehousing began on a more permanent basis.[7] In the troubled times and as protection against the depredations of local Mughal potentates the factories had to be protected—and this led to the creation of independent centres of political and economic power. The acquisition of trading privileges and rights and the desire to forestall other European trading companies led to further conquests. Each of the trading companies intervened in the internecine strife of the eighteenth century, backing this or that local chief, accelerating and exacerbating the Mughal collapse.

Apart from profits from trade Marx notes that even as early as 1689 the English East India Company conceived of establishing a territorial dominion in India and of 'making territorial revenue of their sources of emolument'.[8] Along with the acquisition of political power, of course, went the right to collect the land revenue which, as we have seen, fell to those who could establish their 'right' by the force of arms. This process started to a significant extent from the 1740's onwards when war broke out in the Carnatic and the Company took over there. Subsequently it also took over in Bengal, Bihar and Orissa[9]. The land revenue so collected could be used to purchase the products that the Company sent back and sold in England as well as to finance the ever spiralling costs of maintaining the military.

The rise to power of the British was also the rise to power of those sections of Indian merchant capital who, as we have seen, had survived the collapse of the Mughal system under the protection and as the junior partner of the British. Such hangers-on mediated and made profit on their own account both in the Company's internal trade and in the extraction of land revenue. Thus they too came into conflict with the indigenous receivers of the surplus within Indian society. This clash of interest was most clearly seen in the conflict of the Company with the Nawab of Bengal, Mir Kasim in 1762–65. Mir Kasim was opposed to the rights and privileges arrogated by the Company's servants, and he emphasised that none of the Company's servants agents, gomastahs or other persons employed by them, shall be permitted to hold offices under the Country government, nor to purchase, rent or hold lands, gauges, or markets, nor to lend money to the zamindars or Collectors, as all these are sources of dispute between the Company's people and the governments.'[10]

The Europeans in Dacca took steps to protect their brokers against the Nawab's men and the ensuing victory was a joint one for the Europeans and the Indian Brokers.

This was not simply a dispute over trading rights but also over the direct exploitation of the surplus from the land. In Bengal, for instance, there was a 'dislocation of the ownership of landed property in favour of the rising moneyed class of banyans' as the Company adopted the practice of farming out the revenue by auction to the highest bidder.[11]

The activities of the Company's servants—together with the extremity of the Company's own revenue demands following from its dual need to make a profit and finance its military operations—constituted a very extreme pressure on the direct producers and there was a severe dislocation of production. Henry Verelst in his book 'A View of the Rise of the English Government in Bengal' written in 1772 described how the Company's servants 'forcibly seize the belongings and goods of the peasantry, traders and others at a quarter of their value and by means of violence and oppression they make them pay 5 rupees for goods that are worth no more than one'.[12] The result was a series of famines the worst being that of 1769 but there was little let up in the revenue demand. 'In a year when 35 per cent of the cultivators perished not 5 per cent of the land revenue was remitted and 10 per cent was added to it for the ensuing year (1770–1771)'.[13] By 1787, as one English M.P. William Fullerton put it, 'such has been the restless energy of our misgovernment that within the short space of 20 years many parts of this country have been reduced to a desert.'[14] Nor was this just true of Bengal. In the South of India continual warfare and the heavy exactions of the Company and its rivals led to extensive areas going out of cultivation—physical force had to be used to compel the raiyats to cultivate their lands.[15]

The peasantry rose in continuous rebellion against the British and their agents following the pre-capitalist ruling classes whose very existence was being undermined at a rapid pace.[16] The last desperate rebellion of this type came in 1857. While the rebellion was put down the new government moved to a policy of conciliation to the remnants of the pre-capitalist ruling class—the idea being to turn the aristocracy from enemies to the most steadfast supporters of the British regime. The policy of further annexation of states was dropped and as the Viceroy, Lord Lytton put it, a new policy was instituted 'by virtue of which the Crown of England should henceforth be identified with the hopes, the aspirations, the sympathies of a powerful native aristocracy'.[17] This policy worked successfully and the remnants of the pre-capitalist ruling class were bought off. But the process of conquest up to the Sepoy Rebellion of 1857 had probably led to the elimination of about $\frac{3}{4}$ of the warlord aristocracy and perhaps more than half of the local chieftainry.[18]

The displacement of this big section of the ruling class had implications elsewhere in the old mode of production. 'The downfall of the native courts deprived the skilled workman of his chief market'.[19] Maddison guesses that perhaps three quarters of the domestic demand for luxury handicrafts, with a magnitude of about 5 per cent of the Mughal national income disappeared.[20] This process was accentuated by the fact that the new commercial class that operated as the junior partner to British and the better-off sections of Indian society generally now gradually took over western tastes in consumption. This was deliberately prompted by the British, for instance, in their education policy. One of the aims of education policy was to develop 'an almost inexhaustible demand for the produce of British labour.'[21]

The surplus from the direct producers extracted by the Company and its servants now flowed into different channels from those in which it had flowed under the indigenous ruling classes. In large part it paid for the conquest—otherwise it helped the get-rich-quick activities of the Company and its servants. 'Not a shilling from the revenues of Britain has ever been expended on the military defense of our Indian Empire.' To the extent that the wars and annexations were not financed directly from the current revenues of the Company they were financed by rupee loans floated in Calcutta. Such loans were invested in by the Company servants as safe keeping for their own accumulations taken from the direct producers. In addition the surplus thus accumulated flowed into various plantation mortgages, shares in mercantile and banking establishments and rupee loans which officials and servants of the Company returning to Britain took with them. 'These interests represented simply portions of the Indian spoil and revenue reinvested in India. They did not constitute an export of commercial capital. Only the income from them entered the commercial balances. There it went to swell the annual economic drain upon India—the surplus export of tea, indigo and cotton to England, of textiles to the Continent and of opium to China, to provide for the salaries of London Bureaucrats, pensions and dividends to the East Indian shareholders.'[22]

The heavy exploitation of the peasantry by English merchants' capital after it had displaced a section of the indigenous ruling class provided resources that helped to sustain the process of industrialisation in the metropolis. This is an unfashionable notion but the magnitude of the surplus flow from India to Britain in the years of the Industrial Revolution bears comparison with the rate of capital formation at the same time. J. C. Sinha estimated the drain from Bengal over the period 1757 to 1780 at about £38 millions. East India merchants such as Tucker and Hume put the annual remittable surplus from India in the beginning of the nineteenth century (*c.* 1813) at between £3 and £4 millions.[23] Of course, it should be kept in mind that the flow of wealth into the metropolis also came from other colonial sources. These figures should be placed against a contemporary estimate that put the capital employed in buildings and machinery in the textile industry in Britain at about £1 million in 1783 rising to £9¼ millions in 1802. Deane and Cole estimate that the annual average rate of capital formation was about £10 millions per annum in the early years of the nineteenth century.[24]

It is not alleged that all the plunder from the colonies, extracted in the period of mercantile colonialism, found its way straight into capital formation in the metropolis. Undoubtedly a large proportion would have gone into the luxury consumption of the English ruling class. But this in itself would have set free domestic resources that might otherwise have been consumed. Moreover luxury expenditure by the rich and the rising colonial trade directly stimulated a number of industries.[25]

The 'drain' of wealth from India continued even after the Industrial Revolution. Imports of British goods into India stimulated British industries but the British took out much more than they put in. This wealth became less important to Britain as it continued its industrialisation process but it remained a large burden on India. Robert Knight in 1868 and Dadabhai Naoroji in 1871 estimated the drain from India at £16 millions.[26]

In the interwar years the flow of wealth continued. 'The total drain' due to government pensions and leave payments, interest on non-railway debt, private remittances for education and savings, and a third of commercial profits amounted to about 1.5 per cent of national income of undivided India from 1921 to 1938 and was probably a little larger before that'.[27] This magnitude should be set against net investment which was about 5 per cent of National Income at the end of British rule. Of course, these calculations made by Maddison underestimate the extent of exploitation of India. For instance Maddison takes only a third of commercial profit remittances as 'profits of colonialism'. He treats the rest of profit remittances as 'normal commercial transactions'. This implies a very narrow and undefined view of colonialism which presumably includes merely the privileges coming from direct political rule which state administrators were able to dispense upon British businessmen. Actually direct political rule by British imperialism is merely one level of a general structure of subordination stemming from the whole process of uneven and combined development of capitalism on a world scale. In this structure, one may look as hard as one wants but one will not find in the 'normal commercial transactions' between Britain and India a flow of profit remittances from Britain to India—it was all in the other direction.

The Fate of Petty Handicraft Production

The fate of industrial capitalism, after the period of primary accumulation, had other effects on the pre-capitalist mode of production in India. It is probably true that the East India Company's operations initially had some limited effect in increasing the productivity of labour in certain Indian handicrafts which the Company shipped for sale in Europe. As late as 1882 an English writer could comment how many villages in Bengal and on the Coromandel coast 'still show traces of the times when the East India Company and its continental rivals gathered large settlements of weavers round . . . little forts, and thus formed the only industrial towns that ever existed in India.'[28] However during the latter end of the seventeenth century and during the eighteenth century Indian manufactures and cotton were excluded from the English market and were imported into England only to be sold on the Continent. This was because of the more competitive position of Indian manufacturers at this time. As Marx put it 'the importation of East Indian cotton and silk stuffs was declared to ruin the poor British manufacturers, an opinion put forward in John Pollexfen's "England and East-India: Inconsistent in their Manufactures; London 1697", a title strangely verified a century and a half later, but in a very different sense.'[29] Something of the competitive strength of these Indian textiles may be understood from the evidence given to the parliamentary enquiry of 1813 to the effect that Indian textiles could be sold profitably in the British market at a price 50–60 per cent lower than those fabricated in England. In consequence, British textiles were protected by tariffs of 70 per cent to 80 per cent or by outright prohibition.[30]

The tariffs were important for enabling the nascent British textile industry to get off the ground. Then, once steampower had been applied and Manchester had the advantage of cheap production, the protective tariffs were removed. After the Napoleonic Wars the flow of machine made goods into India multiplied. In 1822–23 cloth imports to the Bengal Presidency stood at a figure seven times that for 1813–14, exports from the same area fell from Rs. 4,600,000 to Rs. 300,000. Spinners were affected not long after. Yarn imports rose from Rs. 81,000 to Rs. 800,000 a year later. The import of other manufactures from Britain also rose sharply.[31] The scale of the consequent disintegration of Indian handicrafts at this time is not known and may have been overemphasised in the past. The village artisans at this stage were largely insulated from the competitive pressures of the market and it was only later when the railways were built across the sub-continent that their position was put under pressure. John Crawford a contemporary observer writing in 1837 estimated 'We furnish the Indians annually with cotton goods which, on the spot, may be worth two millions sterling, that is to say we furnish them to the extent of one-seventeenth part or about 6 per cent of their own manufacture. To the Indian manufacturer the apparent damage done is to that amount and no more . . .' In addition he estimated that Indian exports had fallen by about £$\frac{3}{4}$ million sterling per annum.[32]

Evidence of developments in the early nineteenth century are based solely on eye witness reports. It would seem safe to assume that centres of manufacture for the aristocracy and for export suffered a severe set back but that the majority of artisans who were servants to the village community remained, as yet, largely untouched. But to contemporary observers, however, it seemed a commonplace to note that 'The tide of circumstances has compelled the Indian weaver to exchange his loom for the plough, and has crushed many of the minor handicrafts.'[33] The early British rulers quite consciously pursued a policy of suppressing local manufactures. In petitioning Parliament for certain reforms of the tariff regulations in 1840 it was stated before a Select Committee that:

'This Company has in various ways, encouraged and assisted by our great manufacturing ingenuity and skill, succeeded in converting India from a manufacturing country into a country exporting raw produce . . . The peculiar state of the relation between this country and India and the necessity of extracting from the latter three millions of money for Home Charges . . . and the altered state of Indian industry in it being converted from a manufacturing country into a country exporting raw produce, are circumstances which . . . ought to influence the Legislature to afford every possible protection to its agricultural produce.'[34]

Subsequently, as the railways spread across the sub-continent from the mid-nineteenth century, the village artisans also began to come under competition and their customary relationship to the village community began gradually to be undermined as cheap, machine made goods became available. The change is amply documented in various government publications. 'Improved means of communication have greatly stimulated migration and the consequent disruption of the village community, and by facilitating and lowering the cost of transport of commodities, have created a tendency for industries to become localised. The extensive importation of cheap European piece goods and utensils, have more or less destroyed many village industries. The high prices of agricultural produce have also led many village artisans to abandon their hereditary craft in favour of agriculture . . . The extent to which this disintegration of the old village organisation is proceeding varies considerably in different parts. The change is most noticeable in the more advanced provinces whereas in comparative backward tracts, like Central India and Rajputana, the old organisation remains almost intact.'[35]

One indicator of this disintegration of the artisan industry is found in the increasing deviations in the successive Censuses between hereditary caste occupation and actual occupations for the artisan castes. In the earlier Censuses the fairly close association between caste and occupation are noted. As an example we have the Madras Census of 1881 commenting upon the statistics for 'industrial occupations'. This statistical class more than any other displays 'the special feature of Indian society—the association of caste and occupation. The older and numerically more important traders are still, in a measure, caste callings. The weavers, the leather workers, the barbers and washermen, the metal workers and the carpenters . . . are for the most part following their hereditary occupations.'[36] But even as early as 1881 'with many castes their adherence to hereditary occupations is disappearing'.[37] By 1931 the process of deviation has gone a lot further. The Census comments that 'A general examination of the castes tabulated by occupation enables the position to be roughly summarised as follows: 'In the majority of cases about half the males tabulated retain their traditional occupation and varying numbers up to, but rarely exceeding a quarter have other subsidiary occupations. About a quarter or less of the half that have abandoned their hereditary occupations as their principal means of subsistence retain them as subsidiary.'[38]

The following table for the United Provinces is derived from the 1931 Census Report by P. C. Joshi.[39]

Not all artisan production disappeared. In 1921 16 million workers were still supporting one-tenth of India's population

Principal Occupation of Artisan Castes
Number for 1,000 earners engaged in each caste

Artisan Castes

Occupations	Bharhais	Chamars	Dhunies	Julahas	Kumhars	Lohars	Sonars
Traditional occupation	442	51	191	449	401	357	707
Non-cultivating landlord or tenants	0	0	0	0	0	0	0
Cultivators	427	355	466	278	373	484	191
Agricultural labourers	50	469	166	101	106	73	18
Cattle and sheep breeders etc.	11	24	18	11	18	11	0
Industry, transport, trade and general	45	88	145	144	64	56	55
Others	25	13	14	17	35	12	22
	1,000	1,000	1,000	1,000	1,000	1,000	1,000

Bharhais = Carpenters; Chamars = leather workers; Dhunias = cotton carders; Julahas = weavers; Kumhars = potters; Lohars = Blacksmiths; Sonars = goldsmiths)

(33 million +) by employment in 'industries'. Of these 16 million only 1,266,395 persons were engaged in establishments coming under the Factory Acts although many of these workers included personal service 'trades' such as washermen (1,100,000) as well as sweepers, scavengers etc. ($\frac{3}{4}$ million.)[40] Nevertheless this shows the magnitude, even at this stage, of the 'unorganised' industries vis-a-vis the organised sector. Maddison gives the following table for the relative importance of small scale enterprise versus those employed in factory establishments in the last half century of

British rule.[41] This gives some indication of the stagnation of the artisan sector.

Industrial Growth in the Last Half Century of British Rule
Employment in thousands

	Small scale enterprise	Factory Establishments
Average of 1900 and 1901	13,308	601
Average of 1945 and 1946	12,074	2,983

Taking this in the context of population growth the rate of accumulation in the capitalist sector was roughly sufficient to maintain a constant proportion of a rising population in the industrial sector in the last half century of British rule. The following table shows the number of workers by sector of economic activity.[42]

Employed Labour Force (in millions)

Year	Total Workers	Primary Sector	Secondary Sector	Tertiary Sector
1901	111.4	71.8	12.6	15.6
1911	121.4	79.9	11.1	14.0
1921	117.9	76.0	10.4	13.6
1931	120.6	74.8	10.2	15.0
1941	139.5	72.1	10.6	17.3
1951	188.6	72.3	11.7	16.0

Given the inability of the capitalist sector to absorb more than roughly a constant proportion of a growing population there was a growing pressure of population on the land i.e. in the non-capitalist sector—having important implications in driving up rents and pushing down wages. In the south of India, for instance, there is evidence that there was a tendency for wages to decline from as early as 1875 reinforcing findings that 'it was in this period that the pressure of population on the land began to be felt in certain districts of the (Madras) Presidency.'[43]

Population Growth

As already mentioned the effects of British rule on the peasant economy was different from that on the artisan economy. Broadly speaking the effects of British rule on the agrarian society can be divided into two—an increase in the pressure of population on the land (increase in the man/land ratio) and a transformation in the pattern of property relations within the context of a more commercialised agrarian society.

The increase in the man/land ratio was both a product of the rising trend in population to the total cultivable area and also the lack of alternative industrial employment given the slowness of capital accumulation. The latter variable has already been mentioned and will be dealt with further in the chapter on the development of capitalist production. As far as population growth is concerned we are again hampered by the lack of accurate figures before the beginning of the Censuses in 1872. If we take the commonly accepted estimate of population in 1800 as being 100–125 million then to get to the population of 225 millions in 1872 means a rate of growth of population of 1.0 to 1.3 per cent.[44] This seems very large since the rate between 1872 and 1921 was only 0.4 per cent. It would seem safer to assume a slower rate of population growth in the nineteenth century—though of just what magnitude it is difficult to guess. If one were to project back a 0.4 per cent growth rate from 1872 one would get a population of about 192 millions in 1800.[45] This is a long way from Davis' estimate of 120 million. Maddison guesses at 186 million in 1800 and then extrapolates a 0.4 per cent increase each year to 227 million in 1856.[46]

In general, whatever the exact figures, there was a slow increase in population over the nineteenth century. This was due to the suppression of warfare and banditry, the ending of the ritual suicide of widows and infanticide, and the introduction of some public health measures.[47] The slow increase was, then, partly a recovery from the more unstable times of the eighteenth century. (An instability that British imperialism's actions had been in not a small part responsible for). Talking of South India in 1800 Sir Thomas Munro noted how 'it is reckoned that the population of the country has been diminished one-third within the last forty years'.[48]

But population growth was heavily punctuated by famine and disease and was very sporadic in its nature until the 1920's.[49]

It is after the influenza epidemic of 1918, which more than

doubled the regular mortality rate taking 15 million lives (5 per cent of the population), that the beginnings of the 'population

Indian Population Growth

	% increase during previous decade
1881	·9
1891	9·4
1901	1.0
1911	6.1
1921	·9
1931	10.6
1941	15.0

explosion', so called, are observable. The rate of increase between 1921 and 1941 of 1.2 per cent per annum is fairly modest but a significant increase when compared with the 0.4 per cent per annum increase for the period 1872 to 1921.[50] This increase in the rate of population growth, which has accelerated still further in the Independence period, can best be analysed within the context of the law of uneven and combined development. It has been argued that developments in the 'advanced' capitalist countries permanently affect the conditions of development in the more 'backward' countries. This is also true of population. In pre-capitalist society in the absence of economic and social development both the birth and the death rates are relatively high. Contact with the developed capitalist economies brings the death rate down rapidly but within the context of the stagnation of the existing social and economic structure the birth rate remains at a high level.

'The poor countries of today are benefiting from the accumulated medical knowledge of the past, and are reducing their mortality rates faster than those experienced by the rich countries . . . For example the death rate in India declined from 48.6 per thousand in 1911–20 to 25.9 in 1951–56, a 23 point decline in less than 40 years whereas in England and Wales it took 50 years to reduce the death rate from 32 to 25, and another 110 years to reduce it to 18.'[51]

However, the birth rate remains much more stubbornly at a high level. A large family, for instance, remains the best insurance against old age. An average family of seven children is consistent with having at least one son to look after one in one's old age.[52] Studies suggest that fertility only declines with higher levels of literacy, urbanisation and per capita income—in short with social and economic development.[53] India's high fertility—and hence its high population growth—is thus the *result* of its 'underdevelopment' rather than simply a cause of it.

Birth and Death Rates of India 1901–1950 per thousand[54]

Decade	Birth Rate	Death Rate
1901–10	48.1	42.6
1911–20	49.2	48.6
1921–30	46.4	36.3
1931–40	39.9	27.4
1951–56	40.7	25.9

While the population dependent upon agriculture grew during the British period so did the area sown but increasingly this was not at a commensurate rate. A close study of the extent of cultivation in the Mughal period as compared with today shows that:

'an increase in cultivation . . . has taken place everywhere though in varying degrees. The increase is greatest, amounting to about a hundred per cent in three regions. The first region comprises Ilahabad, Awadh and Bihar and, possibly, parts of Bengal . . . The second region is that of Berar, where cultivation has extended at the expense of the central Indian jungles. And, finally, the Indus valley, where the extension has been due almost entirely to the modern canal system. Beside these territories, the increase in cultivation seems to have varied from one half to one third or only one fourth.'[55]

More precise and accurate figures are available for the twentieth century which show that the total cultivated area rose at less than the rate of population growth. Thus in British India the population grew by 27 per cent between 1920 and 1941 whereas the net area sown increased by only 8 per cent—much of this at the expense of cultivable waste and fallow with total cultivable area increasing by only 4 per cent. With population growing more rapidly than the area sown and the proportion of population dependent on agriculture remaining approximately the same the trend was towards an increase in the man/land ratio. The average number of acres per person was 2.23 in 1891—92 as against 1.90 in 1934—40—a 15 per cent decline.[56]

Changes in the Pattern of Agrarian Relations

The increased pressure of population on the land took place simultaneously with a transformation of the pattern of rural property rights. This transformation reflected a number of influences. One key one was the increased commercialisation of the countryside. The reciprocal relationship between the village artisan and the cultivating peasants was increasingly replaced by a relationship between the peasantry and the manufacturing centres—first in foodstuffs and raw materials in return for manufactured goods. The social surplus in the form of the land revenue had been quite highly monetised in the Mughal era now it became completely payable only in cash. Trade with the manufacturing centres further pulled the Indian peasantry into the vortex of the expanding world market. The growing commercialisation increased the power and influence of the moneylender and trader groups.

Another influence was British land revenue settlement policy. We have already seen that the British together with their Indian commercial junior partners, expropriated most of the Mughal upper aristocracy. The land revenue now accrued to the British imperialist state and was used to finance the expenses of conquest, administration and, under the Company, the need to make a profit. The British settled with those lower down in the hierachical structure of land rights—but did so in ways which changed those land rights in the direction of capitalist private property. These changes involved the expropriation of the rights of some groups and the conferral of these rights on others. By doing this, and by trying to develop a market in land so that it could be bought and sold the British hoped to increase agricultural productivity. Unlike the artisans, the peasantry were the customers of British industry and the increase in the land revenues was a hoped for consequence of agricultural prosperity.

In the early years, however, the stretch on the revenues of the imperialist state meant that the land revenue was kept at a very high level in certain areas. This held back the possibility of any significant increase in production. As we shall see British hopes that western property rights (imposed along with a new system of courts and law and order) would stimulate agricultural productivity also proved fallacious.[57] A westernised flavour was given to Indian parasitism—moreover for reasons of political expediency it proved necessary to introduce legislation to protect certain groups. The loss of land by the remnants of the aristocracy put in danger a valuable ally for the British. The upper sections of the peasantry lost rights both through new land revenue laws and through the operations of the moneylenders. Both the big landowners and upper peasants were pacified by special legislation to protect and, in some cases, to restore their rights.

Land Revenue Policy

The situation varied regionally. In the Bengal Presidency the British settled with the zamindars whose functions were, however, transformed. The zamindars lost their judicial and administrative powers but they gained a property right that was now to be inheritable and transferable without the prior permission of the government. Many of the oldest members of the indigenous gentry were unable to maintain their position when the British pitched the revenue demand at a high level and adopted the practice of farming zamindaris. Their property fell to speculators and members of the banyan and moneyed classes. The result was an agrarian and social crisis which brought a turn round in British policy.[58] In 1793 a permanent settlement of the land revenue was made with the Bengal zamindars. The Preamble to Regulation II of 1793 sets out clearly British objectives in the Permanent Settlement and is worth quoting at some length.[59]

'In the British Territories in Bengal, the greater part of the materials required for the numerous and valuable manufactures, and most of the other principal articles of export are the produce of the lands. It follows, that the commerce and consequently the wealth of the country must increase in proportion to the extension of agriculture.

'. . . To effect these improvements in agriculture, which must necessarily be followed by the increase of every article of produce, has accordingly been one of the primary objects to which the attention of the British Administration has been direct in its arrangements for the internal government of these provinces.

'As being the two fundamental measures essential to the attainment of it, the property in the soil has been declared to be vested in the landholders, and the revenue payable to the government from each estate has been fixed for ever. These measures have at once rendered it in the interests of the proprietors to improve their estates, and given them the means of raising the funds necessary for that purpose.

'When extension of cultivation was production only for a heavier assessment, and even the possession of the property was uncertain, the hereditary landholder had little inducement to improve his estates; and moneyed men had no encouragement to embark their capital in the purchase or improvement of land whilst not only the profit but the security for capital itself was so precarious.'

The Permanent Settlement did not succeed in creating agrarian prosperity—the zamindars took the rental in a purely parasitical fashion. But the Permanent Settlement was successful in creating a stable body of landowners who supported British rule.[60]

Outside of Bengal the financial needs of the imperialist state prevented both further permanent settlements and the sharing of a large portion of the agrarian surplus with zamindari intermediaries. In the Madras Presidency only a little land was settled with zamindars—the bulk was taxed on the so-called ryotwari system. In theory this meant that the government settled directly with the cultivators while bypassing intermediaries. In actual fact ryotwari settlement generally involved dealing with the upper landholding castes in the villages and these castes—like the mirasdars in the Tamil areas, janmis of Malabar or mulawargardars of South Canara—were more than mere cultivators. Such castes would often be receivers of surplus from various kinds of either tenants or agricultural labourers below them.[61] Once again we find that the process of settlement by the British confirmed on these layers rights that they had not previously had. The net result was a movement to a pattern of rights closer to private property. The process of conferral of rights on some meant the loss of these very same rights to others. In Malabar, for example, the kanamdars had had right of occupancy on land that they held under the janmis. The janmis fled in the wars and the rulers of Mysore made their settlements directly with the kanamdars. The janmis returned when the British took over in 1792 and the British made settlements with them which not only restored their former rights but which recognised the janmis as 'landlords' with powers to evict the kanamdars when their leases expired. The deprivation of the customary right of occupancy led to rebellion and litigation among the kanamdars but it was never subsequently restored.[62]

In settling the land revenue in the South the British were concerned not to change agrarian relations too much lest this provoke disturbance. Sir Thomas Munro as Governor General wrote that '(As for) . . . the distribution of landed property . . . we ought to take it as we find it, and not attempt upon idle improvement'.[63] Nevertheless, despite this caution, some change was sought. Munro wished to see a wider land market and he thought that the possession of permanent hereditary property rights with freedom to sublet and transfer might encourage the raiyats to improve their lands.[64] This latter hope was contradicted, however, at least for the first half of the nineteenth century by the high rate of land revenue. With the rate generally exceeding 50 per cent of the gross produce the extent of cultivation remained unchanged for 50 years. A contemporary observer and Company Servant, Francis Brown, noted that the Madras cultivator 'obtains no profit whatever beyond his food after paying his arrears.'[65]

In western India we again find British land policy cutting through pre-existing agrarian relations. Prior to the British the poorer cultivators had been protected by collective institutions like the jatha (family group) and the village community. This was true for instance, for the uprees (cultivators without prescriptive rights to the soil). The meerasdars (hereditary cultivators) organised as a community had been responsible for payment of the land revenue and they had distributed the revenue burden internally to the village community including upon the uprees. In this system the uprees could express their disapproval of an over-heavy burden by migrating to a new village. They therefore had some protection which was inbuilt to the system. But when the British introduced the ryotwari mode of settlement directly with individual cultivators and including upon the uprees the situation changed. The dominant meerasdar castes were able to ally themselves with native officials in the Land Revenue Survey Department and the burden of land revenue was shifted onto the poorer neighbours. The net result was an improvement in the style of life and accumulations in the hands of the dominant groups—at the expense of the greater mass of the cultivators who bore an increasingly crippling burden of debt and whose position deteriorated over time.[66]

Commercialisation and the Structure of Agrarian Relations

The transformation of land rights backed by a new system of courts made for increased transferability of land and the development of a land market. This complemented an increased commercialisation of the economy—due to the high revenue demand in cash and the spread of trade with the railways—to facilitate a greater mercantile/usurious exploitation in the countryside. Buchanan points out that India's experiences in the late nineteenth and twentieth century are better described as a commercial than as an industrial revolution.[67] Thus it was that Indian capital excluded by British hostility from more than a meagre industrialisation, had to orientate to where the profits could be made—on the land. From the mid-nineteenth century an expanding and prosperous market in commercial crops like wheat, cotton and jute developed. Paralleling this a new class of moneylender emerged whose aim was to get hold of these crops at the lowest possible prices. The simplest method was to get hold of the cultivator by enmeshing him in debt, alienating his land and converting him into a tenant-at-will, sharecropper or agricultural labourer.[68]

In their drive to enmesh the cultivator in debt and alienate him from his land the trader-moneylender group was helped by the inelasticity of the British revenue demand when the peasantry now faced not only the fluctuations in production consequent upon the variability of the monsoon but fluctuations in prices consequent upon the trade cycle.[69]

'Without doubt a grave error was made upon annexation, in

suddenly substituting for an elastic kind of assessment a fixed cash settlement—to say nothing of its severity.'[70]

'I have stated my opinion that the origin of the debt which lead to these frequent transfers of property is, in the great majority of cases the pressure of our revenue system. Although the main principles of that system are sound it has, I think, been administered in a very harsh and unbending manner.'[71]

The documentation of these processes can be found in the books of administrators and government publications. Wherever there was agricultural growth and commercialisation traders and moneylenders came too, indebtedness rose and land sales increased. The building of the irrigation works in the Punjab brought increased agricultural production. It also raised the number of bankers and moneylenders (including their dependants) from 52,263 in the 1868 Census to 193,890 in the 1911 Census.[72] From 1866 to 1874 land sales averaged about 88,000 acres a year. In the following quinquennial periods the acres sold averaged 93,000; 160,000; 310,000 and 338,000 a year. Mortgages amounted to 143,000 acres a year in the first period and 212,000; 296,000; 590,000 and 554,000 acres a year in the succeeding quinquennial periods. ('These figures give an exaggerated view inasmuch as they refer to the total area. The total cultivated area may be roughly calculated at half the above.')[73]

The Indian Famine Commission of 1901 reported similar developments in Bombay. 'At least one-fourth of the cultivators in the Bombay Presidency have lost possession of their lands . . . less than a fifth are free from debt . . . and the remainder are indebted to a greater or less extent.'[74] The trend of alienation continued in the twentieth century. Thus in Bombay for the ten years between 1926/27 and 1936/37 five million acres—more than 20 per cent of the total land held by the cultivators—passed into the hands of the moneylenders. The number of actual cultivating owners declined from 1,980,000 to 1,761,000 or by about 9 per cent.[75]

Commercialisation of the countryside can therefore be clearly seen to have had an additional effect on the pattern of land rights involving the expropriation of substantial sectors of rural society. This was not just of the cultivating groups—many higher groups also suffered. We have already seen that the Bengal zamindars had been displaced by commercial elements in the early period of British rule. Usury continued to break up the zamindari estates in the Presidency. In 1772 there were less than 100 landowners in Bengal—a century later in 1872 there were 154,200. Of these '533, or 0.34 per cent, only are great properties with an area of 20,000 acres and upwards; 15,747 or 10.21 per cent range from 500 to 20,000 acres in area; while the number of estates which fell short of 500 acres is no less than 137,920 or 89.44 per cent of the whole.'[76]

The end result of these processes was that, at independence, the areas of greatest commercial development were often those with the highest incidence of sharecropping and leasing. A. Ghosh produces the following table to illustrate such a correspondence.[77]

States	*per cent of population in commerce*	*per cent population in urban areas*	*per cent cultivated area under sharecropping or leases*	*Density per square mile of population in rural areas*
Bengal	9.3	24.80	22.0	610
Punjab	9.1	15.09	21.5	243
Bombay	7.6	23.92	30.6	202
Madras	6.7	15.97	13.2	329
U.P.	5.0	12.46	10.7	453
Bihar	3.9	5.37	10.2	493

(Bengal = West Bengal; Punjab = East Punjab)

He comments: 'The figures indicate that on the whole the ratio of sharecropped or leased area is related to the level of urban commercial development which is the reverse of the density. The conclusion that suggests itself is that commercial penetration of the economy has, instead of bringing about more progressive tenure systems, reintroduced old, wasteful and more oppressive systems in agriculture.'[78]

Sharecropping suited the moneylender-cum-trader landlord who acquired land. 'This type of landlord is already a trader in grains or in jute. It will pay him, therefore, to take as rent the jute or grain from his tenant rather than take cash and then have to buy the raw materials on the open market. In other words he is rationalising the business vertically . . .'[79]

Where they were not turned into sharecroppers the pauperised peasants that had lost rights to the land were either turned into tenants-at-will on fixed rents or into landless labourers. Alternatively they had relations with the landholder intermediary between that of tenant and labourer. By the 1931 Census one-third of the working population in agriculture were returned as wholly or mainly tenant cultivators—one-quarter of the population being tenants cultivating below 5 acres. Two-thirds of these tenant cultivators were in U.P., Bengal, Bihar and Orissa which were the zamindari areas—though tenancy was high in ryotwari areas also.[80] A high proportion of the rural population were agricultural labourers. In 1931 the Census returned 38 per cent of the population supported by agriculture as labourers excluding all those engaged in agricultural wage-labour as a supplementary source of income. If large numbers of 'unspecified labourers' in agriculture are excluded, and just those returned specifically as farm labourers considered, then the proportion reduces to 31.2 per cent which is nevertheless still very high.[81]

Recently Dharma Kumar has attacked the notion that landless labour was insignificant prior to the British conquest and that, in consequence, the effects of British rule can be held responsible for the appearance of landless labour. She points out that in South India probably 12–15 per cent of the population were in the agricultural labour castes in various states of bondage at the beginning of the nineteenth century—10–15 per cent in Malabar, 10–12 per cent in South Canara and in the Tamil areas, 16 per cent in Nellore, and 12 per cent in Salem.[82] Nonetheless agricultural labour did grow significantly under the British—the proportion of agricultural labourers to the total agricultural population in Madras was 36.1 per cent in 1921 and jumped to 52.9 per cent in 1931 'which indicates clearly that the pre-British "slave" labour force cannot be regarded as constituting the main source of the modern labour force.'[83] The situation, of course, varied from region to region. Over half of the 29.8 million agricultural labourers in 1931 were accounted for by Madras, Bombay and C.P. (including Berar). The eastern regions of Bengal, Bihar, Orissa and Assam accounted for another third while U.P., Punjab and NWFP had less than one-fifth of the total between them.[84]

The existence of this landless labour and its employment for wages does not really indicate the existence of capitalism in agriculture. Patnaik coins the term 'dominant landholder' for the landowning interests that employ labour rather than lease out land and who sell the bulk of the product but who nevertheless do not take any entrepreneurial interest or accumulate agricultural capital.[85] In practice the choice of whether to hire agricultural labour or lease out to tenants was purely contingent on the terms for the landowner. Given control over the land and the ample availability of cheap landless labour the landholder was able to pay low wages and extract an adequate income from agricultural labour without any need for productive investment or entrepreneurial effort. Indeed the labourer might be responsible for providing for live-stock, for some of the implements of labour as well as for supervising production. Thus the borderlines between wage labour and tenancy might be blurred in practice.[86]

Agrarian Legislation out of Political Expediency

The process of expropriation of various groups either directly through British land policy or through the moneylender did not proceed without producing acute unrest and instability. The government watched the process affecting different sections of society with a certain amount of anxiety. Sections of society were being ruined that the British wanted to keep as allies like the Sind landlords. Of this group the Revenue Commissioners noted in 1870 that 'Extravagance no doubt has assisted the fall of these Mahomedan gentry; still Government cannot but look with great solicitude on the ruin of the heads of society in a frontier country, conquered but 31 years ago, who have hitherto been conspicuous for their loyalty and good behaviour.'[87]

Unrest would sometimes burst into violence causing action by the authorities. 'Between 1793 and 1882 a series of regulations were passed assuring protection to the ryot and between 1859 and 1885 another series of acts. But behind everyone of these enactments was either a serious famine or a tale of peasants rising in revolt.'[88]

Between 1801 and 1818 in the period of occupation of the North West Frontier Provinces the British settled with a single person whom they recognised as the 'owner' having all the rights and privileges of the English landowner (but subject to a high revenue demand). As a result many gained rights they had previously not had—at the expense of others who lost their rights. The product was mass discontent and the sufferers made no disguise of 'looking forward to the termination of the British government, for the recovery of the Estates'.[89] The British changed policy and in subsequent settlements granted occupancy rights to tenants of 12 years standing. A process of gradual encroachment of tenancy rights upon the rights of superior landholders began.

There are many other such examples. In the 1870's the Bengal tenants were hit hard by depression. Already poverty stricken they refused to pay their rents, disobeyed the dictates of the courts and obstructed evictions. The rising was put down by the government but an Inquiry Committee was set up and the Bengal Tenancy Act of 1885 was subsequently passed. In 1875 there were fierce riots on the Deccan sparked off by the combination of a rigid government demand for revenue and the collapse of the cotton boom at the end of the American Civil War. The slump in cotton prices hit the peasantry very hard and they rose against the moneylenders who, with the aid of the courts threatened them with eviction. The houses of moneylenders were raided, documents of debts were destroyed and some moneylenders were killed.

Once again the government put down the revolt but in response to the situation the Deccan Agriculturists Relief Act was passed in 1879.[90] In the Punjab also, as we have mentioned, the rate of land alienation was extremely rapid and the peasants threatened with loss of their lands rebelled in the last decade of the nineteenth century. This was especially alarming as 'The army was largely recruited from the Punjab castes which were losing land and the contentment of the army was at stake. Furthermore, in many areas the land was passing from Muslim cultivators to Hindu moneylenders so that class tension was compounded by communal antagonisms.' The government responded to this situation by the Punjab Land

Alienation Act of 1900 which had some effect in arresting the process of alienation.[91]

In this way the government was able to buy off the leaders of the peasantry—a privileged upper strata getting occupancy rights and more secure terms for their tenancies.[92] But it should also be noted that much of the legislation that was passed was ignored by the landlords. In the U.P. for instance peasant agitations in 1920–21 demanded that only recorded rent should be paid and that gift payments (nazrana) and forced labour (begar) should not be exorted. These were already part of existing tenancy law but the landlords could safely ignore them as the government policy was to line up behind the landlords. Indeed the U.P. Government took action in alliance with these landed interests to form aman sabha or 'safety leagues' 'designed to rally moderate opinion in the preservation of law and order.' It was in Oudh, above all, that the British imperialists had made concessions to the remnants of the aristocracy out of expediency and by the beginning of the twentieth century a whole doctrine of imperial government was clearly identifiable, known as the 'Oudh School of Statesmenship' or more bluntly 'Oudh Policy, the Aristocratic Policy'. Adherents to the Oudh doctrine regarded the landlords as 'those whom the masses naturally and instinctually regard as their leaders' and therefore 'It followed that the landlords should be supported in order that their influence would be used to underpin British rule, and the "Oudh men" did all they could in their administration particularly in agrarian matters, to bolster the landlords and preserve their local standing and influence.'[93]

It is not without relevance to remember, of course, that after the Mutiny the policy of annexations was dropped and as a result checkerboarded all over the Indian subcontinent vast areas remained under the control of the princes and their retainers. These states—600 in all—contained one-quarter of the population and two-fifths of the area of the sub-continent. Here the most backward patterns of agrarian relations were able to continue. Slavery and forced labour, for instance, continued to prevail in a large number of the Indian states as did the forms of arbitrary social and economic power in the hands of the princes and their governments.[94]

Remnants of the Old Order in the New Pattern of Rights

An analysis of the changes in rural society should go together with a reminder of what remained the same in the old pattern of social relations. It is important to record that relations of dependence—mediated through caste divisions and defined and protected by physical force—did not disappear entirely. In general we still find a close correspondence between social and economic position and caste at the end of British rule. To be sure changes in the economy and land rights made some groups independent of the high castes and this did tend to break down some caste divisions. In his study of Bisipara, a village in Highland Orissa, Bailey describes how economic change 'attacked the superiority of the WARRIORS (caste) from all sides. They lost their monopoly of the land and land itself ceased to be the sole source of wealth as other economic opportunities opened up. British law deprived the warriors of the overt use of force.'[95] Nonetheless the upper castes generally had the best advantages in the new economic structure and so generally managed to stay on top. Numerous anthropological studies at the village level suggest that the caste structure remained in close correspondence to the economic structure. The following table from the 1931 Census of Bengal shows this quite clearly.[96]

Class I consists of landholders and supervisory farmers—i.e. subinfeudatory landlords and the more prosperous non-cultivating or supervisory farmers.

Classes of economic structure	*'Upper' Caste Hindus*	*'Lower' Caste Hindus*	*Saygad Moslems*	*Scheduled Tribes*	*Jolahas*
		(*Nos. in thousands*)			
I	454	120	14	23	4
II	167	981	21	212	63
III	131	264	10	711	14
		Percentages			
I	61	9	31	3	5
II	22	72	47	22	77
III	17	19	22	75	18
	100	100	100	100	100

(Jolahas are a group of Moslem functional castes—having a better position in society than other Moslem functional castes.)

Class II consists primarily of the self-sufficient peasantry—i.e. cultivators (and also artisans and traders).

Class III—sharecroppers, agricultural labourers, service holders and others who depend for their livelihood upon others.

Except in the case of the Jolahas the caste structure maintains a close relation to the economic structure. Corresponding to the maintenance of caste divisions the upper castes continued to maintain considerable social and judicial power over their lower caste dependents. In practice many landlords could still—and still can to this day—act as protectors for and make use of gangs of thugs known as goondas to terrorise the countryside and get the peasants to support their faction. In practice the upper caste landlords could still—and still can to this day—in certain areas (above all where the peasants are economically dependant) exercise juridicial and ritual power over their dependants. Cases continued of punishment by floggings or of the drinking of 'cow dung milk' or human excrement mixed with water.[97] Writing of the Bengali landlord in 1912 Carstairs comments how:

'The lord of each estate was as much its lord as our own medieval Baron was of his. The law prevailing in it was not the law of the land, but the will of the landlord who was master within it.

'Every landlord had his force of retainers . . . They were also his instrument for overawing the villages and for punishing those who had incurred his wrath.'[98]

British Efforts to Develop Agriculture

The analysis of the evolution of the pre-capitalist mode of production in the agricultural sector is incomplete without some further comments about the effects of state policy on the agricultural sector. As should be clear the appropriation of the agrarian surplus by indigenous Indian classes took place as the appropriation of the residual surplus after the demands of the imperialist state for land revenue had been met. In the late eighteenth and early nineteenth century, in particular, the state took an extremely large proportion of the agrarian surplus. The intensity of the state's demand was responsible to a very substantial degree for restraining the productive forces.[99] In Madras, to give a particularly important example, it seems unlikely that there was much expansion of production at all in the first half of the century given the intensity of the revenue demand. The peasantry frequently had to be forced to cultivate.[100] After the Mutiny in the 1860's there was, for a time, a discussion about the feasibility and desirability of fixing a permanent settlement of the land revenue for the whole of India but the proposals fell through on financial grounds. There was too much opposition to income tax. This was introduced for a time but then abolished. There was also too much opposition from the urban classes to import duties quite apart from opposition from the Lancashire exporters. 'Who then was to pay for the increasing cost of administration in India? The only reply was that the agricultural classes must continue to bear the burden.'[101]

The magnitude of the state's demand diminished with time. Other sources of revenue were introduced—e.g. import duties in the twentieth century—and the paucity of state developmental efforts kept its expenditures fairly low. By 1947 the land tax, which had frequently exceeded 50 per cent of the crop, was a mere 2 per cent of agricultural income.[102] The fall was most marked in Bengal where the permanent settlement had fixed the revenue demand in perpetuity after 1793 but it was also true of the other areas. This was something of the nature of a mixed blessing in one sense. As has been shown the increasing residual of the surplus did not accrue to the actual cultivators but to the parasitical landowning groups and the state was able to reduce its demands because it spent so little on development—either in agriculture directly or in other spheres like education and industry that might have stimulated or facilitated agricultural growth directly. This does not mean that the governments' attitude to peasant agriculture was the same as its attitude to competitive industries. We shall deal with the imperialist state's policies to Indian industry elsewhere but it is necessary at this stage to take up some aspects of its policies to agriculture. British capital was, of course, by no means neutral as far as agriculture was concerned. The peasantry were not competitors but were customers for British industry and a certain agrarian prosperity was necessary to ensure social stability in the countryside. We have already mentioned some of the consequent policies with regard to agrarian relations. Additionally to this the state intervened in the construction of irrigation works, the reclamation of wasteland and contributed towards agricultural experimentation, education and extension. The record of the period of merchants' capital and of the East India Company's rule is not a particularly good one. With regard to State Irrigation the Company's 'practice of providing for such projects out of current revenue prevented any regularity or continuity of work and, on the contrary, often resulted in considerable waste from the suspension of valuable works already undertaken.'[103] The irrigation works in Madras were allowed to deteriorate to the detriment of production and the revenues, according to the Commissioners of Public Works for Madras in 1852. Again John Bright (of anti Corn Law League fame) speaking to the House of Commons in 1858 (24 June) commented that:

'The single city of Manchester in the supply of its inhabitants with the single article of water has spent a larger sum of money than the East Indian Company has spent in the last 14 years from 1834 to 1848 in public works of every kind throughout the whole of its vast dominions.'[104] But the Company did not totally neglect agriculture. They needed non-competitive goods to pay for the imports of manufactures and to remit the large volume of 'Home charges' against the Indian revenues. Agricultural experimentation under the British commenced with the establishment of the Botanical Gardens in Calcutta as early as 1786. Other gardens were established later (e.g. in Saharanpore in 1817 and in Dapooree near Poona in 1828) and they imported new plants from abroad and distributed improved varieties among the cultivators.[105]

After the end of the Company's rule state efforts to promote agrarian prosperity became somewhat more substantial—especially in the field of public works. In the last 25 years of the nineteenth century, the area irrigated by Government works increased by 8 million acres to about 18½ million acres for British India.[106] With an increase in private irrigation of over 3 million acres in the same period the total area under cultivation came to 44 million acres in round numbers—out of 226 million acres annually under crops in the irrigating provinces of British India.[107] These figures break down as follows:[108]

		% total irrigated area
State works		42.2
of which: canals	35.5	
tanks	6.7	
Private works		57.8
of which: canals	2.8	
tanks	11.8	
wells	29.2	
other sources	14.0	
		100.0

From the beginning of the twentieth century there is a further increase in irrigation—the Indian Irrigation Commission of 1901–03 recommending a programme of major works to cost Rs. 440 crores spread over 20 years. By the quinquennium ending 1921–22 the average acreage under irrigation by Government works in British India was 25 million acres rising to about 33 million acres for the quinquennium ending 1941–42.[109]

Apart from irrigation agricultural experimentation and extension services were also increased. The first experimental farm was started in Madras in 1865 and two in Bombay in 1869 and 1878. By the 1880's there was an agricultural college in Madras, Poona College of Science had agriculture as one of its branches and Bombay University gave a Diploma in Agriculture. Baroda had an agricultural College affiliated to Bombay University and Punjab a veterinary school.[110] Even so the scale of these efforts should not be overestimated. Government expenditure on agriculture in 1935/36 for instance was only Rs. 27 million—a tiny fraction of the total budget.[111]

Government efforts on irrigation should also be placed in their proper perspective. The main emphasis was, as has been explained, to improve the market—and it seems that expansion of the railways was a preferred method to more direct expenditure on agriculture. Throughout the latter part of the nineteenth century and into the twentieth there was a controversy as to whether railways or irrigation should be given priority in public works policy. R. C. Dutt, an early bourgeois nationalist, in his *Economic History of India in the Victorian Age* (2nd edition 1906) vigorously argued for an expansion of irrigation in preference to the railways. Citing evidence to a Select Committee in

1878 by Sir Arthur Cotton, Dutt pointed out that with a state guarantee of profits at 5 per cent or 4½ per cent on outlay in the building of railways the Treasury made a loss. On irrigation, however, the government made a net gain after interest charges on capital spent in construction.[113] But the government did not spend more on irrigation because:

'the Indian administration is very considerably influenced by the trend of public opinion in England, and not by the opinion of the people of India. Englishmen understand railways and do not understand the importance of irrigation for India. English manufacturers look to the opening of distant markets in India by means of railway extension. English merchants demand fresh facilities for trade with India by new lines of communication. British houses of trade influence Indian administration both through Parliament and by direct correspondence with the Indian Office. Members of Parliament urge the construction of new railway lines by frequent questions in the House of Commons.'[114]

When expanding trade brought a buoyant financial position to the Government of India prior to World War One the Government responded, it is true, with an increase in expenditure on irrigation—but with a far larger expenditure on the railways.[115]

Figures for Gross Investment

	Railways (*Rs. Millions*)	*Irrigation* (*Rs. millions*)
1900–01	83.7	24.1
1913–14	230.6	48.4

Bagchi argues that, looked at from the viewpoint of maximising revenue for the government, or from the viewpoint of providing the overhead capital for the development of agriculture and trade, the expenditure policy in these years was unduly conservative. The major irrigation works at the margin yielded much more than 7 per cent. The Government of India could raise loans in London at an average cost of 3 per cent to 4 per cent and in India at a slightly higher cost (3.5 to 4.5 per cent). 'The Mackay Committee of 1908 went into the question of the safe limits of borrowing by the Government of India in London and found that they could borrow £9 million in normal years, but the annual average of loans raised by the Government of India and the railways together in the London Market works out to £6,303,203 for the 15 years from 1900 to 1914.'[116]

It should also be noted that not all governmental efforts on irrigation were beneficial. The consequences of the public works policies of the British might have been less detrimental had they been concentrated, particularly in their pioneering stages, in uninhabited areas. However, 'the overwhelming proportion of "Saxon energy and British capital" introduced into India in the form of public works was concentrated in immediately productive areas. Schemes for the reclamation of wilderness and barren waste were less attractive to contemporary expansionist zeal.'[117] The disruptive effects on the ecological balances were sometimes extremely costly. Persistent heavy cropping under the stimulus to cultivate valuable commercial crops like sugar cane, opium, cotton and indigo brought a decline in fertility in areas like the irrigated Doab region in the U.P.[118] More serious still the canals disrupted the delicate mechanism of the hydrological cycle causing salination, creating malarial swamps and destroying well irrigation.[119] By the 1890's in the North West Provinces alone the area affected by salinity (reh) was estimated to cover 4,000 to 5,000 square miles. In the midst of this desolate land Voelker, the first agricultural chemist appointed by the Government of India to report on agrarian conditions, found patches of 'valuable' crops like opium, sugar cane, wheat, castor oil plant and cotton. They stood out 'like oases in the salt-covered desert around them.'[120]

The government's development of roads and railways added to the ecological upsets. The use of timber for constructing the railways and for fuel led to extensive deforestation in the Gangetic valley. Railway embankments cut across drainage channels causing swamping.

We have already seen how, in the context of a rising pressure of population on the land and the existing pattern of non-capitalist agrarian relations, British efforts to tamper with the structure of property rights to stimulate agricultural productivity came to nought. The permanent settlement did not produce the hoped for ploughing of private resources into the development of agriculture—rather the zamindars simply lived parasitically from the increasing rental. Again the trend to protect the upper strata of village society by the re-establishment of occupancy right did not lead significantly to expanded production from these groups—but simply their establishment as another intermediary layer between the actual cultivators and the state. In a similar way the government's direct efforts to stimulate agrarian productivity through irrigation, research and extension services were negated within the wider context of agrarian society. Stripped of resources by the moneylender trader and landlord the peasantry could not afford new techniques and new inputs like fertilizers and, living at the margin of subsistence the risk, was too great for them to experiment. New forms of parasitism developed along with the irrigation works—the peasants having to pay not just the Government's Irrigation Departments but also the illegal canal imposts collected by local officials from their 'clients'.[121] Even where irrigation works opened up previously uncultivated areas—where there was a similar pattern of agrarian relations the results were often disappointing. In the Canal Colonies of the Punjab the colonists fell into three catagories—'The small peasant proprietor, who is given a square of land, the yeoman farmer who receives four or five squares, and the landlord, the representative of the landed gentry, who may get anything from six to twenty squares.'[122] (A square is here about 25 acres—quite a large holding for the time.) While the peasant proprietors proved hard working and thrifty 'the other two classes of colonists, the yeoman and the landlord have not so far done very well'.[123] From the start they made indifferent colonists. An early report (which uses the term 'capitalist' to mean landlord) notes how 'With very rare exceptions the last thing the capitalist or yeoman contemplates is the spending of any large sum of money on the development of his grant. . . . They bring their land much more slowly under cultivation, they quarrel with their sub-tenants, they dispute endlessly amongst themselves . . . And it is impossible to get anything like the same amount of work out of them . . . as in the case of the peasant grantees.' Darling commented thirty years later that the situation had not changed much.

Conclusion

In the crisis of the Mughal Empire European merchants'

capital intervened to protect and extend its profits—supporting rival factions, exacerbating and accelerating the collapse of the Empire. British imperialism emerged dominant through the operations of the East India Company expropriating perhaps three-quarters of the warlord aristocracy and a large section of the local chieftainty. They used the revenues of the expropriated group to line the pockets of the English ruling class and to pay for the further expenses of conquest.

Subordination to an expanding industrial capitalist power had a number of profound effects upon the old mode of production. The expropriation of a part of the old ruling class led to the ruination of a section of the artisans catering to the needs of the aristocracy. Subsequently imports of manufactures from Britain began to undermine the position of the village artisans. As railways spread across the sub-continent from the mid-nineteenth century the reciprocal relationship between the village artisans and the peasantry was replaced by trade between the peasantry and the manufacturing centres—at first in Britain and later in India itself. The self-sufficiency of the village economy began to break down and it was sucked into the vortex of the world market and the expanding capitalist metropolis.

Commercialisation and monetisation brought with them increased powers and opportunities for moneylenders and traders who were able, to a much greater extent than before, to batten upon the peasantry as it became caught up in the intricacies and fluctuations of the market mechanism and in the new structure of property laws introduced by the British. By tampering with the structure of property rights the imperialists hoped to stimulate agrarian productivity and hence improve the rural market. They succeeded merely in giving a westernised flavour to the parasitism of rural society. At the top of rural society the remnants of the Mughal aristocracy, the village masters (maliks) and a new trader/moneylender/landlord grouping all waxed strong simultaneously with, and as a consequence of, the ruination of the bulk of rural society.

Imperialist rule brought new burdens to those at the bottom of rural society. Existing rights of possession and cultivation were undermined by the new market in land and the system of property laws introduced by the British. The decomposition of the rural social structure and the ruination of the lower strata in that structure was not accompanied, as in the metropolitan capitalist countries, by a dynamic accumulation process in industry drawing in the reserves of rural poor, expanding the marketing for agricultural products and promoting agricultural capitalism. Capitalist industrialisation was late due to the hostility of British imperialism and when it did come, after World War One it was weak and could not absorb much labour power. Meanwhile, the pressure of population on the land steadily increased—the ruined artisans had nowhere to go but to the land working on inferior terms as tenants or agricultural labourers of various types. The population increased as the death rate fell while the social and economic stagnation of rural society maintained the birth rate at a high level.

Habib describes how in the Mughal era the peasantry would often be able to escape the worst oppressions of the zamindars or jagirdars by migrating to other areas. This option was no longer open to the peasantry in the twentieth century. Where they had lost their rights to the land the peasants were compelled to accept high rents, low wages and high interest payments to the moneylenders given the competition for land jobs and credit.

'To a great extent the cultivator in India labours not for profit nor for a net return but for subsistence. The crowding of the people onto the land, the lack of alternative means of securing a living, the difficulty of finding any avenue of escape and the early age at which a man is burdened with dependants, combine to force the cultivator to grow food on whatever terms he can. Where his land has passed into the hands of his creditor no legislation will serve his need; no tenancy law will protect him; for food he needs land and for land he must plead before a creditor to whom he probably already owes more than the total value of his assets. That creditor is too often a landlord of a different class who has no natural or historical connection with his estate and is only interested in the immediate exploitation of the property in his control.'[125]

In this context agriculture stagnated. The capital stock in agriculture grew at a snail's pace.[126]

Growth of Capital Stock in Agriculture: All India

Years	*Index of Capital* 1950/51 = 100
1920–21	82.14
1925–26	83.26
1930–31	86.70
1935–36	85.55
1940–41	92.01
1945–46	93.94
1950–51	100.00

('Capital' refers to gross durable physical assets excluding land and houses and including irrigation, farm equipment and bullocks.)

From the time that figures for agricultural production became available at the beginning of the twentieth century there is little evidence of any substantial improvement. The main estimates are those of Blyn and Sivasubramonian. If, following Maddison, we combine Sivasubramonian's more optimistic estimate that cultivated area rose by 23 per cent (Blyn estimates 12.2 per cent) with Blyn's estimates of yields we get a roughly constant per capita figure for agricultural output between 1900 and 1946.[127]

NOTES

1 Prabhat Patnaik, 'The Political Economy of Underdevelopment' in *Bulletin of the Conference of Socialist Economists*, Spring 1972, p. 11.
2 Karl Marx, *Capital, Volume I*, p. 786.
3 *Ibid* p. 786.
4 Patnaik, *op. cit.*, pp. 9–13.
5 Jean Bailly and Patrick Florian 'L'exacerbation des contradiction dans les economies semi-industrialisées' in *Critiques de l'Economies Politique*, No. 3, April/June 1971, p. 39.
6 Patnaik, *op. cit.*, p. 11.
7 D. H. Buchanan, *op. cit.*, p. 90
8 Karl Marx in *Karl Marx on Colonialism and Modernisation* Shlomo Avineri (Ed.), Anchor Books, Garden City, N.Y., 1969, p. 102.
9 *Ibid* p. 103.

10 Quoted in B. B. Misra, *op. cit*., pp. 78–79.
11 *Ibid* p. 125.
12 Quoted in Ernest Mandel *Marxist Economic Theory,* Merlin, London 1968, p. 446.
13 W. W. Hunter 'The Annals of Rural Bengal' quoted in Habib, *Agrarian System* . . ., p. 39.
14 Quoted in R. P. Dutt, *India Today,* Left Book Club, London, 1940, p. 116.
15 Dharma Kumar, *op cit.*, p. 8–9, 107–109.
16 See for example the descriptions of rebellions in E. M. S. Namboodripad, *The National Question in Kerala,* Peoples Publishing House, Bombay 1952, Chapter VII—in particular pp. 94–96.
17 R. P. Dutt, *op. cit.*, p. 359. Also Michael Barratt Brown *After Imperialism,* Heinemann, London 1963, pp. 178–179.
18 Maddison, *Class Structure and Economic Growth, India and Pakistan since the Mughals,* London 1971, pp. 54–55.
19 W. W. Hunter, *The Indian Empire. Its History, People and Products,* London 1882, p. 469.
20 Maddison, *op. cit.*, p. 55.
21 Dispatch of Sir Charles Wood in Misra, *The Indian Middle Classes,* p. 155.
22 L. Jenks, *The Migration of British Capital to 1875,* London 1927, pp. 207–208.
23 A. K. Bagchi, 'Some International Foundations of Capitalist Growth and Underdevelopment', *Economic and Political Weekly* Special No. 1972, p. 1563.
24 Phyllis Deane and W. A. Cole, *British Economic Growth 1688–1959. Trends and Structure,* Cambridge 1964, p. 262.
25 Ernest Mandel, *Marxist Economic Theory,* Merlin 1968, p. 444.
26 Bagchi, *op. cit.*, p. 1563.
27 Maddison, *op. cit.*, p. 65.
28 Hunter, *op. cit.*, p. 470.
29 Karl Marx, *Karl Marx on Colonialism and Modernisation, op. cit.*, p. 105.
30 R. P. Dutt, *op. cit.*, p. 124. Hunter, *op. cit.*, p. 448.
31 R. P. Dutt, *op. cit.*, p. 126.
32 Crawford in K. N. Chaudhuri Ed. *The Economic Development of India Under the East Indian Company 1814–1858. A Selection of Contemporary Writings,* Cambridge 1971, p. 241.
33 Hunter, *op. cit.*, p. 469.
34 Quoted in Chaudhuri, *op. cit.*, p. 27.
35 E. A. Gait, *Census of India 1911,* Vol. I, Part I. Report, Calcutta 1913, p. 409.
36 *Report on the Census of British India 1881,* Vol. I, H.M.S.O., London 1883, pp. 399–400.
37 *Ibid* pp. 400–401.
38 J. H. Hutton, *Census of 1931* Vol. I. Part 1. Report, Delhi 1933, p. 296.
39 P. C. Joshi *The Decline of Indigenous Handicrafts in Uttar Pradesh,* Indian Economic and Social History Review, Vol. 1, No. 1, July/September 1963, Table III, p. 34.

40 Buchanan, *op. cit.*, p. 75.

41 Figures from Sivasubramonian quoted in Maddison, *op. cit.*, p. 62.

42 Indian Institute of Public Opinion (I.I.P.O.) *Monthly Commentary on Indian Economic Conditions*, Annual No. 1971, 'A Blueprint for Indian Employment', p. 86.

43 D. Kumar, *op. cit.*, p. 167.

44 K. Davis, *The population of India and Pakistan,* Princeton 1951, p. 42.

45 M. D. Morris, 'Trends and Tendencies in Indian Economic History', *I.E.S.H.R.* Vol. V No. 4, December 1968, p. 368.

46 Maddison, *op. cit.*, p. 164.

47 *Ibid* p. 53.

48 Quoted in Kumar, *op. cit.*, p. 107.

49 Davis, *op. cit.*, p. 28.

50 *Ibid* p. 28.

51 Biblab Dasgupta, 'Population Policy. The Crucial Factor', *South Asian Review*, Vol. 3. No. 4, July 1970, p. 333.

52 *Ibid* p. 337.

53 *Ibid* p. 344. Also Bipan Chandra 'Reinterpretation of Nineteenth Century Indian Economic History,' *I.E.S.H.R.*, March 1968, pp. 72–73.

54 The Table is from Dasgupta, *op. cit.,* p. 332.

55 Habib, *Agrarian System . . .*', p. 22.

56 Davis, *op. cit.*, pp. 207–208.

57 Utsa Patnaik 'On the Mode of Production in Indian Agriculture' *E. and P. W. Review of Agriculture.* September 1972, p. A146.

58 Misra, *op. cit.*, pp. 123–127.

59 Quoted in Bhowani Sen, *Evolution of Agrarian Relations in India,* P.P.H., New Delhi 1962, p. 64. Also see Misra, *op. cit.*, pp. 127–133.

60 Daniel Thorner 'Long Term Trends in Output in India', in Kuznets, Moore and Spengler (Eds.), *Economic Growth: Brazil, India, Japan,* Durham N.C., 1955, p. 124.

61 Kumar, *op. cit.*, pp. 77–78.

62 *Ibid* pp. 87–89.

63 Quoted in *ibid*, p. 81.

64 *Ibid* pp. 81–82.

65 R. C. Dutt, *The Economic History of India in the Victorian Age,* Volume II. Routledge and Kegan Paul, London. Reprint of 1906. Edition, p. 136.

66 Ravindar Kumar, 'The Rise of the Rich Peasants in Western India', in *Soundings in South Asian History,* D. A. Low. (Ed.), London 1968, pp. 25–55.

67 D. H. Buchanan, *op. cit.*, p. 130.

68 Bhowani Sen, *Evolution of Agrarian Relations in India,* P.P.H., New Delhi 1962, pp. 81–88, Utsa Patnaik, 'Development of Capitalism in Agriculture—I', *Social Scientist*, September 1972, p. 19. H. Calvert, *The Wealth and Welfare of the Punjab*, Lahore 1936, p. 246. See M. L. Darling, *The Punjab Peasant in Prosperity and Debt* for the role of the moneylender prior to, and after, the British, pp. 176–185.

69 Elizabeth Whitcombe *Agrarian Conditions in Northern India,*

Volume I. The U.P. under British Rule, 1860–1900. University of California Press, London 1972, p. 14.

70 S. S. Thorburn *Musalmans and Money-Lenders in the Punjab,* William Blackward, London 1886, p. 48.

71 Sir John Strachey in 1859 quoted in Thorburn p. 67.

72 Calvert, *op. cit.*, p. 254.

73 *Ibid* p. 263.

74 *Report of Indian Famine Commission* 1901. G.O.I. Nainital, 1901, p. 168.

75 Figures from S. J. Patel in B. Sen, *op. cit.*, p. 146.

76 Misra, *op. cit.*, p. 131.

77 A. Ghosh *The Impact of Commercial Growth on Agricultural Tenure Systems in India.* Manchester School, Vol. 23, May 1955, p. 187.

78 *Ibid* p. 187–188.

79 *Ibid* p. 186.

80 Utsa Patnaik, 'Development of Capitalism in Agriculture', p. 20.

81 *Ibid* p. 20.

82 Dharma Kumar, *op. cit.*, chapter IV, pp. 62–63.

83 Patnaik, *op. cit.*, p. 20.

84 *Ibid* p. 20.

85 Utsa Patnaik 'Capitalist Development in Agriculture—A Note'. E. and P. W. September 25th, 1971. Review of Agriculture pp. A124–A126. Also in Patnaik, 'Development . . .', p. 21.

86 Patnaik, 'Capitalist Development in Agriculture—A Note', p. A147.

87 Quoted in Thorburn, *op. cit.*, p. 65.

88 Superintendent to the West Bengal Census of 1951 quoted in B. Sen, *op. cit.*, p. 119.

89 Misra, *op. cit.*, p. 138.

90 A. R. Desai, *Social Background of Indian Nationalism,* 3rd Edition 1959, Popular Book Depot, Bombay p. 173. Also U. Patnaik, 'Development . . .', p. 19.

91 John R. McLane, 'Peasants, Moneylenders and Nationalists at the End of the Nineteenth Century', *I.E.S.H.R.* Vol I, p. 71.

92 *The Famine Inquiry Commission,* Final Report 1945, G.O.I. Madras 1945, pp. 250–251.

93 P. D. Reeves, 'Landlords and Party Politics in the United Provinces 1934–1937' in *Soundings in South Asian History* Low Ed., pp. 262–263.

94 R. P. Dutt, *op. cit.*, pp. 394–400.

95 F. G. Bailey, *Caste and the Economic Frontier,* Manchester University Press 1957, p. 269.

96 From R. Mukherjee, 'Dynamics of Rural Society', in Desai, *Rural Sociology in India,* Bombay Popular Prakashan, 4th Edition, 1969, p. 285.

97 Kathleen Gough in *Ibid*, pp. 345–353.

98 Quoted in Walter C. Neal, *op. cit.*, p. 203.

99 Preface to R. C. Dutt, *op. cit.*, pp. x xiii. The heavy nature of the land revenue demand is a recurrent theme throughout Dutt's book.

100 D. Kumar, *op. cit.*, p. 114.

101 B. B. Misra, *op. cit.*, p. 263.

102 Maddison, *op. cit.*, p. 48.

103 Report of the Public Works Department 1860/61 in Helen B. Lamb 'The State and Economic Development in India' in Kuznets, Moore and Spengler, *Economic Growth, Brazil, India and Japan*, Durham, NC, 1955, pp. 470–471.
104 R. C. Dutt, *op. cit.*, p. 364.
105 R. P. Sinha 'Completing Ideology and Agricultural Strategy. Current Agricultural Development in India and China Compared with Meiji Strategy'. Paper to the *Third European Conference of Modern South Asian Studies.* Mimeo 1972. p. 11.
106 *Report of the Indian Irrigation Commission* 1901–03, G.O.I., Calcutta 1903, p. 25.
107 *Ibid* p. 12.
108 *Ibid* p. 11.
109 *Famine Inquiry Commission (1945)*, pp. 129–130.
110 R. P. Sinha, *op. cit.*, p. 12.
111 Lamb, *op. cit.*, p. 490.
112 R. C. Dutt, *op. cit.*, p. 353.
113 *Ibid* p. 365 and pp. 545–546.
114 *Ibid* pp. 545–546.
115 A. K. Bagchi, *Private Investment in India 1900–1939*, Cambridge University Press 1972, p. 41.
116 *Ibid* p. 42.
117 Elizabeth Whitcombe, *op. cit.*, p. 96.
118 *Ibid* p. 8.
119 *Ibid* p. 9
120 *Ibid* p. 11.
121 *Ibid* p. 10.
122 M. L. Darling, *op. cit.*, p. 122.
123 *Ibid* p. 123.
124 Quoted in *Ibid*, p. 124.
125 *Royal Commission on Agriculture in India 1928.* Cmnd. 3123 p. 433.
126 Table cited in Paresh Chattopadyay 'Mode of Production in Indian Agriculture—An Anti-Kritik', *E. and P. W.*, December 30th 1972, *Review of Agriculture*, p. A191.
127 Maddison, *op. cit.*, p. 52.

CHAPTER IV

The Development of the Capitalist Mode of Production

So far we have examined the disintegration and transformation of the old mode of production—the decay of indigenous petty industry and the commercialisation and transformation of the peasant economy. We now turn to the development of capitalism in India itself—to examine the nature of that capitalist development and in particular to explain its limitations and its inability to absorb the surplus population produced by the stagnation and decay of the artisan sector and population growth.

Imperialist rule in India as Marx stressed in his writings on the subject had a dual effect.[1] On the one hand as we have seen the pre-capitalist mode of production would very likely not have developed towards capitalist production and imperialist rule made possible such a development. On the other hand imperialist rule—by subordinating Indian economic development to the interests of the British capitalist class restricted the basis upon which capitalist production could develop in India—above all it restricted competitive industrialisation.

The key element in the subordination of Indian economic development to the interests of the British capitalist class was, of course, the colonial state. Because of the crucial effect of the policies of the colonial state in the development of capitalism in India we shall make this the first item of the analysis.

The Policies of the Colonial State—Between the End of Company Rule and World War One

The rise of the manufacturing interest in Britain brought with it the break up of the Company's trade monopoly and a new stage in the imperialist relationship. It is erroneous to suggest

available to the government given its existing financial commitments—for India had to bear 'preposterous' burdens. The revenues of the Government of India had to meet the costs of the conquest, administration and defence of the sub-continent as well as the debts run up in these projects.

'The cost of the Mutiny, the price of the transfer of the Company's right to the Crown, the expenses of simultaneous wars in China and Abyssinia, every governmental item down to the fees of the charwoman in the Indian Office . . .'[11] These included the cost of a ball for the Sultan of Turkey when he came to London in 1868, a lunatic asylum in Ealing, gifts to members of the Zanzibar mission, diplomatic expenses of Britain of the British in Persia and China, part of the cost of the Mediterranean fleet and of communications between Britain and India. The net result of all this brought into existence a home debt of £30,000,000 between 1857 and 1860 alone.[12]

But the lack of finance was by no means the main problem. If the imperial state had had different priorities India would not have borne such 'preposterous' burdens and resources would have been made available—as they were for the lavish construction of the railways. When the Government of India's financial position was less strained—as in the period up to World War One—the position did not improve substantially. Under the buoyancy of an economy stimulated by expanding trade the Government of India's revenues were swelled and the budget was in surplus for every year between 1898/9 and 1913/14 except for 1908/9. The Government was thus given an opportunity to spend more on industrial development without breaking the canon of sound finance of balancing the budget. In actual fact, however, the aid given to Indian industry in this period of healthy finances was miniscule. Education expenditure rose from Rs. 20.46 millions in 1903/4 to Rs. 24.49 millions in 1905/6 and this in a budget where total expenditure or revenue account was in excess of Rs. 840 millions. The lack of technical education remained a problem for Indian industries. By way of contrast during this period the gross investment on the railways rose from Rs. 83.7 millions in 1900–1 to Rs. 230.6 millions in 1913/14.[13] In the same period Small Departments of Industries were established in Madras and U.P. to provide improved industrial methods and techniques.

However these 'aroused the opposition of the local European commercial community who interpreted them as a serious menace to private enterprise and an unwarranted intervention on the part of the State into matters beyond the sphere of Government'. As a result they were squashed by Lord Morley in 1910.[14]

Colonial Policies during and after World War One

The policy of free trade lasted up to World War One but with the war a new phase in the imperialist relationship opened. British imperialism was progressively weakened and the colonial state could no longer ignore the demands of the Indian bourgeosie. There were basically three reasons for the change in policy and the limited support to industrialisation.

Inter-imperialist warfare made it necessary to introduce a limited industrialisation for military and strategic reasons as well as facilitating that process with a very effective form of protection—in the form of U-boats rather than tariffs.

'Warships and U-boats of the Central Powers lay in around the volcanic island in the Straits of Messina and picked off at their convenience the Allied cargo boats as fast as they came along. Nothing could get through. The English and the French desperately needed steel for use in the East and needed it, so to speak on the spot. That meant Tata's. They vitally needed shells and that meant Tata's too . . .'[15] After the war, Britain had learned its lesson. 'Under the pressure of war necessities (the) Government was driven to abandon its former attitude of aloofness, if not jealousy towards purely Indian enterprise.'[16] The second reason for the change in policy was related closely to the first—for reasons of maintaining inner political stability during the wartime and in the troubled times after the war it was essential to secure the co-operation of the Indian bourgeoisie. For this purpose economic and political concessions were made to them.[17]

The third reason was economic—Britain was in any case losing its grip on the Indian market to foreign competitors. By 1914 Britain's share of the Indian market was already on the decline—from 82 per cent of India's imports in 1874/79 to two-thirds in 1914.[18] In November, 1915 Lord Hardinge wrote in a dispatch to the Secretary of State for India 'It is becoming increasingly clear that a definite and self-conscious policy of improving the industrial capabilities of India will have to be pursued after the war unless she is to become the dumping ground for the manufactures of foreign nations . . .'[19] Tariffs were to help Britain direct and finance development insofar as it did take place. Moreover, the creation of tariffs prepared the way for a policy of imperial preference to protect the Indian market for British manufacturers.[20]

Many of the espoused good intentions of wartime came to nothing after the troubles of war had faded into the background. The policy of 'discriminating protection' adopted by the Government of India was a piecemeal one and no general policy of industrialisation was followed. Effective protection was given sparingly to different industries, the Tariff Board took a long time to process cases for protection, and the Government of India was not bound to accept its conclusions. Effective protection in the twenties was given only to the steel industry and some branches of mechanical engineering, paper and matches.[21]

The hallmark of tariff policy became Imperial Preference just as it had once been Free Trade. At the Ottawa Trade Agreement of 1932 the duty on Japanese and other non-British cotton goods was raised to 50 per cent (and even for a period in 1933 to 75 per cent) while the duty on British cotton goods was lowered to 20 per cent. Though the Indian Legislative Assembly threw out the Trade Agreement of January 1935 (extending the Ottawa Agreement) by a vote of 66 to 58, the vote was overridden by the British Government which enforced the agreement.[22]

Other schemes like the plan for a network of provincial Departments of Industries suggested by the Indian Industrial Commission Report of 1918 came to little. These cropped up in a variety of provinces after the war but they suffered from the beginning from a shortage of staff and were hit by financial retrenchments in 1924. In any case their help went mainly to small scale industries and 'they had neither the financial and administrative resources nor the control over matters of basic policy necessary to make a significant impact on the pace of development of large scale industries.' The recommendations about industrial banking also came to nothing.[23]

In other respects also the Government's policy after the war offset the effects of protection. The war had severely strained the finances of the Government and led to an increase in borrowing which, given inflation and the collapse of a very feverish post-war boom, led to private misgivings about the Government's fiscal policies. The Government of India appointed a retrenchment Committee which recommended drastic cuts in public expenditure. From 1923–24 onwards, partly as a result of improved economic conditions, the Government of India had reasonably large surpluses on its current account but nonetheless its policies remained restrictive.[24] So, for instance, in the 1935/36 budget the total shown below spent on 'nation building' activities came to less than 10 per cent of the budget and as can be seen expenditure on industry was a mere fraction of this.

	Rs. millions
Agriculture	27
Industry	9
Scientific Departments	7
Medical and Public Health	55
Education—mostly at the Secondary and College level	122

In addition, government monetary policy had a deflationary bias—particularly the overvaluation of the Rupee. Following the instability and uncertainty of the value of the rupee after the war the Royal Commission on Indian Currency and Finance recommended that the rupee value be fixed at 1s. 6d. Indian business opinion rejected the 1s. 6d. rate and felt 1s. 4d. more appropriate. They were overruled. A fall in the exchange rate from 1s. 6d. to 1s. 4d. would have been an 11 per cent devaluation and would have given Indian manufacturers an advantage over importers.[26] But the British had other interests. By maintaining the higher level the government minimised the sterling costs of its commitments and its purchases from the United Kingdom. It enabled British residents in India and those on Indian pensions in the U.K. to get 11 per cent more sterling for their rupees.[27] The overvaluation of the exchange rate greatly hindered Indian exports, particularly those sold against Chinese and Japanese competition, and Indian exports fell between 1913 and 1937 from $786 millions to $717 millions.[28] At Independence exports constituted less than 5 per cent of the National Income.

It is also probably true that the overvaluation of the exchange rate could be maintained only by some fiscal and monetary deflation.[29]

With the onset of Depression the deflationary policies were resumed. The Imperial Bank of India raised interest rates from 5 per cent in July 1930 to 7 per cent in August 1931 and finally up to 8 per cent when Britain went off the gold standard. Though rates fell later and though there followed a period of easier money the deflationary policies probably 'largely smothered' extra protective measures that were taken in 1930 and 1931.[30]

The Development of Capitalist Production up to World War One

It is within this context of subordination to the interest of British capital manifested in the policies of the imperialist state that we should understand the low rate of capitalist accumulation and the orientation of this accumulation.

Competitive industrialisation was largely ruled out by the absence of protection to infant industries and the government neglect of necessary infrastructural facilities. Rungta argues that of the annual average import value of Rs. 700 millions for the last decade of the nineteenth century much of what was imported could have been produced in India.

'Assuming that only two-thirds of these imports could have been manufactured locally, this alone would have absorbed capital to the extent of Rs. 1,400 million given the usual capital output ratio of 3 : 1 and ignoring multiplier and accelerator effects. Against this the capital employed in the industrial sector of India at the end of the last century amounted to only about Rs. 400 millions'—in other words there was a possibility of a three to four fold growth.[31]

The only industry of any significance to develop in these circumstances serving the home market was the cotton textile industry based upon Bombay, and this industry developed in the teeth of opposition by British textile manufacturers. When the industry began to develop in the 1860's, when there were a mere 8 mills in Bombay, a strong protest was lodged in the British Parliament. A Member complained of the 'mania for cotton manufacturing in India' and of 'forcing capital into unnatural channels'.[32] But not till the 1870's was the new industry in India seen as a severe threat to Lancashire. In January 1871 the Manchester Chamber of Commerce sent in a strong memorial to the Secretary of State for India about the basis of valuation of the cotton duty and in July 1877 the House of Commons adopted the following resolution *unanimously* 'That in the opinion of this House, the duties now levied upon Cotton Manufactures imported into India, being protective in their nature, are contrary to sound commercial policy and ought to be replaced without delay, as soon as the financial conditions in India will permit.'[33]

A climate of opinion was stirred up which strongly discouraged British entrepreneurs participating in the development of the industry—such persons were regarded as profoundly unpatriotic. Of course, there were divisions of interest in the British capitalist class in so far as machine making firms benefited from, and hence co-operated in, the development of the industry. However, feelings became so strong against betraying 'English interests' that machine manufacturers would sometimes be forced to discriminate against Indian manufacturers. Tata, for instance, reported that an English manufacturer of textile carding machines asked more in India than in England for his machines. When Tata protested 'he answered me bluntly that he must, as an Englishman, decidedly favour Lancashire in his prices compared with the prices he received from his Indian customers.'[34]

Another manifestation of this same opposition came in 1874 when financial requirements led to the reimposition of a general import duty including upon imports of cotton goods of 5 per cent ad valorem. However, to propitiate Manchester a countervailing Excise duty of 5 per cent was placed upon yarns produced in Indian mills which could compete with Lancashire yarns. This was subsequently extended to an excise duty on all Indian woven cloths. In vain did the representatives of the Indian bourgeoisie protest that:

'As an example of fiscal injustice, the Indian Act of 1896 is unexampled in any civilised country in modern times. Most civilised governments protect their home industries by prohibitive duties on foreign goods. The most thorough of Free Trade Governments do not excise home manufactures when imposing a moderate customs duty on imported goods, for the purpose of revenue.'[35]

Nevertheless the cotton textile industry, predominantly under Indian ownership did become established and it continued haltingly to make progress. The necessary conditions for capitalist production under indigenous ownership and control were all present. Firstly the necessary primary accumulations of money capital which could be converted into productive capital were available to the merchants of Bombay from their accumulations acquired in external trade. Bombay did not experience a reckless plundering of its economy in the late eighteenth and early nineteenth century and its merchants were not reduced to the status of mere junior partners to the British. In this respect Bombay differed from Bengal and the difference stems from the fact that the regions neighbouring upon Bombay were not conquered by the Company until into the second decade of the nineteenth century. This was in a period when industrial rather than merchants' capital was dominant in Indian policy. During their struggle with the Marathas the British needed the Parsis and other trading communities as collaborators and sometimes financiers so these trading communities were able to remain in the lucrative import-export trade in cottons and opium. Here they made the necessary accumulations for ploughing into the first cotton mills.[36] The second condition facilitating the start of capitalist production was the availability of the necessary equipment and technology which could be bought abroad despite a certain amount of hostility. Thirdly the necessary supply of unskilled labour existed in relatively plentiful supply. Fortunately the industry required but little skilled labour for this was in a far more scarce supply. Fourthly the industry could find a market for its products. Indian manufacturers had a competitive advantage in the production of coarser varieties of textiles and the demand came from private Indian consumers—they were not dependant upon a state with a niggardly purchasing policy. So a market existed even without tariffs and government purchases.[37] Having said this it should be noted that it was the limitation of the market that acted as the main restraint on the growth of the industry. Difficulty of competing, particularly with higher grades of British products, together with the poverty of the Indian market led to heavy dependence on the Chinese and Japanese markets from as early as the 1870's. The process of expansion had a very halting character. New capacity would be added to the industry and the ability of the market to absorb supply at a profitable level of prices would be overshot. In 1888/89, for example, several mills were formed and the result was that in the next year the Chinese market was glutted with stock. This situation continued till mid 1890 when arrangements to close the mills reduced the stocks in China. In 1890/91 the situation repeated itself again when the number of mills jumped from 114 to 125. Again the mills had to be closed down for two days a week.[38] The market situation became more difficult after the 1890's in foreign markets due to Japanese competition in Japan itself, and in China, in the sale of yarn and crude piece goods. Indian yarn exports to Japan fell from 8,400 tons in 1890 to practically nothing in 1898. Up to the Sino-Japanese War of 1894–5 India supplied 96 per cent of Chinese yarn imports, the U.K. 4 per cent and Japan none. Within three years Japan was supplying one-quarter of Chinese imports and by 1914 India exported less yarn to China than Japan. The decline in overseas sales due to Japanese competition continued during and after World War One. The cotton textile industry had to expand mainly by a slow process of import substitution in the Indian market. In 1896 Indian mills supplied 8 per cent total cloth consumption, in 1913 20 per cent.[39]

In the nineteenth century the cotton textile industry was the only one of any significance orientated to the domestic market. But state policy and the growing dynamic trade relations between Britain and India provided the basis for a sector of capitalist production orientated to the growing external sector which was primarily non-competitive with, and complementary to, the imperial metropolis. Investment took place in the various plantation industries—in tea, jute, coffee and indigo, as well as banking, insurance and steamship companies. There was also some investment in domestic type activities but these, too, actually represented a vertical diversification process supporting the export and import trade at the end of the line.[40] Thus the coal mining companies were initially opened up to provide coal for the shipping and tugboat companies and later for the railways.[41]

The initial money capital for these early ventures was mostly provided by the Company's servants ploughing back not a little of plunder accumulated from their trading activities. 'It would be difficult to find a parallel in economic history anywhere for such direct participation by the military and civil servants of a government in trade generally and in the growth of joint stock companies in particular. The key to this peculiarity lies in the privileged private trade permitted to the Company's servants which enabled them to amass fabulous wealth. As their gains could not always easily be sent to England, they sought safe and profitable investments in India.'[42]

The size of European investment grew significantly only after the complete abolition of the Company's monopoly in 1833. A drive was made to encourage European investments in the plantations industry so as to find the counterbalance in which to pay for the rising import of finished manufactures from Britain and also the supply of goods in which to remit the 'Home Charges' which accounted for the balance of exports over imports sent to Britain. The Charter Act of 1833 permitted Europeans to buy land though the Company was at first reticent over this. Not till 1837 did the Company issue orders granting lands to Europeans and even at this stage Europeans purchasing land were not allowed to be absentee landlords.[43]

The main field for investment at the beginning of the nineteenth century was indigo. The history of the indigo industry is an interesting one because it illustrates the principle that the establishment of capitalist production must involve the expropriation of the means of production and subsistence from the hands of the direct producers.[44] While the primary accumulations of money capital were available to the planters from their own trade profits, from Indian and European Houses of Agency, the social preconditions of capitalist production were not present at the beginning of the century. In the main areas of indigo cultivation the peasants still possessed their own means of production. For this reason the planters had to use violence and oppression to get the peasants 'to produce indigo at prices much less than remunerative'. The mode of exploitation was essentially that of merchant's capital. Thereafter a process of expropriation of the peasantry got under way. In order to fully control the agricultural operations a variety of schemes were tried to bind the peasants to the will of the planter. The principal one was that of debt bondage. Naturally the peasantry wanted to be left alone and debt bondage had to be forced upon it. 'The success of the debt system was possible only by the practice of both deceit and oppression.'[45] There were periodic rebellions but these were to no avail. The 'civilising mission' of capital could not be held back and as a result of a long process the peasantry were expropriated by the capitalists. 'From independent merchants buying finished indigo, the indigo dealers had become, by a gradual process of evolution covering roughly a century, owners of land and independent producers with every stage of the process under their control.'[46] Then capitalist competition took its own toll. Synthetic dyes replaced indigo and the whole business passed into extinction.

In response to the growing export demand tea, coffee and rubber plantations were also established. Tea was the most important. Much of the tea land was reclaimed from unused jungle so there were not the same problems in the tea industry as in indigo. However, the tea industry was a labour intensive one and there were problems of labour recruitment because the plantations were situated in the thinly populated areas of Assam. All kinds of trickery and deception were used to get coolies to go to the plantations. Once they were there they were treated 'not unlike prisoners.'[47] The planters were given powers of criminal prosecution to keep the coolies on the estates and they flogged and killed dissenters. But, as enlightened employers know, contented cows give more milk, so conditions improved.

It is interesting to note that, once again, the key limitation on the expansion of the tea industry was the market. The growth of the tea industry frequently exceeded the growth of demand and brought several periods of acute depression.

Apart from tea, the other major industries of Bengal in the nineteenth and early twentieth century were jute and coal. The jute industry was also restrained by the lack of markets and grew slowly in the face of competition from Dundee and the limited world demand for jute manufactures.

The industry ran into difficulties with over-production from 1884–5 onwards, some mills were closed down and for five years from February 1886 the mills worked only 4 to 4½ days instead of seven. It ran into similar problems (compounded by earthquake, famine and plague) from 1896.[48]

As this industry was actually established in competition with British manufacturers its establishment in India (as an extension of the production of raw jute there) calls for some explanation. Its establishment may possibly have been due to higher wages in Britain 'trade union organisation and the growing solidarity of the British workers in the nineteenth century were forcing the jute manufacturers to yield to the demand for better wages and more humane conditions, they found that by transferring their capital to India and building jute mills there, they could increase the rate of exploitation by getting destitute Indian ex-peasants to work for them for almost nothing . . .'[49] the jute industry represented a kind of industry typical in 'underdeveloped' countries—instead of crude primary products being exported the primary product is processed and the manufactured goods exported.[50]

As has already been mentioned the coal industry represented a derived demand from the other industries and the needs of the navigation companies and the railways. It grew as these industries did and also when high freight rates for coal fell with the building of the railways.[51]

By the end of the nineteenth century India's capitalist sector had expanded considerably—but considering this was an expansion from a negligible base it was still tiny in relation to the economy as a whole. The industrial pattern was largely based upon coal mining, cotton textiles, jute textiles, railways and allied workshops, some foundries and metallurgical plants and ordinance factories. There was also a relatively rapid growth of tea plantations, shipping and dockyards, insurance and banking facilities.[52] The paid up capital of Joint Stock Companies in operation in 1902–3 was as follows:[53]

	£,000
Banking and insurance:	3,308
Trading and shipping:	4,861
Mining and Quarrying:	1,671
Mills and presses:	12,714
Tea and Planting:	2,438

This growth of the capitalist production was consolidated in the first decade of the twentieth century and up to World War One with a stimulus to investment in such industries as jute manufactures, tea and coal coming from expanding exports and foreign trade. Both total exports and total imports of India expanded by more than 100 per cent over the period 1900–13 and the net gross barter terms of trade improved considerably. In cotton textiles Japanese competition in foreign markets was offset by rising import substitution and possibly rising per capita incomes, though foodgrain prices were rising in the period and this must have hit poorer groups.[54]

Before World War One in 1912 the Indian Steel industry was established by J. N. Tata in Jamsedpur. 'It is indeed difficult to imagine the Tata venture, which was to prove a roaring success eventually as anything but a happy historical accident. Two early failures, the enormous task of organisation (of both technical know-how and finance) and prospecting for a suitable site—all these would have ruled out any entrepreneurical attempt except the visionary.'[55]

Capitalist Production during and after World War One

The war brought with it an expanded demand for the products of capitalist industry—jute, coal and steel feeding the war machine—and providing an effective protection for the Indian market—stimulating cotton textiles which expanded with the absence of textile imports. However, war protection for the Indian market stopped supplies of imported means of production getting through and so restrained the growth of capacity in industry. After the war, as has been shown, government policy towards industrialisation had changed (albeit very stingily with the government's other economic policies offsetting the beneficial effects of tariffs) and this had some effect in stimulating the growth of industry catering for the internal market. The cotton textile industry remained the most important internally orientated industry expanding its share of the domestic market for cloth from 20 per cent in 1913 to 62 per cent in 1936 and 76 per cent in 1945.[56] In addition factory industry had expanded and diversified into minerals and metals; food, drink and tobacco; chemicals and dyes; paper and printing; processes relating to wood, stone, glass, skins and hides within a decade after the war.[57] While industries under Indian control orientated to the Indian market expanded in the interwar period the export orientated sector primarily based upon Bengal and under British ownership (coal, tea, jute) was badly hit by the doldrums of the twenties and thirties and stagnated. The world agricultural recession had already set in by 1926 and the total exports of India that had increased after the war up to 1924/25 declined thereafter and stagnated till 1928/29 after which they declined drastically.[58]

By contrast the domestically orientated industries remained surprisingly buoyant in some years of the depression: 'aggregate private investment in real terms during some years of the depression was higher than during the middle years of the twenties and the aggregate internal demand for certain commodities such as refined sugar and cotton piecegoods was surprisingly well maintained.' The explanation is probably in terms of the drastic change of the terms of trade between industry and agriculture in favour of industry, the fact that the commodities sold by industry were in the nature of necessities and hence had a low income elasticity of demand, the fact that in any case agriculture was still largely uncommercialised so was not too badly hit by price falls and, of course, the effects of increased protection in the 1930's.[59]

The Second World War brought another short lived stimulus to demand but once again this increased demand could not be converted into investment in expanded capacity due to transport bottlenecks in the imports of producer goods.

The following brief table taken from Sivasubramonium[60] sums up the expansion in capitalist production in factory establishments in the last half-century of British rule.

	Employment (thousands)	*Value Added (in 1938 Rs.)*
Average 1900 & 1901	601	379
Average 1945 & 1946	*2,983	2,461

*incl. plantations

In terms of value added the important industries in 1946 is cotton textiles (46.01 per cent of value added in the 1946 Census of Manufacturing Industries)—jute textiles (17.49 per cent of value added) sugar, vegetable oils, iron and steel and general engineering. In terms of employment the same industries were prominent—cotton textiles providing 44.38 per cent and jute textiles 22.22 per cent.[61]

The Relations between British and Indian Capital and the Genesis of the Indian National Bourgeoisie

So far in our analysis of Indian capitalist development little mention has been made of the division of ownership and the direction of that development between British and indigenous capital—and the relations that existed between the two. It should be evident however that imperialist capital was mainly well established in the externally orientated sector—in plantations, jute and coal and the trading and banking infrastructure established to service this sector. The predominant form of business organisation underlying this development and perpetuating the subordination of Indian to British capital was that of the managing agency system. The managing agencies began basically as traders and later became organisers and managers of industry —trade surpluses being employed in the extension of industrialised enterprise under the management and control of the pioneering firm.[62] The managing agencies which thus grew out of the key dynamic element of the economy—international trade mainly under foreign control—retained their power through their quasi-monopoly in the access to sources of funds, supplies and markets via their close links with British banks, insurance and shipping companies. The initial advantage of the managing agency system was that it provided centralised sources for procuring staff, equipment, finance and a variety of specialised services in a country new to capitalist enterprises where these were not available.[63] The managing agencies provided the advantages of self-sufficiency within their own group and provided a substantial market within their own operations. Thus 'Martin Burns' steel output went largely into their railway engineering workshop which served their large railway interests, alternatively into their constructional activity which found further support in their cement interests and so on. Andrew Yules' jute mills required electricity and coal supplies which in turn required engineering facilities, transport and a host of ancillary materials and services to be found within that complex.'[64]

So the managing agencies were initially a logical outgrowth of the colonial economy lacking infrastructural development and geared to foreign trade—but they were able to retain their dominance at the expense of Indian capital by virtue of their monopolistic positions and links with the colonial government. Even where Indian enterprise did succeed in establishing industrial enterprise it was largely staffed by Europeans appointed by managing agencies. In 1895 42 per cent of the managerial and supervisory staff of the Bombay textile mills were English even though the plants were owned by Indian capital. As late as 1925 the proportion was still 28 per cent.[65] While Indian managing agencies with a greater emphasis on industry in their interests also developed the British ones remained very powerful. This is revealed from the following table derived from evidence to the Tariff Board's Cotton Textile Enquiry of 1927. The table covered 99 per cent of Bombay's cotton mills.[66]

	Mills	*Spindles*	*Looms*	*Capital (in million Rs.)*
Cos. with English Managing Agents (9):	27	1,112,114	22,121	98.9 (50.3%)
Cos. with Indian Managing Agents (32):	56	2,360,528	51,580	97.7 (49.7%)

The agencies were often able to take decisions favourable to their own interests rather than the interests of the shareholders—many agencies were remunerated for their managerial services by a commission on output rather than a share of profits. This tended to result in output being expanded beyond the limits of the market resulting in chronic overproduction. During World War One, however, there was a tendency to change in the period of boom to a percentage of profits so as to allow the agents a larger share of war time profits.[67] Again in the depression 'There have been a few cases in which these agents have turned their loans to the mills into debentures, with the result that the concerns have passed into their hands and the shareholders have lost their capital invested in the undertaking.'[68]

The operation and domination of the managing agencies in many ways typifies the whole relationship between British and Indian capital—a relationship that took time to erode. The structure and operation of the banking system in relation to Indian capital is another example of this—the Banks of Bengal and Madras had no Indian directors between when they were constituted as Presidency Banks, and their amalgamation into the Imperial Bank of India in 1921 except for a year or two at the end. For reasons already explained the Bank of Bombay did, however, have Indian directors and these, moreover, often had a majority. The other major banks were all mostly owned and controlled by Europeans and were in any case geared to foreign trade rather than to the needs of industry.[69] Additionally Indian business frequently had to suffer racial discrimination in the allocation of funds:

'Some complaints have been made about racial discrimination on the part of the Officers of the Imperial Bank of India when considering applications for credit. It has been suggested that the European managers of the Bank on account of their methods of living and social habits have greater opportunities of coming in closer personal contact with European clients than with Indians and that this personal informal contact results in more favourable treatment being accorded to European concerns than to Indian concerns. It is generally believed that the Bank lends to European concerns more freely than to Indian concerns . . .'[70]

Nor was racial discrimination simply a problem in finance. The Royal Indian Engineering College established to fill the 'superior ranks' of Public Works Departments in India laid down, among other things that candidates for admission must be 'British subjects of European race.'[71] 'As late as 1938, Murray's Handbook for Travelling in India, Burma and Ceylon (15th Edition, 1938) pointed out specifically that among the clubs listed (numbering 12 in Bombay, 10 in Calcutta and 9 in Madras), only the Calcutta club was open to Indians and Europeans, though Willingdon Club in Madras was open to Indian and European ladies.'[72]

In this way the European business community linked together with predominantly European colonial administration in its own insulated old-boy network was able to carve out its business arrangements to the exclusion of Indian capital.

However Indian capital made headway in the interwar years. Excluded from foreign trade it had perforce to orientate to the domestic market and gained from the change in government policy in the interwar period. British capital, by contrast, suffered badly from the depression and stagnation of the export economy and there was a considerable repatriation of capital from the economy in the 1930's—possibly also reflecting the growing political insecurity for imperialist capital. Kidron notes that strict comparison between the positions of foreign and Indian capital 'is impossible, but where a list of companies founded by Indian managing agencies shows a heavy concentration during the late 1930's and the war then, after a hiatus, during the modern planning period, a group of 32 of the largest foreign houses shows a steep decline in the number of newly incorporated managed companies from 79 in the 1900–19 decade, to 55 in the twenties, 28 in the thirties, 13 in the forties, and 5 between 1950 and 1956. Between 1936–7 and 1942–3 non-Indian companies increased their paid-up capital by 1 per cent compared with 17 for Indian companies.'[73]

Wartime profits that could not be converted into productive capital proved an important source of funds to buy out British interests. 'Hampered by the non-availability of machinery imports during the war, unable to invest in any large measure in new industries, this huge mass of accumulated capital in Indian hands gravitated inevitably to industries already established in this country under foreign ownership. Complete or partial buying out of British concerns by Indian interests became a significant phenomenon during the war and immediately after and to the British interests concerned was not unwelcome in view of the uncertain political future of India and Asia generally.' (Capital Dec. 22, 1949).[74]

The process of change over time—as well as the distribution by social origin of the various communities of the Indian bourgeoisie can be gleaned from the following table:[75]

As can be seen up to 1911 by far the most important role was played by the British except that in the western sector where the

Industrial Control by Community

	No. of Cos.			No. of Directors		
	1911	*1931*	*1951*	*1911*	*1931*	*1951*
British	282	416	382	652	1,335	865
Parsis	15	25	19	96	261	149
Gujaratis	3	11	17	71	166	232
Jews	5	9	3	17	13	–
Muslims	–	10	3	24	70	66
Bengalis	8	5	20	48	170	320
Marwaris	–	6	96	6	146	618
Mixed Control	28	28	79	102	121	372
Total	341	510	619	1,016	2,282	2,622

Parsis, Jews and Gujarati Hindus held the ground fairly successfully. This group came mainly from trade to industry.

The most striking rise, however, as the table shows, was of the Marwaris—the most important business community in present day India. This group up until the early nineteenth century had been mainly petty moneylenders. Throughout the century they thrived greatly from the growing commercialisation of the Bengal region acquiring both wealth and power in their traditional pursuit of moneylending and dealing in grain, butter, cloth, oilseeds, jute, gold and opium. After World War One several Marwari families moved into industrial activity opening textile mills and other industrial enterprises in a number of cities particularly Calcutta. They did not, of course, immediately abandon their other activities—far from it—'it is a noteworthy fact that even the Birla family, the foremost industrialists in the Marwari community, with considerable recent emphasis on heavy industry is actively engaged in commercial, usurious and speculative operations.'[76] It is noteworthy then that the industrial bourgeoisie retained considerable links with the mercantile and usurious bourgeoisie from which it had emerged. Capital tends to move to where it makes the highest return. With the growth of industry restrained by limitations of the market and lack of governmental assistance the bulk of Indian capital remained outside the sphere of production altogether as a parasite upon pre-capitalist production. The Indian Industrial Commission Report of 1918 commented on how, in general, Indian capitalists had remained in rural trade and moneylending taking advantage of the effects of expanded communications and trade 'merely to extend the scale of their previous operations. In trade and moneylending and, to a less extent, in financing village artisans, the trading classes found that large and certain gains were to be made, while modern industries required technical knowledge and offered only doubtful and, in most cases, apparently smaller profits.'[77] There is no doubt that such operations promised high profits. Whereas the income tax paid by the entire corporate sector in the two years 1895–6 and 1899–1900 came to Rs. 1,144,670 and Rs. 1,329,586 respectively, the corresponding figures for unincorporated banking and moneylending alone amounted to Rs. 3,594,570 and Rs. 3,821,430.[78]

Parasitical capital in the spheres of trade and usury remained far more substantial than capital rooted in production—despite the industrial expansion of the interwar years. If we take the figure for rural indebtedness to represent the capital of the rural moneylenders this alone came to an estimated Rs. 900 crores for British India at the end of the 1920's.[79] By contrast Indian capital in the 'organised sector' remained much more limited. In 1928–29 the 6,330 joint stock companies registered in India with Rupee capital had a paid-up capital of only Rs. 279 crores.[80]

A chain of intermediaries linked the 'organised' and unorganised sectors in the commercial and usurious exploitation of the peasantry and what remained of the artisans.

'The village moneylenders supplement their capital by borrowing from the urban moneylenders and rarely take deposits from the public. Some of the urban moneylenders, on the other hand do take deposits and sometimes borrow from the indigenous bankers. Merchants and traders have dealings with Joint Stock Banks as well. It is said that some of the itinerate moneylenders in Bihar and Orissa add to their resources by borrowing from co-operative societies of which they are members in their own districts.'[81]

The Movement for Independence

In discussing the nature of the nationalist movement we should distinguish between the social base of the movement—those classes and social groups from which the movement drew its members, support and even its leadership—and the programmatic basis of the movement which articulates the interest of the social class having hegemony over it. (By programme is meant here not simply the written programme but the entire way in which the movement organises itself, educates its members and so on—in short the actual social role that the movement fulfills.) The movement for independence in India, as with all nationalist movements, found its social base in various classes and groups who aspired to remove the obstacles impeding the realisation of their aspirations but it was the national bourgeoisie that 'put its own class impress on the movement, filled it with the content of its own class needs and aspirations subordinating those of other classes to its own.'[82] This was despite the fact that the social origins of the bulk of the leadership was in the urban professional and middle classes and the mass base of the movement was in the peasantry and to a lesser extent in the working class. This apparent contradiction is partly explained by the fact that it was the national bourgeoisie who financed Congress. But the main explanation lies elsewhere—in fact the programmatic basis of the nationalist movement could only have been either support for capitalist development and hence logically for the national bourgeoisie or a development under the leadership of the proletariat and the destruction of capitalism in the commanding heights of the economy. There were no other possibilities. The urban professional and middle classes did not of themselves represent an alternative mode of production. Their role was thus determined for them by the logic of their social position. If they supported a nationalist movement that remained within the bounds of private property this meant steering Congress in ways that facilitated the development of capitalism and which protected private property. This was despite the fact that such a course might necessitate measures that would cut across the need to maintain a base of support in the masses. This is clearly manifested in the policies of the Congress ministries established prior to Independence. In Bombay, for instance, though the Congress ministry had been elected on a manifesto which had included a guarantee of the workers' right to strike, the same ministry enacted the Bombay Trade Disputes Act in 1938 which restricted the freedom to strike and laid down rules for the registration of trade unions which the labour unions considered advantageous to the unions sponsored by the employers. 'The Bombay Provincial Trade Union Congress organised a protest strike. In the firing by the police that took place one person was killed and a number of others were wounded.'[83] Again 'The Congress government promulgated section 144 and others in Ahmedabad when the workers went on strike. In Sholapur, a number of labour leaders were arrested on the 'Release of Political Prisoners Day' when they organised a demonstration. Some of them were subsequently tried and imprisoned. The Congress Government of the North West Frontier Province . . . (made) use of the Criminal Law Amendment Act when the peasants launched a struggle against the Raja of Tour.'[84]

The alternative for the middle classes was to go over to the Communist camp—to fight for the establishment of a post-capitalist mode of production. But severe repression and more importantly the ineptitude of the Communist Party and its subordination to the disastrous shifts and turns of the Comintern prevented the proletariat from taking the leadership of the movement for Independence.[85]

The necessary condition for throwing off foreign rule to any nationalist movement was gaining the support of the peasantry as the most populous class bearing the burdens of British rule. The peasantry is too fragmented a social class to itself have the cohesion to lead a revolutionary movement—its fragmentation consisting of an enormous heterogeneity of interests, geographical dispersal and the fact that its mode of production being individual rather than social (i.e. little division of labour) it tends to produce political movements based on individual acts (terrorism). The main class aim of the peasantry is the expropriation of landlord property and trader/moneylender capital, and the division of the land to the actual tillers themselves. But the leadership of the peasantry in India fell to the national bourgeoisie and the Indian national bourgeoisie was not prepared to lead such an upheaval. For one thing it was inextricably mixed up itself in the exploitation of the peasantry through its links with the landed interests and through its mercantile and usurious operations in rural areas. Above all the bourgeoisie was afraid, especially after 1917 in Russia, that a full scale attack against landlord property might well rebound into an attack on bourgeois property itself.[86]

The Congress thus performed an extended balancing act—trying to use the masses to pressurise the British to hand over power while restraining the masses from full scale revolt. In this balancing act the leadership of Gandhi was of great importance—calling off the mass movement in periods of upsurge when armed rebellion was on the agenda and limiting the revolt to non-class issues like the salt tax while upholding the sanctity of landed and bourgeois property.[87]

To summarise, while the social base of the nationalist movement was muti-class—the class whose interests hegemonised Congress and ultimately determined its programme (policies and role) was that of the national bourgeoisie. This is clear from the way that negotiations and non-violent pressure were the tactics used against British imperialism so as to avoid a mass upheaval in which establishment property rights might be put in question. At the same time, however, Congress ministries used coercive means against the workers and poor peasants when they moved into struggle. In the mass upsurges in World War Two and after the workers and peasants were left leaderless. The Indian Communist Party under orders from Moscow turned to support for British imperialism when Russia came under attack by the fascist powers. Only later in the 1940's did the Communist Party take up armed struggle. The Congress cleverly absolved itself from leadership of the struggle. D. D. Kosombi, reviewing Nehru comments how 'When the All India Congress Committee met in Bombay, the members knew that arrest was imminent and most of them had prepared for the event . . . What strikes this writer as remarkable is that not one of these worthy and able delegates, though aware that the British adversary was about to strike ever thought of a plan of action for the nation as a whole . . . Why is it that knowledge of popular dissatisfaction went hand in hand with the absence of a real plan of action?

'. . . One may notice that on a class basis the action was quite brilliant . . . The panic of the British government and the jailing of all leaders absolved the Congress from any responsibility for the happenings of the ensuing year; at the same time the glamour of jail and concentration camp served to wipe out the so-so record of the Congress ministries in office, thereby restoring the full popularity of the organisation among the masses . . .'[88]

Despite such leadership British imperialism had been gravely weakened by World War Two. It was compelled to hand over power with Congress having to put up no strong fight. The Labour Government gave independence because they had to do so. Lord Ismay, as Mountbatten's Chief of Staff in India, wrote in his biography 'There was in fact no option before us but to do what we did.'[89]

NOTES

1 Karl Marx in *Karl Marx on Colonialism and Modernisation*, pp. 132–133.
2 M. D. Morris, 'Towards a Reinterpretation of Nineteenth Century Indian Economic History', *Journal of Economic History*, Vol. XXIII No. 4, 1963, p. 615.
3 Bipan Chandra, 'Reinterpretation of Nineteenth Century Indian Economic History', *Indian Economic and Social History Review*, March 1968, pp. 64–69.
4 Karl Marx, *op. cit.*, p. 107.
5 Chandra, *op. cit.*, p. 64.
6 A. K. Bagchi, *Private Investment in India 1900–1939*. Cambridge University Press 1972, p. 167.
7 L. H. Jenks, *op. cit.*, p. 222.
8 R. S. Rungta, *The Rise of Business Corporations In India 1851–1900*, Cambridge University Press 1970, pp. 129–130.
9 *Ibid* p. 130.
10 A. K. Bagchi, *op. cit.*, pp. 76, 170.
11 Jenks, *op. cit.*, pp. 223–224.
12 *Ibid* p. 224.
13 Bagchi, *op. cit.*, p. 37.
14 *Report of the Indian Industrial Commission 1916–1918*, Calcutta 1918 p. 70.
15 J. N. Bhagwati and Padma Desai. *India: Planning for Industrialisation, Industrialisation and Trade Policies since 1951*, Oxford University Press 1970, pp. [illegible]
16 Sir Valentine Chirol in *The Observer*, April 2, 1922. Quoted in R. P. Dutt, *op. cit.*, p. 151.
17 *Ibid* p. 155.
18 *Ibid* p. 144.

19 A. R. Desai, *Social Background of Indian Nationalism*, 3rd Edition 1959, Popular Book Depot, Bombay, p. 98.
20 *Ibid* p. 101.
21 D. H. Buchanan, *op. cit.*, p. 164; M. Kidron, *Foreign Investment in India*, Oxford University Press 1965, pp. 13–14.
22 R. P. Dutt, *op. cit.*, p. 157–158.
23 Bagchi, *op. cit.*, p. 55; R. P. Dutt, *op. cit.*, p. 156.
24 Bagchi, *op. cit.*, p. 44.
25 H. Lamb, *op cit.*, pp. 489–490.
26 D. H. Buchanan, *op. cit.*, pp. 473–476.
27 Bagchi, *op. cit.*, pp. 64–65; Maddison, *op. cit.*, p. 60.
28 Maddison, *op. cit.*, p. 59.
29 *Ibid* p. 60.
30 Bagchi, *op. cit.*, p. 66.
31 Rungta, *op. cit.*, 267.
32 A. K. Sen 'The Commodity Pattern of British Enterprise in Early Indian Industrialisation 1854–1914' in *2nd International Conference of Economic History 1962*, Paris 1965, p. 795.
33 *Ibid* p. 796.
34 *Ibid* p. 798.
35 R. C. Dutt, Vol. II, *op. cit.*, p. 543.
36 Ranajit Das Gupta *Problems of Economic Transition. Indian Case Study*, National Publishers, Calcutta 1970, pp. 28–29; Bagchi, *op. cit.*, p. 182.
37 Bhagwati and Desai, *op. cit.*, pp. 25–26.
38 Rungta, *op. cit.*, pp. 161–162.
39 Maddison, *op. cit.*, pp. 57–59.
40 Bhagwati and Desai, *op. cit.*, p. 26.
41 Rungta, *op. cit.*, pp. 173–175.
42 *Ibid* p. 20. See also B. B. Misra, *op. cit.*, pp. 114–115.
43 Misra, *op. cit.*, p. 84.
44 The following account is taken from Buchanan, *op. cit.*, pp. 36–51.
45 *Ibid* p. 45.
46 *Ibid* p. 51.
47 Tea Commissioners Report of 1868 quoted in *Ibid* p. 61.
48 Rungta, *op. cit.*, p. 168.
49 Beauchamp quoted in *Ibid*, p. 10.
50 Prabhat Patnaik, 'Political Economy of Underdevelopment', p. 15.
51 Rungta, *op. cit.*, pp. 173–175.
52 Bhagwati and Desai, *op. cit.*, p. 30.
53 Figures from Misra, *op. cit.*, p. 233.
54 Bagchi, *op. cit.*, pp. 73–75.
55 Bhagwati and Desai, *op. cit.*, p. 28.
56 Maddison, *op. cit.*, p. 57.
57 Bhagwati and Desai, *op. cit.*, p. 33.
58 Bagchi, *op. cit.*, pp. 89–90.
59 *Ibid* pp. 89–90.
60 In Maddison, *op. cit.*, p. 62.
61 Bhagwati and Desai, *op. cit.*, p. 43.
62 Kidron, *op. cit.*, p. 57.
63 Buchanan, *op. cit.*, pp. 165–168.
64 Kidron, *op. cit.*, pp. 6–7.

65 Maddison, *op. cit.*, p. 56.
66 R. P. Dutt, *op. cit.*, p. 169.
67 Buchanan, *op. cit.*, p. 166.
68 Central Banking Enquiry Committee Report quoted in R. P. Dutt, *op. cit.*, p. 169.
69 Bagchi, *op. cit.*, pp. 171–172.
70 *Indian Central Banking Enquiry Committee, 1931*. Part I, Majority Report, p. 272.
71 Bagchi, *op. cit.*, pp. 151–152.
72 *Ibid* p. 166.
73 Kidron, *op. cit.*, p. 41.
74 *Capital,* December 22nd, 1949. Quoted in A. R. Desai, *Recent Trends in Indian Nationalism,* Popular Prabashan, Bombay 1960, p. 32.
75 Misra, *op. cit.*, p. 250.
76 R. Das Gupta, *op. cit.*, pp. 30–31.
77 *Indian Industrial Commission 1916–18*, p. 64.
78 Rungta, *op. cit.*, p. 181.
79 *Central Banking Enquiry Committee Report,* p. 55.
80 *Ibid* p. 261.
81 *Ibid* p. 81.
82 A. R. Desai *Social Background of Indian Nationalism,* p. 51.
83 *Ibid* pp. 346–347.
84 *Ibid* p. 347.
85 Lasse and Lisa Berg, *Face to Face. Fascism and Revolution in India,* Ramparts Press, Berkeley 1970, pp. 135–141.
86 L. Trotsky, *Results and Prospects* and *Permanent Revolution,* Pathfinder Press, New York 1970.
87 Desai, *op. cit.*, p. 340.
88 Desai, *Recent Trends in Indian Nationalism,* pp. 37–38.
89 Quoted in Michael Barratt Brown, *After Imperialism,* Heinemann, London 1963, p. 191.

CHAPTER V

Capitalism and Combined Development

A Resumé of the Argument

It is now possible to recall the introductory discussion at the beginning of this book and the issues and questions raised there. It should be clear after the historical analysis of India up to 1947 that it is correct to argue that 'underdevelopment' is an inappropriate term for a partly created condition in which, unlike in the advanced metropolitan countries, capitalism emerges as a rather weak growth in an unhealthy environment. Further it should be clear that India's evolution cannot be similar to that experienced by today's advanced capitalist countries.

The whole preceding analysis has made clear that when capitalism developed in historically belated countries, like India, it developed under different and more unfavourable conditions from those in the pioneering capitalist countries. The first capitalist countries subordinated other societies to facilitate their own development by gaining access to the markets and resources of these other societies. The societies thus subordinated, like India, faced this same process as a barrier to their own capital accumulation process. In contrast to what was the case in the first capitalist countries the Indian capitalist class found it difficult even to get access to its own home market against the established competition of British industry. British imperialism took away resources that could have sustained India's own development and the colonial state neglected to provide the necessary overheads for competitive industrialisation.

Once capitalism did get under way in India it was because the ties of subordination had been weakened—but they had not been broken altogether and the process was in consequence, a slow one. Capitalism was now developing at a late stage and its establishment created a combined socio-economic formation validating Trotsky's observation that 'The development of historically backward nations leads necessarily to a peculiar combination of different stages in the historic process. Their development as a whole acquires a planless, complex, combined character.'[1] Capitalism thus developed alongside the pre-capitalist mode of production. At the same time the pre-capitalist mode of production was not isolated from the evolving dynamic of developing world capitalism, on the contrary it was profoundly affected by this process. As was showed, a process of combined development took place within the old mode of production leaving certain of its old features unchanged but transforming others. In particular the reciprocal relationship between the artisans and the cultivating peasants within the village community was increasingly replaced by a trading relationship between the industrial centres—first in Britain, later in India—and the peasantry. The peasantry supplied foodstuffs and raw materials and received in exchange industrial goods. What went with all this was a greater commercialisation and monetisation within the old mode of production and a change in the pattern of land rights, produced by this and by the efforts of the British to increase the agrarian market and their sources of land revenue. The remnants of the pre-capitalist mode of production became a key market for industry and a key source of inputs and resources.

Other important changes in the pre-capitalist mode of production need to be noted. Another product of an advanced culture displaced into a backward one was rising population growth. Taken together with this was the low rate of capital accumulation and industry's adoption of a technology from the advanced countries at a high level of labour productivity. The overall combination producing a rising pressure of population on the land.

It should be clear, then, that India's socio-economic formation is considerably different from today's advanced countries in the early stages of their capitalist economic development. Given this it is relevant to raise the questions—can capitalism develop the productive forces in the Third World to a degree sufficient to meet the needs of the vast majority of the Indian population? Does the pattern of social relations as it has evolved hinder or promote the development of the productive forces? To answer these questions we shall examine Indian economic development after 1947.

The Limits of Combined Development in General Terms

In the same chapter in his 'History of the Russian Revolution' where Trotsky elaborates upon the theory of Uneven and Combined Development he also makes a qualification about the process of combined development. 'The possibility of skipping over intermediate steps is, of course, by no means absolute. Its degree is determined in the long run by the economic and cultural capacities of the country, the backward nation, moreover, not infrequently debases the achievements borrowed from outside in the process of adapting them to its more primitive culture.'[2] The experience of India's industrial development richly validates these perceptive remarks.

At Independence the 'economic and cultural capacities' of India were limited by its condition of historic belatedness and the retardation implicit in the 200 year dominance of British imperialism. This has acted as a significant check on capital accumulation in the industrial sector. There are two kinds of problems faced by individual enterprises. One is that the industrial base is too narrow to sustain expansion. We have seen that the British neglected to build up the economic base for sustained expansion. In consequence periods of rapid growth run up against bottlenecks which check further forward movement. This problem is manifested in all sorts of ways—shortages of educated and trained manpower, shortages of indigenous capital goods, absence of indigenous sources of electricity, transport bottlenecks and so on. To take just two of these—at independence in 1947 there was a serious shortage of educated labour power. In a population of about 350 million people only 2,700 graduates with degrees and diplomas were being turned out each year and only 6,600 students were being admitted to technical colleges and professional courses each year.[3] Moreover even this education system was geared to the production of the junior administrators, lawyers and other functionaries of a colonial regime rather than to producing technicians, scientific and other workers needed in a developing economy. In the investments goods industries we find a high degree of dependence upon foreign supplies. This may be judged from the ratio of domestic production in the supply of industries producing primarily investment goods which was 47 per cent in 1950/51.[4]

The kind of bottlenecks created by this weakness had been evident in the war when rapid increases in demand, production and profits could not be carried back into the creation of industrial capacity. In the 1950's, the problem reappeared. When industrial expansion began in response to rising demand after 1954 shortages of basic metals, coal, electricity and a variety of capital goods all held back the upsurge and by 1957/58 foreign currency reserves had declined by nearly a half compared with 1955/56 despite lavish borrowings from the I.M.F.[5]

Where inputs cannot be obtained then the result is excess capacity. Just before devaluation in 1966 the World Bank argued that 'capacity standing idle for want of materials and components . . . could contribute an increase of Rs. 10,000 million in the national income over four years.'[6]

The second kind of problem faced by industrial enterprises seeking to expand in the Indian context is the narrowness of the domestic market. The all round lack of investment and general development up to 1947 means that the demand for products is very limited. Demand is not meant here in the Keynesian sense but in the classical sense of supply to offer in exchange on the market. In this respect it should be noted that India has a tiny market for manufactured goods. In fact, while Denmark has a population which is only 1 per cent that of India it has a market for manufactured goods which is the same size as the Indian market. Lack of demand makes for substantial problems of excess capacity (see Appendix I) and the narrow market makes for a high degree of concentration which has further unhealthy consequences.[7]

Fundamentally both the limitations of the industrial base and of the market stem from the same source—the transplantation of production processes developed in the advanced capitalist countries into the backward nation with its limited 'economic and cultural capacities.' These production processes have a particular and important feature—they are designed to fit into an existent interdependent whole. Capitalism socialises production to a greater and greater degree—i.e. it involves a higher and higher interdependence between specialised processes. This is the anti-thesis of pre-capitalist production which is based on a narrow division of labour and hence the relative self sufficiency of the productive units. What this means for latecomers is that they cannot reproduce individual production processes without having the problem of having to try to create the complementary processes of the whole of which they are a part.

From one angle this appears as a problem of acquiring inputs. The establishment of a factory poses the need to acquire the necessary sources of trained and educated labour—implying an established educational system; the necessary sources of basic inputs, say of steel—implying an established supply of steel from a steel industry, the necessary sources of power, say of electricity—implying an established electricity network and so on. From the other side there is the problem of complementary outputs for production—this is obvious enough for producers' goods. The establishment of producer goods industries without a sufficient complementing growth in consumer goods industries will obviously lead to excess capacity. The Indian experience is clear cut in this respect.

'In 1969 many capital goods industries were working well below capacity even though capacity itself was well below what was intended. In some cases low output was due to almost total lack of demand. The worst cases were industries producing capital goods for heavy industry. In 1968 the government plant making heavy machine tools was working at 3 per cent capacity, the foundry and forge at 7 per cent and heavy machine building at 13 per cent. The Mining and Allied Machinery Company worked at 6 per cent of capacity.'[8]

But it is not just producers' goods that have to have complementary outlets. As has just been said the market for consumer goods is small because of lack of supply to offer on the market—i.e. is a correlate of the all round industrial underdevelopment. As a result, as we shall see, the rural market is particularly important as an outlet for industrial consumer goods.

The processes of combined development clearly give rise to problems utterly different from those experienced in today's advanced capitalist countries in the early stages of their development. The ability of the state to overcome these problems in the interest of the bourgeoisie is obviously of critical importance to the analysis. First, however, two particular features of Indian economy flowing from the above analysis deserve further attention. One is the high degree of industrial concentration and the implications flowing from this. The other is the heavy dependence of industry on agriculture both as a market and as a source of inputs.

Senility in childhood—monopolisation and oligopolisation in Indian industry

The high degree of concentration of capital due to the narrowness of the domestic market as compared with productive capacity is a particularly striking feature of the process of uneven and combined development. In the early stages of capitalist development the industrial structure already displays the unhealthy feature of a high degree of monopolisation—a characteristic of capitalism in its later stages in the metropolitan countries. Baran's comment about this is amply validated by the Indian case.

'Setting out to supply commodities similar in quality and in design to those previously brought in from abroad, they created single large scale modern plants sufficient to meet the existing demand . . . The amount of capital required to break into the monopoly's privileged sanctuary, the risks attendant upon the inevitable struggle, the leverages that the established firms could use to harass and to exclude an intruder—all tended to decimate the inducement for merchant capital to shift to industrial pursuits. The narrow market became monopolistically controlled, and the monopolistic control became an additional factor preventing the widening of the market . . .'[9]

Empirical data on the degree of concentration may be taken from the Monopolies Inquiry Commission Report of 1964. Out of a total of 1,289 products 437 had only one producing firm in each case and 229 products were produced by 2 firms (i.e. 17.5 per cent of the products by duopolists). 87.7 per cent of the products were produced by 10 or less firms for each product. Except for food products, cotton textiles and jute textiles the textbook categories of monopoly, duopoly and oligopoly are in evidence throughout Indian industry.[10] In international comparisons Indian industry tends to be highly concentrated. Bain's comparison of 16 Indian manufacturing industries with counterpart industries in the U.S.A. in terms of seller concentration shows this clearly. For this sample the degree of concentration of control of individual industries by ostensibly independent firms was significantly higher in 13 out of 16 cases, about the same in one, and significantly less in 2 cases only.[11]

High concentration, a limited and slowly growing market gives rise to problems of surplus capital. Profits are not automatically ploughed back into those sectors from which they have been extracted since this would lead to rising production capacity which, if used, could only lead to rapidly falling prices in the absence of a rapid growth in the market. In the oligopolistic sectors increased production and falling prices would disrupt the existing set up. The 'live and let live' regime between existing competitors would be broken up. Accordingly surplus capital has to find the outlets where it will earn the most profitable rate of return.[12]

One tendency is towards diversification. This is likely to be stronger 'the lower the elasticity of demand in the original product, the greater the excess capacity and the lower the degree of specialisation of the firm's productive facilities. It is not unreasonable to expect all three to combine in the conditions of an undeveloped economy.'[13] The tendency to diversification is most marked in the oldest established capitalist sectors where demand has grown very slowly and where continued expansion of existing traditional business does not promise a competitive return. This is true for the cotton, jute, sugar and tea companies. In cotton the government restrictions and the inadequacies of the domestic and export markets did not offer expansion opportunities comparable with other industries. In jute the situation is broadly similar. 'The two industries are none too prosperous if taken as a whole but many units within them, especially those controlled by certain leading groups, have excess financial and managerial capacity. A similar situation has arisen in the tea and sugar industries also.'[14]

Where the market is too small and grows too slowly and where diversification does not provide an outlet for surplus capital then funds tend to leave the organised sector for the higher profit rates available in the non-capitalist sector. Bettelheim describes this process as a 'financial and commercial overgrowth'[16] and he puts it down to 'the monopolistic domination of industry and the weak domestic market . . .'. The Indian industrial capitalist class emerged, as we have seen, from communities of trading and moneylending capitalists—this tendency reinforces and reproduces the ties between the two. Evidence for the flow of resources into the usurious activities in the countryside was provided by the Rural Credit Survey of the early 1950's. In Malabar, Quilon and Nizambad the proportion of credit ultimately coming from urban sources was, respectively 57 per cent, 29 per cent and 22 per cent of total debts. 'In many other districts the proportion varied between 10 per cent and 20 per cent at the time of the R.C.S. enquiry.'[17]

Because of its emergence as part of a process of combined development the Indian bourgeoisie displays a physiognomy very reminiscent of those countries discussed in the introduction to the book. Japan is an obvious comparison. It will be remembered that the industrial revolution in Japan 'proceeded under the dominance of the haute bourgeoisie of privileged great merchant industrialists; thus Japanese capitalism right from its origin, had an oligarchic and monopolistic character'. The tendency towards diversification is reminiscent of the zaibatsu that completely span the organised sector in Japan. Moreover the ties of the bourgeoisie in the mercantile usurious exploitation of the countryside is another point of similarity—another mark of a bourgeoisie that in its formation did not desire to radically overthrow the old order because 'it itself already belonged to the old society, representing not the interests of a new society against an old, but renewed interests in a superannuated society'.

The Interdependence of Industry and Agriculture

Of particular importance in the ability of industry to make necessary forward and backward linkages to sustain its growth is the performance of agriculture. 'In the Indian economy the performance of the industrial economy is largely dependent upon the agricultural sector's performance in more than one way.

Agro-based industries, which constitute 30 per cent of the organised industries, contribute two-thirds of the foreign exchange earnings. On the other hand, the food commodities produced by the agricultural sector influence not only the available income which may be spent on industrial products but in times of short supply and higher prices also increase labour costs of production and help jack up cost-push inflation.'[18] Given the lack of development of the capitalist sector itself the market in the countryside is a key one and the most important aspect of the integration between the capitalist mode of production and the non-capitalist mode of production lies precisely in the exchange of industrial products for foodstuffs and agricultural raw materials. In 1960–61 the rural market for industrial consumer goods was Rs. 4,600 crores as compared with an urban market of only Rs. 1,600 crores. Of this rural market it is the rich peasants/landlords who purchase most of the industrial consumer goods—the richest 10 per cent in rural areas took 34.6 per cent of the Rs. 4,600 crores cited above.[19] In return these wealthy peasants supply the bulk of the marketed surplus of agricultural output as the following table shows.[20]

1960–61—Percentage Distribution of:

Size class of holding (acres)	*Population*	*Output*	*Marketable Surplus*	*Marketable share of output*
0–2.49	36.59	9.39	2.39	8.88
2.5–4.9	21.35	15.19	8.69	18.77
5.0–9.9	20.32	22.11	15.31	22.76
10.0–14.9	8.93	12.48	10.62	27.93
15.0–19.9	4.24	10.66	15.46	47.57
20.0–24.9	2.56	5.75	7.04	40.12
25.0–29.9	1.68	4.50	6.26	45.66
30.0–49.9	2.88	10.62	16.65	51.44
50 and above	1.45	9.30	17.54	61.87
All	100.00	100.00	100.00	32.80

(Sources: Utsa Patnaik Social Scientist, No. 2, p. 27.)

As can be seen 47.49 of the marketable surplus is provided by just 8.57 per cent of the population (with holdings of sizes 20 acres and above). The bottom layers of rural society are, by contrast, of very marginal significance. 57.44 per cent of the rural population, either owning no land at all or less than 5 acres, provide a mere 11.08 per cent of the marketable surplus. From the standpoint of capitalist development this sector matters only in so far as its labour continues to enrich the rural plutocracy who are the key economic partners to the industrial bourgeoisie.

But the rural plutocracy are themselves far from being an ideal partner. It would seem for example, that for foodgrains at least, the marketed surplus responds perversely to changes in price. Thamarajakshi finds a negative regression coefficient between marketed surplus of agricultural output and the net barter terms of trade for agriculture—however, his coefficient is not significant at the 10 per cent level.[21] Sau finds a more significant relationship between μ, the marketed surplus of cereals and P the relative price of cereals to the relative price of manufactures

$$\mu = 8.70 + \frac{0.0921}{P}$$

$r^2 = 0.42$ Significant at 2 per cent level.[22]

Other studies also argue that there is a negative relationship in which a movement of the terms of trade against agriculture tends to stimulate the size of the agricultural marketed surplus—and vice versa. Sau hypothesises that what is involved here is a situation in which there is a handful of landowners and money-lenders who provide the bulk of the marketed surplus who have a consumption pattern fixed in the short run and who 'look for a more or less fixed amount of industrial goods in exchange for their agricultural produce.'[23] Thus when industrial growth drags up prices of agricultural goods relative to industrial goods not more, but less supply comes forth—a situation hardly conducive to industrial growth.

Of course the volume of marketed surplus must also be examined in terms of other variables and not solely relative prices. In this respect the overall volume of agricultural output is obviously very important. This is indicated in Thamarajakshi's equations for the period 1951–52 to 1965–66[24] where μ = marketed surplus, P = terms of trade, O = agricultural output and t = time.

$$\mu = 60.9887 - \underset{(0.2767)}{\overset{(a)}{0.3568P}} + \underset{(0.2178)}{\overset{x}{0.68020}} + \underset{(0.6219)}{\overset{xx}{1.1658t}}$$

figures in brackets are standard errors.
(a)—not significant at the 10 per cent level
x—significant at 1 per cent
xx—significant at 10 per cent

The importance of the overall volume of agricultural output is demonstrated in the way that industry tends to be markedly affected by the size of harvests and the variability of the monsoons. The record harvests of 1953–4 due to excellent weather conditions helped expand the domestic market for textiles and other industrial goods. In the first years of the Second Plan there was a low rate of industrial expansion and relative stagnation in agriculture. This in turn, was followed by the good harvests of 1958/59 again accompanied by rapid industrial growth. Thereafter in the early 1960's the situation was slightly modified with poorer harvest going together with industrial expansion. The reasons for this change in the general pattern was basically the massive step up of state expenditure in the Second and Third Plans. The sources of this will be examined later but it should be noted that in the mid 1960's the pace of the government's efforts could not be sustained and this, together with the effects of 2 catastrophic harvests, sent industry into a deep recession.[25]

Such fluctuations in agricultural output, and concomitantly the demand for industry/supply from agriculture, have taken place against an overall trend which has not been encouraging. Over the period 1951/52 to 1965/66 the yearly rate of growth of the net marked surplus of agriculture was 2.90 per cent, that of agricultural production 2.70 per cent.[26] Much of the increased volume of agricultural output is, moreover, accountable to increases in the area under cultivation which cannot continue at the rate of the past.

The failure of agriculture will be probed later—its consequences have been most manifest in the industrial fluctuations mentioned and in the increasing import of foodgrains and other agricultural inputs. This has used up foreign exchange and run up foreign indebtedness.

Net Import of Cereals (in million tonnes)[27]

1st 5 Year Plan		*2nd 5 Year Plan*	
1951	4.80	1956	1.44
1952	3.93	1957	3.65
1953	2.04	1958	3.22
1954	0.84	1959	3.87
1955	0.71	1960	5.14
3rd 5 Year Plan			
1961	3.50	1966	10.36
1962	3.64	1967x	8.67
1963	4.56	1968x	5.69
1964	6.27	1969x	3.87
1965	7.46		

x Provisional figures.

By its failure—and the consequent use of foreign exchange and growth of foreign indebtedness agriculture hits industry indirectly since foreign exchange is vitally necessary to obtain a whole variety of inputs for industry.[28]

State efforts to Complement Capital Accumulation

State efforts to ensure the necessary supply of inputs and infrastructure and to ensure the growth of the market—i.e. to ensure the necessary complements to the capital accumulation process—are obviously of the utmost importance to the successful development of capitalism when transplanted into India. Building up the economic base for development is often out of the reach of private capital because of the large scale of the investments required and because the payoff period on many of the necessary productive facilities is too long. The major part of the public investment has been in sectors which would contribute to increases in output after a significant time lag. 'For instance, public sector investment in iron and steel programmes in the third plan envisaged that target production would be forthcoming only towards the end of the third plan. The same is true of investment in basic producer goods industries in the development of which the public sector is assigned a key role.'[29] The result of this time lag is that the shift in investment in favour of the public sector (54 :46 in the 2nd Plan and 61 :39 in the 3rd Plan) is not fully reflected in the relative contribution of that sector to total output. Since output is, in its turn, the counter part of financial resources, the public sector does not have much in the way of its own resources. 'Thus the public sector investment will have to depend essentially in the initial stages of development on the surpluses of the private sector.'[30] The problem, however, is how to get hold of these surpluses—this will have to be looked at later.

To the extent that the state can get access to resources and spends these building up the economic base of the economy it generates demand and alleviates the market blockage. The state is an important outlet for several important industries—for example 37 per cent of the orders of engineering goods and 46 per cent of the demand for cement came from the government in the 60's.[31] The rapid speed up of industrial production in the private sector in the Second and Third Plans largely paralleled the growth of state expenditure and the collapse of funds available to the government leading to a decline in its expenditure in the mid 60's severely hit many sectors of industry. In its mid year appraisal of the economy in 1967 the Indian Institute of Public Opinion noted that for 2 years 'the industrial economy did not respond despite incentives in the post-devaluation period, by way of liberalisation of imports of necessary industrial raw materials and other maintenance goods, because Government outlays during this period were reduced resulting thereby in subdued industrial activity.'[32] The situation has not much changed thereafter. The stagnation of public investment creating problems both of lack of demand and of bottlenecks in certain essential sectors. In fact had investment conformed to the scheduled targets of the original 4th Plan then at the end of 1972 the country would have been using up about 12 million tonnes of ingot steel as against the actual figure of 6 million tonnes, 3.3 lakh tonnes of aluminium as against 1.6 lakh tonnes, Rs. 102 crores worth of machine tools as against Rs. 43 crores worth. Additionally the railways would have been carrying 308 million tonnes of freight as against 200 million tonnes and installed capacity for power generation would have been 30 million KW as against an actual generated figure of 17 million KW. The

Economic and Political Weekly editorialised that 'The enormous gap between where the economy should have been and where it in fact is, must be attributed above all, to the government's failure to step up the rate of planned investment'.[33] In previous post war years rapid leaps of industrial production of 8 to 9 per cent have been attained but these coincided with large increases in public sector plan investment outlays. These outlays cannot be sustained over a long period for lack of finance hence the present stagnation in industry which is likely to continue until such time as the resources for another spurt in public investment can be found.

The feebIness of the state's public investment record poses the question of the actual power of the Indian state to promote economic development and capital accumulation. A common approach of bourgeois economists is to search for bottlenecks or constraints in the development process and then to prescribe appropriate state action to remove the identified problem. But this leaves open the real problem. As Myrdal notices the state in South Asia is 'soft' and it may not be capable of dealing with the constraints upon economic progress.[34] The state is not itself autonomous from the society that it is supposed to intervene in to change. Rather the Indian state reflects a particular correlation of the ruling social forces. In this correlation the bourgeoisie does not exercise a complete hegemony and its relative weakness in society is reflected in its position in the state which mediates between the contending interests of the various ruling groups. The state follows up the interests of none of the groups too forcefully if this runs up against the interest of any other group. Accordingly it is unproductive to call, for example, for radical land reform legislation because the legislative assemblies responsible tend to be dominated by landlords. Independence weakened the grip of the imperialist powers and gave the Indian state a changed character, capable of stepping up an increased development effort. Nevertheless the state is still a decidedly weak instrument to promote capital accumulation and the interests of the bourgeoisie.

Nature of the post-colonial state

The political superstructure in India reflects the integration of the economic base—the coexistence of the capitalist mode of production with the non-capitalist mode of production is reflected in the state apparatus by power being wielded by a bloc of the capitalist class together with the landlord/malik interest—rather than by the capitalist class on its own.[35] Moreover it should be noted that the state bureaucracy operates with a certain degree of autonomy for its own particular interests which we shall examine later. So it is clear that the bourgeoisie does not wield complete hegemony over the Indian state—how much power then does it have?

In a country where the vast majority of the population are unable to get access to a sufficient income to maintain an adequate diet the wealthy and cultured bourgeoisie exercise power beyond the dreams of the workers and poor peasants. The bourgeoisie exercises a substantial control over the national press and is thereby able to mould 'public opinion'. It is the source of funds for Congress and other political parties. In the 1967 elections the following members of the bourgeoisie donated to Congress—Birla Rs. 16 lakhs; Tata Rs, 11 lakhs; Sri Rams New Delhi Cloth Mills Rs. 6 lakhs; Sahu Jains Rs. 6.20 lakhs; Martin Burn Rs. 5.70 lakhs.[36] Such contributions do not go unrewarded. Big business houses get, at the very least, a hearing on a high administrative and possibly political level on their more or less inevitable and continuous appeals to the government for necessary permits. Big business has frequent and sustained access to the executive and bureaucracy for lobbying when policy is being made and bribing when it is being implemented. As with other capitalist countries corruption and rottenness prevails throughout[37] the highest levels of society and is a frequently noted feature of political and business life. Official enquiries into corruption in the bureaucratic hierarchies like the Sanathanam Committee have noted this.[38]

But big business does not get everything it would like, and it does not rock the boat too much if it is unhappy with state policy—lest the ruling class as a whole capsize. Prior to the 1967 elections a growing big business—government divergence led many individual representatives of Big Capital to intervene actively in the election campaign and there was a decline in financial support for Congress. Partly as a result of this and partly as a result of general class polarisation and antagonism in this period the Congress majority fell sharply, a Communist United Front dominated government emerged in West Bengal and a period of instability and paralysis ensued. In this situation the recalcitrant members of the big bourgeoisie moved back behind Congress and there was a general mood of reconciliation. The Federation of Indian Chambers of Commerce and Industry refused 'to react too strongly over the issue of bank nationalisation' and it provided much support to Indira Ghandi in the 1971 elections despite the nationalisations.[39]

That Big Capital should concur with bank nationalisation without too much fuss is a fact worthy of note because ownership of the banks has been important in enabling Messrs. Tata, Birla, Thaper et al in extending their industrial empires. The Mahalanobis Committee drew attention to the way in which money deposited by millions of small depositors had often been used for purposes of intercorporate investment and acquiring control of companies.[40] Bank nationalisation actually reflects the interests of smaller capital and the rural kulak group within the ruling class bloc—this is evident because, after nationalisation, an obligation was put on the banks to extend their funds to 'hitherto neglected sectors such as export, agriculture, small industries, small traders and other men of small means'. From June 1968 to March 1971 bank advances to small scale industries rose from Rs. 195 crores to Rs. 544 crores taking the proportion of advances to this sector from 6.27 per cent to 10.58 per cent.[41]

We shall have call later to analyse the evolving structure of socio-economic and political power in the countryside but we may now briefly mention those groups with which the bourgeoisie has shared power. The rural elite of landlords and maliks (masters) are able to exercise influence particularly at the level of the States of the Union in India's federal political structure. It is the States that have power over those things that are key to the kulaks—e.g. land reform legislation and agricultural income tax. Thorner, in a tour of 117 co-operative credit societies scattered throughout India, found that the co-operatives were generally dominated by the 'big people' in the villages—and it was just the same better off families that generally provided persons to the legislative assemblies. 'The people in power in the capitals of the various states are pretty much the same people in the seats of power in the villages, only occupying larger chairs.' They are able to exercise this power through a variety of means.[42] It may be relatively simple a process. In Kumbapettai in Tanjore, Kathleen Gough describes how, in the all-India elections, the Brahmins marshalled their non-Brahmin tenants and Pallan labourers on voting day and instructed them to vote for Congress.[43] It may involve a more extended fight. In Madhopur in U.P. after Independence the Chamar caste fought and won power in the village panchayat elections. But the Thakurs, on whom the Chamars were economically dependent were able to make the victory ineffectual. The village council could not enforce its own ordinances, or collect its own taxes against the wishes of the Thakurs. Court action against the Thakurs was too expensive. The tenant party was disrupted by bribery and expensive law suits brought against it. 'The low castes and particularly the Chamars, lacked the economic base for a long term fight against the Thakurs on whom they were dependent for a livelihood.' Thus the Thakurs retained dominance.[44]

In addition to the rural elite, small business men and town merchants as well as professional groups who are not direct exploiters but who are integrated into the class structure like lawyers and managers provide the power base of the State—usually mediated through Congress, at the local level. This group is anxious to preserve its position vis-a-vis Big Capital and it is the smaller business men and the rural kulaks who have, as we have seen, benefited from bank nationalisation. The limitation on the power of Big Capital which they represent in the ship of state is also reflected in the continuance of a large sector of public ownership in the economy. Large scale state expenditure was, of course, an initial necessity, especially in heavy industries as sufficient resources were not available to private enterprise for the establishment of these industries. However, whereas in Japan, the State bore the burden of expenditure and subsequently sold the plant thus established at knock down prices to private enterprise—in India this has not been the case. In India such a step would 'benefit the monopoly houses; and the smaller bourgeoisie supported by the petty bourgeois class would oppose it.'[45]

The leverage of the bourgeoisie over the state and thereby

over the economy is also reduced by the important semi-autonomous interests of the state bureaucracy itself. The importance of the bureaucracy is partly an inheritance from the colonial regime.

'The colonial state is . . . equipped with a powerful bureaucratic military apparatus and mechanisms of government which enable it through its routine operations to subordinate the native social classes . . . At the moment of independence weak indigenous bourgeoisies find themselves enmeshed in bureaucratic controls by which those at the top of the hierarchy of the bureaucratic-military apparatus of the state are able to maintain and even extend their dominant power in society being freed from metropolitan control.'[46]

The autocratic power structure set up by the British was, of course, on the other side in the struggle for independence and it is not to be wondered at that Nehru should feel that 'no new order can be built up in India so long as the spirit of the I.C.S. pervades our administration and our public services . . . Therefore it seems to me quite essential that the I.C.S. and similar services must disappear completely, as such, before we can start real work on the new order.'[47] After 1947, however, the trend was, if anything, in the other direction to that called for by Nehru. It was too dangerous for the ruling class to take apart the structures which held the country together in conditions of acute social instability and British imperialism pressed for the maintenance of the privileges and position of the higher echelons of the civil service. Thereafter the weakness of the bourgeoisie, compelling its reliance on state support, further strengthened the bureaucracy. Because, for reasons already explained, the state sector could not be hived off to big capital the power of the state bureaucracy has continued to grow unabated.

Being based upon a coalition of social classes the Indian state is too weak to make decisive developmental efforts where these contradict the interests of any member of the coalition. This is manifest in a number of spheres the most important being in the raising of resources for development and in the attempt by land reform to change the pattern of non-capitalist agrarian property relations. The latter will be evident when we come to discuss changes in agriculture—as far as the former is concerned this is crucial. As the discussion above showed public investment expenditure is necessary both to build up complementary sources of inputs and the economic infrastructure and to provide demand for the expansion of the industrial sector.

The Inability of the State to Raise Resources for Development

The problem of getting access to sufficient resources to sustain development became serious with the initiation of the Second 5 Year Plan in 1956. Public expenditure on development rose from Rs. 19,600 millions in the 1st Plan (1951–56) to Rs. 46,720 millions in the 2nd Plan (1956–61) to Rs. 86,280 millions in the 3rd Plan (1961–66).[48] Under the 4th Plan the total public sector development outlay is projected at Rs. 143,980 millions. Ideally the resources for increased public (and private) investment would be raised through an increase in the rate of domestic saving—with an important part of the surplus of the private sector being siphoned off by the government in increased taxation to finance its own programmes. However the rate of domestic savings has not been raised significantly since the mid 50's and the government has not succeeded in substantially increasing its revenues from the propertied classes.[49]

That the resources do exist that could be used for development is undeniable—it is especially clear in the figures for income distribution. One scholar has calculated that for the 1950's 'The size distribution of income in India is more unequally distributed than in any of the developed countries.' More precisely he found that while the bottom 20 per cent of income recipients got 3.7 per cent of India's national income the top 20 per cent got 64.7 per cent.[50] But much of this income goes into unproductive consumption. Perhaps it can be argued that we have here just another manifestation of the same general problem—i.e. that once development has taken place elsewhere this permanently affects the possibility of development of historically backward countries. In this case consumption standards set in the advanced capitalist countries are copied by the wealthy in the more backward countries in what has been termed the 'international demonstration effect'. Resources are thereby channelled into the so-called 'U-sector' that could have been used in ways more conducive to development.[51]

The state's taxation revenues are small both because of widespread evasion and also because of the limited coverage of the direct tax net. As far as evasion is concerned this is very considerable. The Income Tax Investigation Commission of 1947 investigated 1,058 cases and discovered concealed income of the order of Rs. 48 crores.[52] In 1956 Kaldor's *Indian Tax Reform: Report of a Survey* discussed how much income was concealed as a proportion of income assessed to tax. 'Conversations with individual businessmen, accountants and revenue officials reveal guesses which range from 10–20 per cent of assessed income at the minimum to 200–300 per cent at the maximum'.[53] Where the figures were most reliable for making estimates—in the mining and factory industries—the ratio of assessable incomes to assessed incomes was almost 2 : 1. 'If these figures are anywhere near the truth, the amount of income tax lost through tax evasion is more of the order of Rs. 200–300 crores than the Rs. 20–30 crores that is sometimes quoted in this connection.[54] (It should be noted that in testifying before the Direct Taxes Administration Enquiry Committee of 1958–59 Kaldor explained that the Rs. 200–300 crores estimated represented the loss of tax not just through evasion but also through avoidance[55]—this does not, of course, affect our argument about the inability of the state to raise revenues through direct taxes.) The most recent data is from the Direct Taxes Enquiry Committee of 1972 (Wanchoo Committee).[56] The Wanchoo Committee Report concluded that previous measures taken to reduce tax evasion had not made the slightest dent on the problem. By the very nature of the problem reliable statistics are not available but the Committee estimated that the income on which tax was evaded was Rs. 811 crores in 1961–62, Rs. 1,216 crores for 1964–65 and Rs. 1,400 crores for 1968–69.[57] So for 1968–69, for example, the extent of income tax evaded would be of the value of Rs. 470 crores—being one third of Rs. 1,400 crores.[58] It is also instructive to note that as one of the measures to deal with the problem of tax evasion the Wanchoo Committee recommended a reduction in tax rates! Apart from evasion of direct taxes it should be noted that agricultural income—constituting about 50 per cent of the G.N.P. —is outside of the central governments tax net altogether.[59] The rural elite that dominates at the state level where agricultural income tax can constitutionally be levied is unwilling to put a heavy tax burden upon itself. The following table shows the position for the first half of the 1960's.[60]

Contribution of Agriculture to the Public Revenues

	1960/61	1963/4	1965/6
Agric. income tax, land revenue and irrigation revenues (Rs. m.)	915	1174	730
As percentage of public revenues	5.2	4.0	2.6
As percentage of tax revenues	8.0	6.0	3.2

(N.B. Most agricultural income tax is paid by the plantations.)

Nor has the situation improved since the mid 60's—despite the rapid increase in agricultural production and the anxiety of big capital that agriculture pay its fair share. The problem of raising taxes in rural areas is not a technical one—as some authors suggest—but a social one. It is true that there are problems of assessing and collecting income tax in the countryside, particularly when a large proportion of the agricultural product is non-monetised.[61] However this was also, indeed more, true in periods of Mughal and early British rule when an extremely large volume of the agricultural product was screwed out of the countryside. What is different now, however, is that people in power at the state level are the very people who would be hit by agricultural taxation—as a result the land tax is now a mere 0.8 per cent of farm income.[62] This is not all. While the States have been unwilling to increase their taxation revenue they have persistently overspent with the result that either they have compelled the Central Government to give substantial assistance or they have run up huge debts.[63] In January 1972, for instance, the States governments had overdrafts with the Reserve Bank of India of over Rs. 470 crores due to higher than expected plan and non-plan outlays.

'It has been . . . emphasised by Mr. Subramananian that additional resources should be mobilised for implementing Plan schemes and efforts should also be taken to reduce non-Plan expenditure. It has been added that plan outlays will have to be reduced suitably if there were no matching resources though this step is undesirable. The states are in a position to raise fresh resources by taxing agricultural incomes and making better use of the irrigation and power projects'[64]— But such sentiments have been expressed for over a decade to no effect. Another possible source of revenues is from the surpluses of public sector enterprises. As has already been argued—by the very nature of the states activities there would be insufficient to finance development due to the long pay off period of public investment (indeed if they were sufficient then private capitalists would be able to do the job). At the same time it should be noted that the profitability of the government sector is maintained at a low level by the pricing policies of the government—in order to cheapen the inputs for the private sector.[65] Once again we have the same unwillingness of the propertied classes to bear the burden of development.

If the propertied classes are unwilling to bear the burden of an increase in the rate of national saving then there are only 3 options left. Firstly the poor can be made to pay more. Secondly the government can borrow more domestically. Thirdly the government can borrow resources from abroad.

As far as the first option is concerned it should be noted that the dominant feature of tax policy followed by the Government has been an increasing reliance on indirect taxes which fall quite heavily on articles of common consumption. Indirect taxes as percentage of total tax revenue (direct and indirect) increased from 50 per cent in 1950–51 to 86.8 per cent in 1971–72 (Budget estimate).[66] The following table gives details of where the taxes are levied.[67]

(Rs. lakhs) *Commodity-Wise Description of Union Excise Duties*

	1964–65	*1971–72*	*1972–73*
Sugar	5105	13345	14170
Tobacco	8968	22923	24768
Kerosene	3967	13450	14200
Cotton Fabrics	4874	5562	5730
Paper	1794	2623	2820
Cement	2731	4961	5460

The common man experiences such indirect taxes as a rise in the price of necessities. He experiences in a similar way the effects of government deficit financing.

The following table gives the volume of deficit financing.[68]

Deficit Financing by Centre and States

	Rs. Crores	
	Proposed	*Actual*
1st 5 Year Plan	290	260
2nd 5 Year Plan	1,200	1,177
3rd 5 Year Plan	550	1,133
Planning Interregnum		
1966–7		189
1967–8		224
1968–9		269
1970–1		429
1971–2		631

Over the decade up to the end of 1972 total supplies as measured by the growth of real output increased by 3.5 per cent per annum while the money supply increased by about 10 per cent per annum over the period. As a result the Union Finance Minister Y. B. Chavan had to admit in the Sabha in August

Prices indices as in—Base year 1939 = 100

Article	*1949*	*1956* (June)	*1966*	*1972*	Residual purchasing power expressed as per cent of 1949 value	per cent of erosion since 1949
Cereals	235	472	763	1232	19.0	81.0
Pulses	512	434	923	1537	33.3	66.7
Sugar and Jaggery	416	318	628	1238	33.3	66.7
Vegetable oils	711	615	1809	1811	38.2	61.8
Kerosene	170	182	311	453	37.5	62.5
Textiles	325	425	564	898	36.2	63.8
Metals	286	398	673	1590	18.0	82.0
Building Materials	191	550	762	1160	16.5	83.5[70]

1972 that the purchasing power of the Rupee was 42.4 per cent of its 1949 level.[69] In fact, the decline in the value of the Rupee is probably greater for the bulk of the population taking into account price rises for commodities of essential consumption.

Apart from soaking the poor the government has been able to borrow some resources domestically. The following table for the first 3 Plans shows total domestic borrowing in relation to the total domestic resources raised for the government's development outlays.[71]

	1st Plan	*2nd Plan*	*3rd Plan*
Total domestic resources	17,710	36,320	62,120
Domestic borrowing	8,720	23,070	30,560

(Rs. millions at current prices.)

Increasingly this borrowing has been from the financial institutions—largely on a compulsory basis. This is a trend which illustrates the difficulty of getting access to funds.

Percentage of total government marketable debt owned by:

	1956	*1967*
Financial Institutions (excl. banks)	33.6	67.2
Commercial and co-operative banks	24.7	22.9
Non-government public	41.7	9.9[72]

This lack of success in raising domestic resources for development expenditure is exacerbated by rising non-developmental expenditure. A prominent one is 'defence'. This rose from Rs. 168 crores in 1950/51 to Rs. 312.39 crores in 1961/62. The Sino/Indian border war brought with it a rapid increase to Rs. 816.12 crores in 1963/64. Following the Indo-Pakistan war of 1965/66 the defence budget rose again to Rs. 1,100 crores in 1969/70. It increased yet further after the Bangla Desh crisis.

The Inability of the State to Eliminate the Foreign Exchange Gap

Just as the state cannot raise sufficient resources to sustain the development process without recourse to foreign borrowing and squeezing the poor, so it cannot sufficiently control the development process to eliminate the foreign exchange gap. Indian foreign exchange reserves were relatively high in the early years of independence. In 1950/51 they stood at Rs. 1,029.2 crores (excluding the gold reserves). Thereafter they depleted rapidly. Between 1954/55 and 1956/57 there was a net capital inflow of Rs. 487.6 crores and a further Rs. 489.1 crores in 1957/58. Despite this the reserves had fallen to Rs. 303.4 crores in 1957/58.[74] The general trend can be judged from the growing size of the current account deficit.

Current Account Deficit. Annual averages in Rs. crores

Up to end of 1st Plan	80.5
During 2nd Plan	329.2
During 3rd Plan	511.5
1966–67	958.5
1966 to 1969–70	685.5[75]

Within the present structure of property relations Indian foreign exchange gap appears principally as a problem on the one hand of a relatively inflexible demand for imports and on the other hand of the relatively slow growth of world demand for India's exports.

As far as the demand for imports is concerned it is necessary to restress one of the key points of this book—that once capitalist development and industrialisation has been pioneered the conditions of historically belated development can never be the same. In historically belated countries on the contrary, to a certain degree it is inevitable that, instead of development proceeding through all the intermediary stages of social and economic evolution, development must proceed by leaps with the direct import of foreign equipment, foreign know-how, trained personnel and so on. The point is so obvious that it might be missed—whereas Britain's industrialisation was not greatly dependent on foreign supplies of equipment and technology India's must be to a much greater degree—thus for example the import component of investment in capital equipment for the period 1959–1966 was as high as two thirds.[76]

This would not present itself at a problem if exports could be expanded sufficiently rapidly to balance the requirement for foreign exchange. Whereas some backward countries—the oil producing states are an obvious example—have commodities for which there is a high and growing world demand this is not true of India. As has been explained in the section on the pre-Independence period—India's exports were restricted to a particular range of commodities. Firstly there are those primary commodities which were non-competitive with the products of the imperialist countries. Tea is an important example accounting for over 21 per cent of India's exports in the late 50's.[77] Primary products might be processed prior to export—jute manufactures is the key example of this accounting for about 20 per cent of India's exports in the 50's.[78] Secondly there were exports of basic consumer goods industries—industries which had branched into exporting because of the limitation of domestic markets. An important example here is of cotton textiles which made up 10–13 per cent of India's export earnings in the 50's.[79] For each of these products the growth of world demand and world trade has been sluggish and there has been competition, for example in the export of tea, from other ex-colonial countries who are anxious to increase their own foreign exchange earnings. In the case of tea India has faced a declining volume of exports due to competition from Ceylonese and East African producers and a decline in the average price of tea sales abroad.[80]

Exports of Tea[81]

		Price at London auctions Indian tea per. kg.	
Year	*Volume* in *m. kgs.*	*shillings*	*pence*
1956	237.5	10	11
1957	200.8	10	1
1958	229.5	10	3
1959	213.7	10	0
1960	193.1	10	5
1961	206.3	10	0
1962	211.8	10	6
1963	223.5	9	10
1964	210.5	9	10
1965	199.4	9	5
1966	179.2	9	4
1967	213.7	9	8
1968	208.4	8	10
1969	168.7	8	2

But the foreign exchange problem cannot simply be reduced to being the product of an economic structure in which there is an inflexible demand for imports and a paucity of export outlets. India's dependence on foreign imports reflects, it is true, a certain inevitable situation stemming from its historical belatedness. But the need to import foreign equipment, components, know how and so on also varies with the particular kind of development. A development that caters to the needs of the wealthy will throw up industries having a higher import dependence than a development catering to private necessities. A development in which the government cannot squeeze the consumption of the wealthy in line with its own increasing expenditures will generate incomes that are spent on imports—by contrast if the government could have increased its squeeze on the rich, imports would have been smaller and a margin of available capacity in domestic industry could have been used for exporting rather than for the satisfaction of a high level of domestic demand. If the government was capable of taxing agriculture, in particular, and thereby procuring a bigger supply of foodgrains; if, moreover, it had been capable of resorting to rationing in period of harvest failure, then much of the foodgrain imports might not have been necessary. Nor would such foodgrain imports have been necessary, of course, if agriculture were more dynamic. If development were less dependent upon foreign private firms it would be less expensive in terms of foreign exchange since the foreign private sector is, on balance, a net user rather than a contributor of foreign exchange. It should be noted, moreover, that foreign private capital tends to put restrictions on Indian collaborator's freedom to export. To top all of this the foreign exchange gap has been met by extensive foreign borrowing and this borrowing, while proving a short term pain killer for the balance of payments, is in the longer term a poison involving a mounting debt servicing burden which acts as a serious drain on foreign exchange earnings.

A number of these questions, which all have their fundamental root in the present structure of India's property relations, and its subordination to the advanced capitalist countries have been, or will be, dealt with elsewhere. Thus the reasons for the import of agricultural produce have already been examined and at a later stage an examination will be taken up of the effects of foreign private capital and the magnitude and implications of public 'aid'. At this stage of the argument, however, we will take up merely the issue of the state's inability to restrict the real consumption of the wealthier strata of the population either by procuring increased savings or by increased taxation. Given the increased expenditures of the government incomes have been generated which have either pulled in luxury goods directly or which have led to the establishment of new industries having high import requirements. The import component of production appears to be largest where the industries established are producing luxury goods. This is clear from the following table compiled by Bagchi from some data of Hazari.[82]

Import component in total consumption of luxuries and necessities
(as percentage of total consumption)

	1961–62	*1962–63*	*1963–64*
Luxuries	11.2	11.2	11.6
Necessities	5.8	6.6	6.4

(There is always a difficulty of precision in delineating what are luxuries and what necessities. It should be noted that in his table of necessities Hazari includes electric fans, clocks and watches, typewriters, thermos flasks, wooden furniture and fixtures and other items that for millions of workers and poor peasants would constitute unimaginable luxuries.)[83] More data on the import—either direct or in the form of components and other inputs—for luxury good industries have been compiled by K. N. Raj. For 1964 he finds that imports of raw cotton for producing superior varieties of cotton for domestic consumption came to about Rs. 50 crores; imports of yarn, pulp and chemicals for the art silk industry amounted to about Rs. 22 crores. In addition the gross value of output of industries producing other non-essentials like plastic goods, cosmetics, steel furniture, refrigerators, air conditioners and electrical gadgets amounted to not less than Rs. 50 crores in 1964 and probably the foreign exchange cost for these industries would amount to one third to one half. A careful examination of the consumption expenditure of the upper income groups will enlarge this list very considerably . . . A total foreign exchange leakage of about Rs. 200 crores per annum does not seem to be, therefore, an overestimate.[84] (Rs.

200 crores at the pre-devaluation rate would be about Rs. 300 crores at the post-devaluation rate of exchange.)

What is occuring here then, is a process of what Bettelheim calls 'pseudo-industrialisation' in which new industries are established which are often 'big importers of raw materials and semi-products, their existence means an increase rather than a decrease in the charges weighing on India's current balance of payments'.[85] The establishment of such industries tends to negate the whole purpose of the programme of import substitution initiated by the government to stem the inflow of foreign supplies. A viable programme of import substitution would have involved the establishment and growth of industries which, on balance, tend to eliminate imported supplies. But this process of 'pseudo-industrialisation' involves the establishment and growth of industries which, on balance, require foreign supplies of various kinds—they, therefore, drag back the drive to self sufficiency.

The actual progress to self sufficiency is the subject of some debate. There is some empirical work which tends to suggest that, overall, there has been progress. The following figures, for example, are taken from the work of J. Ahmad.[86]

Proportion of Domestic Production in Total Supplies

	1950/51	*1955/56*	*1960/61*	*1965/66*
Industries primarily producing consumer goods.	0.90			0.96
Industries primarily producing intermediate goods.	0.83			0.92
Industries primarily producing investment goods.	0.47	0.49	0.63	0.79

(Figures from Table 1, p. 360 Int. Dev. Studies, April 1968.)

The table may, however, be misleading because it is about domestic production and therefore it excludes imports where there is no domestic industry producing products competing with such imports. Now such imports may remain important inputs into industries that have apparently made progress towards self sufficiency by replacing imports in final supplies. Say, for example, that there was import substitution in that all of the assembly of the imported components of a particular product was done domestically whereas no assembly was done at some prior date. This might look like 100 per cent import substitution but would not be so if in both periods all components had to be imported.[87]

Another method of trying to assess the progress towards self sufficiency has been devised by V. V. Desai by examining changes in the structure of manufacturing output during the period of the 3 Plans.[88] To measure such changes the various items of manufacturing output are divided into 3 broad groups according to the stage of production at which they stand: finished stage goods, intermediate stage goods and primary or basic stage goods. The classification is somewhat arbitrary and open to revision but 'Generally, the degree of processing undergone by the product and also the degree of further processing required before it is used, has been a guiding consideration in this classification. Therefore, the finished goods—capital or consumer—are in the nature of final stage goods as they are used in such a manner that they do not become physically incorporated in the production of other goods. For this reason, machinery belongs to the finished stage goods along with a number of other goods of a very different nature. The products at intermediate stages of production serve essentially as inputs for other outputs and include goods like spun yarn, forgings and castings etc. Further the production of iron and steel, heavy chemicals etc. is included in the basic stage goods.'[89] Now if development was moving towards self sufficiency there would be a change in the structure of production towards a greater proportion of output being produced in the basic and intermediate stage goods—'To the extent that this does not happen the expanded production of final stage goods needs to be sustained by imports of the goods belonging to the earlier stages of production.' The following table seems to show that it has not taken place to any great extent and that there has been no great shift in the structure of production to basic and intermediate stage goods.[90]

Changes in the Relative Position of the 3 Groups of Goods 1951–1964
(percentages)

Group		*1951*	*1956*	*1961*	*1964*
I	Basic Stage Goods	12	11	14	14
II	Intermediate Stage Goods	15	16	16	14
III	Final Stage Goods	73	73	70	72
	Total	100	100	100	100

The implication seems to be that the move towards self sufficiency has not been as great as might be suggested by the other table.

Thus the creation of import controls may have had some, but limited, success in transforming the productive structure in such a way as to reduce dependence on foreign imports. The relative lack of success is related to the whole problem of 'pseudo-industrialisation' and the inability of the state to curb the growth of industries catering for the well off. On top of this it should be noted that import and foreign exchange controls in any case leak like a sieve and the wealthy are able to get access to foreign exchange on the black market relatively easily. The Government of India 'Study Team on Leakage of Foreign Exchange through Invoice Manipulation' estimated that the total amount of foreign exchange leaking into unauthorised channels during 1969/70 was Rs. 240 crores. In reality the sum is probably a lot higher. Thus the report estimates that the leakage of foreign exchange through gold smuggling is Rs. 160–170 crores but 'the estimate in trade circles is about Rs. 300 crores. Added to this is the large scale smuggling in of watches, synthetic fibres and a host of commodities which fetch a high premium in the country'.[91]

Conclusions

To conclude, capitalism cannot develop in backward countries in the same way as it did in today's advanced capitalist countries. India has not simply been left behind by the advanced capitalist countries—rather its development has taken the combined form natural to backward societies. But the socio-economic formation that has thus emerged does not hold out the prospect of dynamic development. The transplantation of production processes, developed and adapted to the advanced capitalist economies, into India creates special kinds of economic problems. India's industry is highly monopolised, it is plagued by excess capacity due to infrastructural bottlenecks, shortages of inputs and lack of demand. The bourgeoisie is too weak to ensure the necessary complementary development in the form of an economic infrastructure, a flow of demand and inputs from agriculture and a healthy balance of payments. Had the state not been so 'soft' it would have been able to increase the degree of productive utilisation of the social surplus instead of allowing it to be dissipated in the luxury consumption of the wealthy. Then, for example, a high agricultural income tax might have ensured a sufficient flow of foodgrains and other inputs to sustain a government development programme—thereby also providing government demand for sustained industrial growth. Again, a higher rate of taxation on the propertied classes generally—cutting down on their consumption expenditures—would have prevented the pseudo-industrialisation process which acts as a drain on the foreign exchange reserves. But neither has proved possible.

The way out of this situation for the bourgeoisie has been on the one hand to draw upon resources from abroad in the form of public 'aid' and private capital. On the other hand there has been an attempt to open up and develop more fully the rural market by inducing the maliks to modernise the agrarian structure. The next two chapters will deal respectively with the influence of the imperialist countries on India's economic developments and the developments in the agricultural sector—which is the principal remnant of the old pre-capitalist mode of production.

NOTES

1 Trotsky, *History of the Russian Revolution* pp. 26–27.
2 *Ibid* p. 27.
3 Bhagwati and Desai, *op. cit.*, p. 52.

4 J. Ahmad. 'Import Substitution and Structural Change in Indian Manufacturing Industry. 1950–1966' *Journal of Development Studies*, April 1968, p. 360, Table I.

5 Kidron, *op. cit.*, p. 124.

6 Kuldip Nayer, *Between the Lines* New Delhi 1969, p. 74. Also John P. Lewis, 'Wanted in India: A Relevant Radicalism' *Economic and Political Weekly*, Special Number 1970, p. 1213.

7 M. Merhav, *Technological Dependence, Monopoly and Growth*, Oxford 1969, p. 28.

8 Maddison, *op. cit.*, p. 116.

9 Paul Baran, *The Political Economy of Growth*, Monthly Review Press, 1957, p. 175.

10 Aurobindo Ghose, 'Monopoly in Indian Industry: An Approach' *Economic and Political Weekly*, Annual Number 1972, p. 385. See also *Report of the Monopolies Inquiry Commission*, 1965, Vol. I, Chapter III.

11 Joe. S. Bain, *International Differences in Industrial Structure: 8 Nations in the 1950's*, London 1966, p. 106.

12 Merhav, *op. cit.*, Chapter 2.

13 *Ibid* p. 89.

14 R. K. Hazari, *The Structure of the Corporate Private Sector. A Study of Concentration, Ownership and Control* Asia Publishing House, London 1966, p. 372.

15 See Chapter I.

16 Charles Bettelheim, *India Independent*, Monthly Review Press, New York 1968, pp. 72–79.

17 *Ibid* p. 75.

18 Indian Institute of Public Opinion (I.I.P.O.) *Quarterly Economic Report*, Vol. XVIII, No. 1, September/October 1971, 'The Changing Structure of Growth of India's Industries. 1960–1970', p. 18.

19 Ranjit K. Sau, 'Indian Economic Growth: Constraints and Prospects', *Economic and Political Weekly*, Vol. VII, Nos. 5.7, Annual Number 1972, p. 368.

20 Utsa Patnaik, 'Development of Capitalism in Agriculture'. Part 1, p. 27.

21 R. Thamarajakshi 'Intersectoral Terms of Trade and Marketed Surplus of Agricultural Product, 1951–52 to 1965–66', *Economic and Political Weekly*, Review of Agriculture, June 1969, p. A.98.

22 Sau, *op. cit.*, p. 366.

23 *Ibid*, p. 366.

24 Thamarajakshi, *op. cit.*, p. A98.

25 Bettelheim, *op. cit.*, pp. 238–239.

26 Thamarajakshi, *op. cit.*, p. A99.

27 B. R. Nayar, *The Modernisation Imperative and Indian Planning*, Vikas Publications, New Delhi, 1972, p. 187.

28 *Ibid* p. 186.

29 T. K. Velayudham 'Financing Public Sector Investment with Special Reference to the Role of Domestic Borrowing and Small Savings: A Case Study of India' in United Nations' *Economic Bulletin for Asia and the Far East* (EBAFE), Vol. XIX No. 2, September 1968, p. 49.

30 *Ibid*, p. 50.

31 I.I.P.O. *The Changing Structure of Growth of India's Industries*, p. 18.
32 *Ibid* p. 18.
33 *Economic and Political Weekly*, December 9th, 1972.
34 G. Myrdal, *Asian Drama*, Vol. 1. Allen Lane, London 1968, p. 66.
35 Prabhat Patnaik, 'The Political Economy of Underdevelopment', pp. 17–18. Also Prabhat Patnaik 'Imperialism and the Growth of Indian Capitalism' in *Studies in the Theory of Imperialism*, Ed. Sutcliffe and Owen, Longman, 1972, p. 215–217. For a crude critique of Marxist positions based on misunderstanding see A. H. Hanson, *op. cit.*, Chapter VII.
36 R. Das Gupta, *op. cit.*, p. 222.
37 Stanley A. Kochanek 'The Federation of Indian Chambers of Commerce and Industry and Indian Politics', *Asian Survey*, September 1971, pp. 884–885.
38 R. Das Gupta, *op. cit.*, pp. 223–224. Myrdal, *op. cit.*, Chapter 20.
39 Kochanek, *op. cit.*, pp. 880–881. See also B. R. Nayar 'Business Attitudes Towards Economic Planning in India', *Asian Survey*, September 1971, pp. 850–865.
40 *Report of the Committee on Income Distribution and Levels of Living* (*Mahalanobis Committee*) Part I, Government of India Planning Commission 1964, pp. 33, 46–47, 48.
41 I.I.P.O. *Monthly Commentary on Indian Economic Conditions*, Annual Number 1971, 'A Blueprint for Indian Employment' p. 99.
42 Daniel Thorner, *Agricultural Co-operatives in India. A Field Report*, Asian Publishing House, London 1964, p. 11.
43 Gough in Desai, *Rural Sociology in India*, p. 350.
44 B. Cohn in *Ibid*, pp. 354–363. On the 'ruling Triumvirate' of Moneylenders, landlords and Traders in the countryside, see also Lasse and Lisa Berg, *Face to Face. Fascism and Revolution in India*, pp. 42–44.
45 Patnaik 'Imperialism . . .' p. 215.
46 Hamza Alavi, 'The State in Post-Colonial Societies—Pakistan and Bangla Desh', *New Left Review*, No. 74, July/August 1972.
47 Myrdal, *op. cit.*, p. 262.
48 Velayudham, *op. cit.*, p. 60.
49 A. K. Bagchi 'Long Term Constraints on Indian Industrial Development 1951–1968' in *Economic Development in South Asia*, Robinson and Kidron (Eds.), IEA. 1970, pp. 179–182.
50 Subramanian Swamy, 'Structural Changes and the Distribution of Income by Size. The Case of India'. *Review of Income and Wealth*, Series 13, No. 2, June 1967, pp. 169–170, Table 12.
51 Bagchi, *op. cit.*, p. 184. See also B. U. Krishna Murti 'The Plan and the U-Sector', *Economic Weekly*, September 24th 1960 and Kersi Doodha 'Capital Formation in the U-Sector', *Economic Weekly*, October 29th, 1960.
52 *Report of the Direct Taxes Administration Enquiry Committee 1958–1959*, Government of India 1960.
53 Nicholas Kaldor *Indian Tax Reform. Report of a Survey*, Dept. of Economic Affairs, Ministry of Finance, G.O.I. 1956, p. 103.
54 *Ibid* p. 105.
55 *Direct Taxes Administration Enquiry Committee*, Chapter 7.

56 The following account of the Wanchoo Committee Report is taken from I.I.P.O., *Monthly Commentary on Indian Economic Conditions*, Vol. XIII, No. 9, April 1972, Blue Supplement on 'Taxation Policy and the Wanchoo Report'.
57 *Ibid* p. 11.
58 *Ibid* p. 6.
59 Velayudham, *op. cit.*, p. 58.
60 *Ibid* p. 58, Table 7.
61 R. J. Chelliah, 'Tax Potential and Economic Growth in the Countries of the E.C.A.F.E. Region', U.N. EBAFE, Vol. XVII No. 2., September 1966, p. 32. Also C. R. Thiagara Varma 'Taxation in Developing Countries', *Eastern Economist,* Feb. 18, 1972, p. 268
62 Maddison, *op. cit.*, p. 109.
63 A. H. Hanson, *The Process of Planning. A Study of India's Five Year Plans,* pp. 108, 328, 340, Oxford, 1966.
64 *Eastern Economist*, February 18th, 1972, p. 259.
65 Bettelheim, *op. cit.*, p. 168.
66 *Social Scientist,* Volume 1. No. 4, p. 69.
67 *Ibid* p. 69.
68 Figures from *Ibid*, p. 68 (for 1970–71) and B. R. Nayar, *The Modernisation Imperative and Indian Planning,* Table 13, p. 192.
69 Social Scientist, *op. cit.*, p. 68.
70 *Ibid.*
71 Velayudham, *op. cit.*, p. 60, Table 9.
72 *Ibid* p. 72, Table A.
73 R. Das Gupta, *op. cit.*, p. 85.
74 A. K. Bagchi, *op. cit.*, p. 176.
75 N. K. Chandra, *Western Imperialism and India Today* Mimeo 1972. p. 6, Table 1.
76 R. K. Hazari in Ranjit Sau, 'The New Economics' *E. and P.W.* Special Number 1972. Vol. VII, Nos. 31–33, p. 1572.
77 M. Singh, *India's Export Trends,* Oxford, 1964, p. 56.
78 *Ibid* p. 37.
79 *Ibid* p. 73.
80 'Problems and Prospects for Indian Tea Exports During the Fourth Plan' *Reserve Bank of India Bulletin* (*RBIB*), March 1971, pp. 332–351.
81 *Ibid* Table 1, p. 337.
82 Bagchi, *op. cit.*, p. 178.
83 B. R. Hazari, 'Import Intensity of Consumption in India', *Indian Economic Review,* n.s. II, No. 2 (1967), Table 2, pp. 164–165.
84 K. N. Raj in Sau, *op. cit.*, p. 1579.
85 Bettelheim, *op. cit.*, pp. 253, 301–304.
86 Ahmad, *op. cit.*, p. 360, Table 1.
87 N. K. Chandra, *op. cit.*, p. 16.
88 V. V. Desai, 'Pursuit of Industrial Self Sufficiency. A Critique of the First Three Plans' *E. and P.W.* May 1st 1971, p. 915.
89 *Ibid.*
90 *Ibid* Table 1, p. 915.
91 Nandia Pant, 'Leaking Foreign Exchange Tap', *E. and P.W.* July 22, 1972, p. 1413.

CHAPTER VI

The Effects of Foreign Imperialism

Public 'aid'

The weakening of British imperialism directly accounts, as has been shown, for the stepping up in the rate of economic growth after World War One. The exit of British imperialism from direct control of India in 1947 accelerated the process and the pace of economic development speeded up yet further. But it soon ran up against all those contradictions described in the previous chapter. These were bridged in part by 'aid' from abroad. To put it crudely India's industrialisation has been sustained, to a significant degree, on foreign credit. But foreign credit is not given out of altruism but on conditions, it has to be repaid with interest and cannot go on mounting for ever.

The following figures give some idea of the magnitude of 'aid'.[1]

Annual averages

	Gross aid		*Debt Servicing*	
Period	*Rs. crores*	*As % of National Income*	*Rs. crores*	*As % of Exports*
Up to end of 1st Plan	40.3	0.4	4.8	0.8
During 2nd Plan	286.1	2.3	23.9	0.4
During 3rd Plan	573.3	3.2(3.1)	108.5	14.5
1966/67	1054.9	(4.2)	274.5	25.4
1966/67–1969/70	1004.9	(3.4)	348.8	27.5

(figures in brackets are per cent of 'revised' estimates of national income—otherwise of conventional estimates of national income.)

The breakdown of Aggregate External Assitance into its different forms and sources is as follows.[2]

Aggregate External Assistance Utilised up to March 1971
(figures in $m, figures in brackets are %s.)

	Loans	*Grants*	*PL 480/665 and 3rd Country currency assistance*	*Total*
International Bank for Reconstruction and Development	2047	–		2,047 (12.9)
International Development Ass.				
U.S.A.	3955	353	4,149	8,457 (53.4)
U.S.S.R.	893	14		907 (5.7)
West Germany	1110	27		1,137 (7.2)
U.K.	1124	15		1,139 (7.2)
Japan	451	1		452 (2.9)
Others	994	699		1,693 (10.7)
Total	10,574	1,109	4,149	15,832 (100.0)

Before looking at the implications of foreign aid it is highly relevant to look at its actual face value so as to see how far this corresponds to its real value. For one thing, as is evident from the table shown above there is a mounting burden of debt servicing to be born which is eating progressively into the real value of aid. For another it is well known that aid tying costs reduce the real value of aid to the recipient country. No detailed estimates of such costs are available for India though figures for 1967 by Mahbub Ul Haq estimated that the worlds official aid total is reduced by 20 per cent in value due to aid tying costs.[3] Another set of data shows that freight on U.S. flag ships under tied credits runs at 43–113 per cent above the lowest quotation on international bidding. The U.S.A. requires 50 per cent of aid shipments to travel in American ships at a cost greatly excessive by world standards.[4]

One wonders—who is 'aiding' who by accepting credits—which of course have to be repaid with interest—tied to the purchase of commodities that are overpriced and uncompetitive in world markets? '. . . some of our tied exports would simply not occur if it were not for foreign assistance financing. This is most easily seen in the case of a number of U.S. commodities that are priced above world levels but which are nevertheless exported because AID funds are restricted for purposes of their purchase. The cost of some commodities we finance may run considerably above world market prices.'[5]

Apart from being aided by having to buy the most expensive commodities available on the world market there are other important implications of foreign aid. Principal of all is that India has lost a considerable margin of autonomy vis-a-vis its creditors in the advanced capitalist economies—for foreign aid is used as an instrument of control. President Kennedy put it baldly but truthfully:

'Foreign aid is a method by which the United States maintains a position of influence and control around the world, and sustains a good many countries which would definitely collapse or pass into the Communist bloc.'[6]

The U.S. works out what it wants its debtors to do and then tells them. The AID formulates for the principal aid receiving countries a Long Range Assistance Strategy which spells out U.S. economic, political, and security interests in the countries in question together with the conditions necessary for their attainment.[7]

It was precisely for this type of reason that the Indian government had tried to attract private foreign capital in the first few years after Independence with little success. It was very wary of accepting foreign official aid. Experience of American pressure on India to modify her neutral stand during the Wheat Loan negotiations of 1950 led the Planning Commission to the following conclusions when it came to formulating the First Five Year Plan.

'External assistance is acceptable only if it carries with it no conditions explicit or implicit, which might affect even remotely the country's ability to take an independent line in international affairs. There are obvious risks in excessive reliance on foreign aid which depends on the domestic political situation in lending countries and which might be interrupted by any untoward international development.'[8]

This hostility was possible given the relatively stable internal political situation in the 50's after the chaos of Independence and partition and given, also, the low level of the developmental effort which left a relatively easy domestic resources and foreign exchange position. But the situation deteriorated with the Second Plan and the 1957/58 drain on the foreign exchange reserves thrust India into a totally new dependence on foreign support.

The Growth and Effect of Foreign Private Capital

The aid givers have influenced the Indian states policies in a number of important respects. Probably most importantly they have put pressure on the government to widen the sphere of operation for private capital in general—and for foreign private capital in particular. This is most vividly illustrated by the letter of the World Bank's Chairman Eugene Black to the Minister of Finance T. T. Krishnamurty of September 1956.

'In making my own comments, I should like to emphasise once again that India's interest lies in giving private enterprise, both Indian and foreign, every encouragement to make its maximum contribution to the development of the economy particularly in the industrial field. While I recognise that the Government of India itself must play an important role in India's economic development, I have the distinct impression that the potentialities of private enterprise are commonly underestimated in India and that its operations are subject to unnecessary restrictions there . . . We feel that we would have to consider the pace and scale of our further loan operations in India from time to time in the light of economic conditions and prospects and taking into consideration the economic policies pursued by your Government . . .'[9]

This was before the full force of the foreign exchange crisis and the government for a brief time was able to take a relatively independent line. While foreign capital was invited in there was a reluctance to compromise with foreign interests. 'For example, the Government shied away from concluding an Investment Guarantee Agreement for which the United States were pressing throughout this period.' But after the foreign exchange crisis the government's attitude changed significantly. The government relaxed the majority Indian ownership rules (the so-called '1 per cent rule'), an Indo-U.S. Convertibility Agreement was signed in September 1957 and the first of a series of tax concessions to foreign firms were made—affecting salaries (May 1957), wealth tax (July), and super tax (September). Foreign firms were invited to take up the more profitable parts of state reserved industries—in drugs, aluminium, heavy electrical equipment, fertilisers and synthetic rubber. The World Bank responded with a relief operation which brought India more than $600 million in six months.[10]

Attracted by these—and a continuing stream of concessions as well as by the rapid growth of the Indian economy under the stimulus of the Second Plan expenditure, private foreign capital began to flow in increasing quantities.

Nor was it simply the state that now favoured an increased inflow of foreign private capital. From a period of hostility to foreign private capital reflecting their experiences prior to Independence the Indian industrial bourgeoisie now swung round to a position eager for collaboration with foreign capital. The very structure of the economy bequeathed by imperialism pushed in this direction. Certain inputs could be provided only from abroad and collaboration provided the foreign exchange costs of expansion programmes. The know-how and necessary trained personnel were available only in the metropolitan countries—collaboration with a foreign firm secured the necessary access to these vital inputs.[11] For every individual capital collaboration with a large foreign firm strengthened it vis-a-vis its domestic rivals. A particularly striking example of this latter factor has been the growth of the Mafatlal group. The Monopolies Inquiries Commission had shown that the group occupied 15th place among the largest business houses in 1963–64 with assets amounting to Rs. 46 crores. Within the brief space of only 3 years the assets of the group had increased by 176 per cent to Rs. 127 crores. This was done largely by expanding its interests in chemicals with foreign collaboration.[12]

The following table gives an impression of the growth of private foreign investment between 1948 and 1968. It aggregates direct investment and portfolio investment in all their different forms, but is restricted to industry and commerce and excludes the financial sector.[13]

Foreign Investment in India (in Rs. crores)

Sector	*1948*	*1955*	*1961*	*1968*
I Plantations	52.2	87.2	103.8	122.5
II Mining	11.5	9.3	12.4	9.6
III Petroleum	22.3	104.0	152.5	196.4
IV Manufacturing of which	70.7	129.1	295.0	821.6
a. food, drinks etc.	10.1	29.0	36.1	44.1
b. transport equipment	1.0	5.6	13.0	84.8
c. machinery	1.2	5.0	14.0	49.6
d. metals	8.0	11.1	95.1	155.3
e. chemicals and allied	8.0	20.3	54.1	241.4
V Services	107.9	112.8	117.3	392.7
Total	246.6	442.4	681.0	1542.8

As can be seen there has been a more than sixfold increase in foreign private capital since independence and the increase is mainly centred on the most dynamic sectors of the economy—in the manufacturing sector. This is at variance with the old colonial pattern of private foreign capital in the plantations, mines and services. Such investments have increased at a much slower pace. Chandra has worked over Reserve Bank of India studies on the finances of foreign and Indian companies to find the relative importance of foreign private capital to Indian private capital. He concludes '(1) The share of sales, fixed assets or total capital employed, controlled directly from abroad through Foreign Branches or Foreign Controlled Rupee Companies have been around one quarter; including the Companies Indirectly Controlled by Foreigners, the extent of foreign dominance generally varies between one third and one half. (2) In terms of practically every index the foreigners share has improved over the sixties. The extent of progress is generally modest, but in view of a mere 7 year span, it is by no means negligible. (3) It can be said that the foreigners have displayed a greater efficiency in exploiting the market. Thus their share of sales is higher than their share of fixed assets or of total capital employed. A far clearer indication is provided by the gross profits indicator . . . By 1968, foreigners' direct share stood at 45 per cent, overall i.e. direct and indirect (controlled companies shares of profits) was as high as three quarters for all companies and four fifths for manufacturing.'[14] (Chandra's criteria for Companies Indirectly Controlled by foreigners is any rupee company having foreign equity holdings. He argues 'It would be strange to find foreigners, individuals or institutions, willing to invest in Indian held companies just for the sake of dividends . . . These foreign companies are usually international giants who cannot be expected to behave like a junior partner.'[15]

Collaboration agreements between foreign and domestic capital are another method of penetration by foreign capital. Such collaboration agreements, multiplied rapidly from the Second Five Year Plan, reflecting the rising tempo of economic activity. Between 1948 and 1955 284 collaboration agreements were approved by the government. In 1956 there were 82, in 1957 81, in 1958 103. The figures then leapt to 150 in 1959 and 380 in 1960. Since then there have been between 300 to 400 each year.[16] A Survey of Foreign Collaboration Agreements in Indian Industry as of March 1964 by the Reserve Bank of India found that of 1,055 agreements in force machinery and machine tools, electrical goods and chemicals accounted for 55 per cent of the agreements.[17] Pure technical collaboration was relatively more important in textiles, machine tools and machinery, metals and metal products while agreements also involving subsidiaries and minority participation companies dominated in petroleum, transport equipment, electrical goods and chemicals.

The Distorting effects of Foreign Private Capital

Penetration by imperialist capital—whether in the form of investment, or in the form of technical collaboration agreements distorts Indian economic development in a number of ways. Firstly the operations of imperialist capital tend to considerably exacerbate the balance of payments constraint. The foreign private sector is a net user rather than contributor of foreign exchange.[18]

The foreign oil companies are a particularly notable drain on the foreign exchange reserves. To take the example of the three foreign owned refineries built in the 1950's. '. . . the total investment on these amounted to approximately Rs. 600,000,000 of which about one-third was in foreign exchange; whereas between 1955 and 1961 in seven years, these three companies earned a net profit of Rs. 345,000,000 including heavy depreciation, development rebates and dividend taxes. A large part of this

Foreign Exchange Contributions of the Branches of Companies (FB) and Foreign Controlled Rupee Companies (FCRC)

Annual averages in Rs. crores

	1954–55	*1956–61*	*1962*	1963–4 to 1967–8 *FB's only*	1963–4 to 1967–8 *FCRC's only*	1963–4 to 1967–8 *Total*
1 Gross inflow	19.1	35.2	32.1	–	32.0	–
a. Retained earnings	11.6	13.7	7.8	–	16.4	–
b. Non-cash inflow	6.0	17.0	25.8	–	12.6	–
c. Cash inflow	1.5	4.0	–	–	3.0	–
2 Gross outflow	–5.0	–12.2	–9.3	–	–0.4	–
3 Net inflow (1–2)	14.1	23.0	22.8	–6.3	31.6	25.3
4 Profits distributed	–24.2	–26.2	–31.2	–11.2	–37.8	–49.0
5 Overall contribution (3–4)	–10.1	–3.1	–8.4	–17.5	–6.2	–23.7
6 Contribution in Foreign Exchange (3–4–1a)	–21.7	–16.8	–16.2	–	–22.6	–

profit was remitted by 1961 and the rest was a contingent liability on India's foreign exchange reserves . . .'[19]

The foreign companies' participation in Indian economic development is now directed primarily to the internal market and as foreign capital has operations elsewhere it has no particular desire to see its Indian subsidiary or Indian partner exporting to markets either that it supplies on the spot or that it supplies from the parent company. Additionally it is not unnatural that the parent company takes preference when it comes to purchase of inputs of various kinds. In 1951–52 the exports of foreign controlled firms in India exceeded imports by these firms by an average of nearly 70 per cent—reflecting the export orientation of the old colonial pattern of foreign firms. By 1956–8, however, foreign controlled companies were running an import surplus of 10 per cent on average.[20] Foreign collaboration agreements also frequently contain restrictions on the Indian collaborators right to export. According to the RBI Survey already referred to 43 per cent of all agreements in 1964 had export restrictions.[21] The Government has tried to limit such agreements but there is a limit to what the government can do. Where necessary firms 'replace formal agreements to limit exports with informal, but enforceable ones; sales networks abroad can be denied Indian products; and recalcitrant firms may rest assured in the knowledge that the Government will carry its feud with business or an individual firm well short of the point at which production would have to cease.'[22] And of course collaboration is not free to the Indian partner—royalty payments and technical fees have to be paid on patents and licencing agreements. In 1966/67, for instance, the foreign exchange costs of royalty payments on private sector collaboration agreements came to Rs. 8.0 crores, technical fees came to Rs. 28.7 crores and dividend remittances associated with collaboration agreements came to Rs. 36.7 crores. Once again the government has tried to impose restrictions on royalty payments on patents and licensing agreements.[23] Royalties have been limited to a maximum of 5 per cent of net sales and agreements are generally not allowed to run for periods exceeding ten years. But such restrictions can easily be evaded by charging higher prices for equipment, taking higher lump sum payments for technical collaboration and so on.[24]

Foreign capital also has a very bad record over pricing. The oil companies and the drug companies are particularly notable in this respect. The government appointed an Enquiry Committee in August 1960 under the Chairmanship of K. R. Damle to look into the question of oil product prices. It reported in 1961—taking into account Soviet prices in the Indian market at 20–25 per cent below those offered by the major companies. The committee recommended a price ceiling discounting Persian Gulf prices by 10 per cent for kerosene and high speed oil, 5 per cent for motor spirit and 9.4 per cent and 3 per cent for light diesel oil and furnace oil respectively. The oil companies threatened stoppage of product imports if the Damle prices were imposed upon them and it took a year before all the majors agreed to Damle prices. But oil product prices were still high—so high that another price enquiry committee was established under J. N. Talukdar. This submitted its report in September 1965 and asked for large discounts on Persian Gulf prices—10 per cent on furnace oil, 12 per cent on motor spirit, kerosene and light diesel oil and 15 per cent on jet fuel.[25] The oil companies have also charged very highly for imported crude oil. Early in 1960 the Government concluded a contract with the U.S.S.R. to purchase 3.5 million tons of crude oil at a reported 20–25 per cent discount on Persian Gulf prices—to be paid for in rupees. But the government had no refinery of its own to process the crude oil and the oil companies refused to process imported Soviet crude when the government requested that they do so. The government had to break off its agreement with the U.S.S.R. and purchase from the companies who did, however, discount their crude prices.[26] The situation is still not satisfactory. The Shah Committee Report of 1969 called for a 25 per cent reduction in crude oil prices and large reductions in the companies' selling prices to cut gross receipts by Rs. 19.3 crores.[27]

The record on drugs prices is also a very bad one. Foreign subsidiaries (with 50 per cent or more equity) control about one half of the private sector sales. An American Senate Committee found that 'prices in India for the broad spectrum antibiotics, Aureomycin and Achromycin, are among the highest in the world. As a matter of fact, in drugs generally, India ranks among the highest priced nations in the world—a case of an inverse relationship between per capita income and the level of drug prices.'[28] The government again has been ineffective in controlling this situation. There was supposed to be a price freeze on drugs in the wake of hostilities with China but this was never operative. Hazari showed that in 1964 the then wholly foreign owned drug companies earned a cash profit sufficient to fetch their investment back in just 2 years. The rate of profit in foreign majority companies was such as to recoup their profits in a little over 4 years.[29] *The Economic and Political Weekly*, in May 1970 editorialised that price control on drugs was at last operative but by August 1971 they had another article detailing the difficulties in the control of drug prices. While prices of some essential life saving drugs have come down—this has been more than compensated for by a rise in the price of mass consumed but less essential products.[30]

The cases of drugs and oil outlined above both make clear the strength of foreign capital vis-a-vis the Indian state. To take another example from the drugs industry the companies have been able in the past to induce the Government 'to change decisions (such as further collaboration with the U.S.S.R. in the field of drug manufacture) which might be detrimental to their interests.'[31]

Foreign Technology in India's Development

Most serious of all the foreign sector acts as a channel for the import of a technology inappropriate to Indian conditions. In the discussion in the previous chapter it was argued that the transplantation of individual production processes from the advanced capitalist countries to India created problems of forward (i.e. market) and backward (i.e. imports and infrastructure) linkages. The feasibility of a solution based upon stepping up the resource flow through the government which could itself provide the necessary complements was examined. But it was found that the state did not have sufficient leverage over the economy given the social classes upon which it was based. Another possible solution not discussed there is to change the technology used in the development process to reduce, as far as possible, the problem of linkages. In other words to adapt the technology used in production to local resource availabilities and conditions and to the size of the local market.

It is quite erroneous to see technology as being rigid and predetermined. As Engels puts it 'If technique largely depends upon the state of science, science depends far more still on the state and requirements of technique. If society has a technical need, that helps science forward . . . The whole of hydrostatics (Torricelli etc.) was called forth by the necessity for regulating the mountain streams of Italy in the sixteenth and seventeenth centuries.'[32] (Letter to H. Starkenburg) But the technology used in the colonial and semi-colonial countries is but little adapted to their specific needs.

To make this point clearer and to ram home its relevance the following hypothetical illustration is distilled from an article by Urs Muller-Plantenberg.[33] This succinct essay shows both the potentially harmful effects of using technology adapted to conditions in the advanced capitalist economies and also the potentially beneficial effects of using a technology adapted to the needs of an economy like India. Muller-Plantenberg's starting point is a product, P, produced by machine, A, at cost of 17.5 units of value in an advanced capitalist economy and 15 units of value in an underdeveloped economy. The cost of production is cheaper in the underdeveloped economy because labour-power is assumed (realistically) to be cheaper—in fact wages are assumed to be two-thirds of those in the advanced capitalist economy. In addition it is assumed that the under-developed economy has to import machinery in the absence of a developed producer goods industry, but that raw materials are domestically produced in the underdeveloped economy. The cost of production for 10,000 P using machine A breaks down as follows:

	Advanced Capitalist Economy	*Backward Economy*	
	50,000M	50,000M	(M = machine)
	50,000R	50,000R	(R = raw materials)
	75,000L	50,000L	(L = cost of labour-power)
Total	175,000	150,000	
Cost for 1P	17.5	15.0	

Muller-Plantenberg then assumes the development of a machine, C, adapted to the needs of the advanced capitalist country. Specifically this machine is designed to cut down labour costs which are higher in the advanced country and to replace a part of the raw materials by cheaper synthetic inputs. Machine C has a 6 fold increase in production capacity and the following characteristics:

Cost for 60,000P in Advanced Capitalist Economy.		
	300,000M	
	150,000R	
	100,000S	(S = synthetic inputs)
	300,000L	
Total	850,000	
Cost for 1P	14.17	

However, if C were to be used in the backward economy where, we shall assume, the market is limited to 30,000 P then the cost of production will be as follows :

	300,000M	
	75,000R	
	50,000S	
	1000,000L	(i.e. $\frac{1}{2}$ of 300,000 = 200,000 at $\frac{2}{3}$ of labour costs = 100,000)
Total	525,000	
Cost for 1P	17.5	

It should be clear that in terms of costs the use of 3 of machine A would be more economical in the narrow market with a cost of 15 for 1P. But this is not the only disadvantage of using C as against A. Assuming that the synthetic input, S, is not available domestically then the import bill will more than double. Use of 3 of machine A would require imports of 150,000. Use of C will require 300,000M + 50,000S. In terms of domestic resources the cost of fixed capital rising to 300,000 from 150,000 is also a big hike. The use of the synthetic input S has reduced the demand for the domestic product R from 150,000 for 30,000P to 75,000. Moreover the number of people employed has fallen by a third—with 3 of machine A the wage bill would be 150,000—with C it is 100,000. Use of machine A thus leads to unemployment and effects the structure of demand.

To make the point clearer Muller-Plantenberg hypothesises the development, by a team of technologists, of a machine, B, to replace A that is actually adapted to the conditions of the backward economy. Machine B does not change the consumption per unit of P of labour and raw materials but, because of the lack of local resources (in terms of savings and foreign exchange) to go into the establishment of productive capacity, the aim of the technologists is to reduce the cost of the machine itself in relation to production.

Cost for 30,000P (B) In Backward Economy	
	100,000M
	150,000R
	150,000L
Total	400,000
Cost for 1P	13.33

In this example the employment of labour and domestically produced raw materials have not been hit. It should be noted that the use of B would not be economical in the advanced economy—the cost of production for 1P is 15.83 as compared to 14.17 with the use of C.

These examples are all hypothetical, of course, and so they do not prove anything. They do, however, serve to illustrate well the general significance of the type of technology used on the cost of establishing productive capacity, the structure of employment and demand, the size of the import bill and so on. There is enough empirically observable evidence to suggest that these examples reflect a real situation.

Much productive equipment is imported that is not adapted to either the size of the local market or the size of the production runs.

In a tour of a number of plants in India in 1965 Kidron describes how in almost every plant visited in which foreign collaborators had a significant equity stake new equipment could be seen standing idle. 'In some cases it was fork lift trucks, at Rs. 30,000–40,000 apiece in foreign currency, replaced by one ton pedal lifts made locally and selling at between Rs. 300 and Rs. 400. In others it was automatic lathes, replaced by very much cheaper capstans.'[34] When asked for the reasons for this management readily spoke of short runs not justifying the use of the imported equipment.

Foreign technology is inappropriate to indigenous availabilities of inputs. In theory at least a certain readaption of imported technology to the specificities of local resources endowments could be made but in practice this does not occur. This is most evident in the stipulations in many collaboration agreements that the product should only be manufactured according to the strict specifications of collaborators and that no change in the design should be made without the collaborators' prior approval. The reasons for this are obvious enough—the foreign collaborator thereby maximises his returns from the sale of know-how by forcing the Indian producer to purchase imported inputs suitable to the technology being used.[35]

'The point for emphasis is that when there is a likely collusion between equipment suppliers and designers, there is always the possibility of pumping in wasteful imports of materials and equipment at marked up prices.'[36]

The need to import components is exacerbated by the absence of standardisation. Imported machinery and equipment varies from plant to plant within the same industry as it has been supplied by collaborators according to their own convenience. In the absence of standardisation ancilliary industries do not find it economic to manufacture spares and parts required by Indian industries. This probably accounts in large part for the enormous maintenance import requirements. According to a study by the National Council of Applied Economic Research of 50 industries—these industries would require an annual maintenance import of Rs. 677 crores by 1970.[37]

Even where an effort is made to use Indian raw materials these raw materials have to be additionally processed to meet the necessary specifications for use with foreign equipment at considerable cost and wastage.[38]

The most important aspect of the inappropriateness of foreign technology to domestic resources endowments is its inability to utilise and absorb the surplus population in the colonial and semi-colonial economies like India. 'Certes, le progrès technique est une nécessité pour les economies capitalistes developpées dans la mesure où la défense des intérêts des travailleurs est relativement organisée et où joue la concurrence intercapitaliste. On pourrait alors penser que le progrès technique n'est pas nécessaire pour les economies semi-industrialisées, puisque l'offre du travail est rélativement elastique, car il existe un grande réservoir de main d'oeuvre (certes insuffisamment qualifiée), et que la concurrence est peu violente. Mais en fait, l'insertion des économies semi-industrialisées dans le processus productif mondiale ruine ce schéma, ça c'est la situation internationale qui guide le développement (le fonctionnement même) de ces économies, et, par conséquent, elles sont constraintes de suivre l'évolution des techniques des économies capitalistes developpées, elle sont «condamnées» à adopter les innovations téchnologiques des metropoles impérialistes; il y a transmission internationale du progrès technique du centre vers la peripherie.'[39]

The following tables give a broad indication of the trends

involved in employment in the factory sector and the mines.

	1951	*1955*	*1960*	*1965*[40]
Total employment in factories and mines (millions)	3·45	3·69	4·45	5·39
Increase in employment in factories and mines (millions)		0.24	0.76	0.94
Investment in the organised sector incl. power and mining (Rs. m at current prices)		5470	20300	36320
Employment-Investment Ratio in the Factory sector and mines Rs. per additional job		1:22792	1:26710	1:38638

(From RBIB July 1971 p. 995 Table I)

Compound Growth Rates % p.a.[41]

	Factory Employment	*Industrial Production*
1st 5 Year Plan	1.7x	7.4x
2nd 5 Year Plan	3·9	6.6
3rd 5 Year Plan	4·7	9.0
1951–1968	2.9	6.5

x 1951 base year.
(from RBIB July 1971 p. 994)

As can be seen the trend growth of employment in the factory sector has been very slow—much slower than the growth in industrial production. The amount of investment required to produce a new job rose from Rs. 23,000 in the 1st Plan to Rs. 27,000 in the 2nd Plan to Rs. 39,000 in the 3rd Plan.[42] Of course it is true to say that this trend reflects not just the shift in technology in each individual industry to less labour intensive techniques but also a shift in the productive structure away from the traditional industries towards modern, fairly sophisticated capital goods industries. For instance, the share of Textiles Group in total employment of the factories and mines fell from

38.5 per cent in 1951 to 26.0 per cent in 1968 and there were also declines in groups such as sugar, edible oils, tea and bidi.[43]

The trends in technology have also had an effect upon the type of increased employment generated with the fastest increases in technical and professional employment. In the manufacturing sector the proportions of different types of employees in 1967 as compared to 1961 are as shown below.[44]

Types of Employees	*% to total employment*	
	1961	*1967*
Technical and professional	1.9	2.9
Clerical and related	6.3	6.7
Administrative and managerial	1.0	1.0
Skilled	63.7	60.7
Unskilled (including office workers like peons)	25.8	23.1

In absolute terms the number of skilled workers declined from 13.5 lakhs in 1961 to 13.4 lakhs in 1967. The numbers of unskilled workers increased only marginally from 14.5 lakhs to 14.6 lakhs. 'That not much reliance can be placed on large scale manufacturing industries for a massive expansion of employment opportunities should be obvious.'[45]

Reasons for the Adoption of Inappropriate Technology

If it is true that the technology adopted is inappropriate to Indian conditions then an explanation has to be made as to why business and government use it. In particular there has to be an explanation for the adoption of a technology sparing in its use of labour in a labour surplus economy and an import intensive technology in an economy constrained by a foreign exchange gap.

A few words are necessary first on technological developments in the imperialist countries. Since World War Two all the imperialist countries have experienced a stepped up rate of capital accumulation in consequence of a secular upward shift in the rate of profit. This created favourable conditions for a rapid process of technological innovation which in turn maintained and reinforced the pace of the expansion.[46] Additionally the armings of the imperialist countries against the bureaucratised workers' states has also produced a spin-off of technologies relevant and profitable for application in the 'civilian' economy.[47] Finally another feature of the imperialist economies has been the tendency of giant corporations to diversify into newly developed product lines as markets for existing products become saturated due to a declining income elasticity of demand and the trusts are left with surplus capital needing new outlets for accumulation.[48] A McGraw Hill Survey of Research on Development activity in American manufacturing in 1962 found that in all manufacturing industries combined 'about 47 per cent of the firms reported . . . that their main purpose was to develop new products, 40 per cent that it was to improve existing products and only 13 per cent reported that it was to develop new processes.'[49]

The time horizon on the profit calculus of the giant corporations is very short '39 per cent of the large firms in a survey expect their R and D expenditures to pay off in less than 3 years and another 52 per cent of large firms in more than 3 but less than 5 years.[50] This rapid pace means a rapid obsolescence of machinery, equipment, know-how and trained personnel and the implications are that 'A market has to be found for . . . relatively obsolete elements, otherwise technical progress itself would suffer. In fact the areas of increasing foreign investments and technical collaboration are precisely those where the rate of technological progress abroad is relatively fast.' Electrical equipment and chemical industries are particularly noted for R and D expenditure on innovations in the U.S.A. and electrical equipment and chemical industries in India are major recipients of foreign investments and technical collaboration.[51]

Metropolitan capital wishes to push its know-how, its technical expertise and its technology as it is embodied in equipment into the Indian economy. This alone is a very potent reason for the import of inappropriate technology—for what is profitable and in the interests of the giant international corporations does not necessarily coincide with the needs of Indian economic development. As far as the corporations are concerned maximum profitability is attained by the maximum possible utilisation of productive technologies created at great expense and becoming rapidly obsolete. Even where this is not the main reason for technology being pumped into India by the corporations these giant companies are not likely to adjust and adapt their techniques for a relatively minor sphere of their operations within the small Indian market. Such considerations as these cover roughly a third to a half of the entire private corporate sector that is controlled either directly or indirectly by foreign capital.

To a very considerable extent it is inevitable that foreign technology should be imported and used in India. In the absence of an adequate domestic producer goods industry development necessitates an import of foreign capital goods which embody the technology of the country in which they are produced and to whose conditions they are most likely adapted. It should be kept in mind that imports constituted as high as 56.5 per cent of total supplies of capital goods in 1951 and in 1961 the figure was still 42.4 per cent.[52] Tying aid has a similar effect—only a particular range of goods brought from the metropolitan country that is the source of aid can then be acquired. No official data of aid tying is available but a semi-official computation reported by Bhagwati and Desai shows the proportion of tied aid in aid utilised rising from 66.3 per cent in the second to 82.5 per cent in the Third Plan.[53] For other reasons as well, it is very likely that foreign technology will tend to be imported and used—just as the absence of an indigenous capital goods industry necessitates the import of capital goods, at least in the crucial initial stages of development, so the small size of the scientific and technological establishment bequeathed by an apathetic British imperialism initially necessitates the import of foreign technical experts and specialists. These people are, of course, trained in, and used to, different conditions from those of India.

'Foreign technologists and foreign consultants are geared to foreign equipment and materials. Foreign consultants and equipment suppliers show a marked preference for imported machinery and equipment even when comparable indigenous equipment is available or where it is possible to fabricate it in India.'[54]

Moreover, such technical experts pass on their ideas to local scientists and technologists either through participation in local scientific and technical education or in the training of indigenous manpower in the colleges and universities of the metropolis. As an example we may look briefly at the United States links with Indian technical education. The U.S. has provided equipment and funds for 5 engineering colleges, and between 1958 and 1968 more than 500 Indian engineering educators received advanced training in the United States. The Indian Institute of Technology in Kanpur 'one of Asia's premier technological universities' is aided by a consortium of nine American Universities. Nearly 30 American professors teach there, the U.S.A. supplies a considerable volume of its equipment. The U.S. governmental scientific institution, the National Science Foundation has made consultants available to India's National Council of Science Education. These are just some of the links that inevitably bring with them imported productive techniques not always adapted to local conditions.[55]

Another reason for the use of inappropriate foreign technology is that private costs do not adequately reflect social costs. The use of labour-power that would be otherwise unemployed involves no cost to society but the capitalist purchasing the labour-power of necessity has to pay a wage. The over valuation of the exchange rate artificially lowers the cost of imported investment goods (even after the devaluation of the rupee—in 1966—the black market rate in 1969 was $1 = Rs. 12 whereas the official rate was $ = Rs. 7.5).[56] Official intervention in the market for loans has, moreover, lowered interest rates to industrial borrowers below the free market interest rate. Finally both businessmen and state bureaucrats feel safer using techniques tried and tested abroad rather than untested, and possibly unreliable, Indian technologies.

To be sure a change in state policy might be able to deal with some of these reasons for the foreign technology imports and the state could possibly make greater efforts to develop an indigenous Indian technology. It is difficult to believe, for instance, that more expenditure could not be put into research. India spends only about Rs. 80 crores on research compared with the Chinese figure of Rs. 600 crores.[57] But the fundamental issues are beyond the bounds of the Indian state—given the considerations governing metropolitan capital covering one third to one half of the manufacturing sector—there are severe limitations upon the ability of the state to bribe and bully the corporate sector to develop new techniques of production or to shift to more labour intensive industries by shadow pricing schemes of one sort or another. It has already been noted how weak the state is when it tries to cut across the interest of foreign private capital.

The question of the adoption of foreign technology not adequately adapted to Indian conditions is bound up integrally with India's subordinate position in the world capitalist economy. This subordinate position cannot in turn be dealt with unless by revolutionary changes within Indian society or else radical changes in the metropolitan capitalist countries themselves.

NOTES

1 Chandra, *op. cit.*, p. 6, Table 1.
2 RBIB, *Annual Report 1971*, p. 55.
3 Chandra, *op. cit.*, p. 4.
4 K. U. Gowda 'U.S. Aid. A Critical Evaluation', *Commerce*, November 30th 1968, p. 24.
5 Harvard Business Review article quoted in Harry Magdoff *The Age of Imperialism: The Economics of U.S. Foreign Policy*, Monthly Review, London 1969, p. 132.
6 Quoted in *Ibid*, p. 117.
7 *Ibid* pp. 142–143.
8 Planning Commission 1st Plan p. 26, quoted in Kidron, *op. cit.*, pp. 99–100.
9 Quoted in R. Das Gupta, *op. cit.*, p. 276.
10 Kidron, *op. cit.*, pp. 156–160. Patnaik, 'Imperialism and the Growth of Indian Capitalism', p. 222.
11 Kidron, *op. cit.*, p. 178.
12 Patnaik, *op. cit.*, p. 218; Das Gupta, *op. cit.*, p. 201.
13 Chandra, *op. cit.*, p. 18, Table 4, (from RBI Surveys).
14 *Ibid* p. 21, Table 1.
15 *Ibid* p. 25.
16 Patnaik, *op. cit.*, p. 218.
17 'The Role of Foreign Private Investment in Economic Development and Co-operation in the ECAFE Region', *U.N. Economic Survey of Asia and the Far East*, Bangkok 1970, p. 60.

18 Chandra, *op. cit.*, Table 5. p. 20.
19 B. Dasgupta, *The Oil Industry in India*, Cass, London 1971, pp. 139–140.
20 Kidron, *op. cit.*, p. 245.
21 In 'The Role of Foreign Private Investment . . .' p. 60.
22 Kidron, *op. cit.*, p. 312.
23 Chandra, *op. cit.*, Table 7, p. 28.
24 H. K. Bagchi, 'Aid Models and Inflows of Foreign Aid', *E. and P.W.* Annual Number 1970, p. 229.
25 B. Dasgupta, *op. cit.*, pp. 163–164.
26 *Ibid* p. 186.
27 Chandra, *op. cit.*, p. 23.
28 Quoted in Kidron, *op. cit.*, p. 251.
29 *E. and P.W.* May 30th, 1970.
30 *E. and P.W.* August 21st, 1971.
31 Bagchi 'Aid Models and Inflows of Foreign Aid', p. 229.
32 Engels, 'Letter to H. Starkenberg in Marx/Engels', *Selected Works*, Vol. II, Moscow 1962, p. 504.
33 Urs Muller-Plantenberg 'Technologie et Dependance' in *Critiques De l'Economie Politique*, No. 3, April/June 1971, pp. 68–83.
34 M. Kidron, 'Excess Imports of Capital and Technology' in *Foreign Collaboration* R. K. Hazari (Ed.), Bombay 1967, p. 264.
35 K. K. Subramanian 'Indiscriminate Import' in *Seminar* No. 131, July 1970, p. 27.
36 *Ibid.*
37 B. Prasad, 'The Problem' in *Seminar*, No. 131, p. 13.
38 M. N. Dastur, 'Implications' in *Seminar*, No. 131, p. 38.
39 Jean Bailly and Patrick Florian 'L'exacerbation des contradiction dans les economies semi-industrialisées' in *Critiques de l'Economie Politique*, No. 3, April/June 1971, pp. 31-32.
40 RBIB. July 1971. 'Trends in Employment Generations in the Factory Sector in India 1951–1968', Table 1, p. 995.
41 *Ibid* p. 994.
42 *Ibid* p. 995.
43 *Ibid* p. 999.
44 I.I.P.O., *Monthly Commentary on Indian Economic Conditions*, Vol. XIII No. 5, December 1971, 'A Blueprint for Indian Employment' p. 69.
45 *Ibid* p. 69.
46 E. Mandel. 'Laws of Motion of Capitalism and History of Capitalism' Paper to the Tilburg Conference on 'Capitalism in the Seventies' Mimeo.
47 M. Kidron, *Western Capitalism Since the War*, Weidenfeld and Nicolson, London 1968, pp. 35–37.
48 Sean Gervasi 'Arrested Development and Multinational Corporations' Paper to Seminar on Theories of Imperialism. Oxford 1970. Mimeo. See also: M. Merhav, *op. cit.*, pp. 80–96.
49 Ranjit Sau, 'Indian Economic Growth Constraints and Prospects', pp. 370–371.
50 *Ibid* p. 371.
51 *Ibid* p. 370.
52 I. Little, T. Scitovsky, M. Scott, *Industry and Trade in Some*

Developing Countries. A Comparative Study, OECD/O.U.P. London 1970, p. 60, Table 2.8.

53 Bhagwati and Desai, *op. cit.*, Table 10.9, p. 201.

54 M. N. Dastur, *op. cit.*, p. 38.

55 P. K. Kelkar, 'U.S. Assistance to Technical Education' *Commerce*, November 30th 1969, pp. 64–66.

56 Maddison, *op. cit.*, p. 123.

57 M. M. Suri, 'Deliberate Choice', *Seminar*, July 1970. p. 21.

CHAPTER VII

Agriculture and Rural Society

Economic change in India's rural society after 1947 had two fundamental sources—on the one hand the upheavals and intensified class conflict coming with and after Independence when the British prop was pulled away from under the social structure. On the other hand industrial growth had necessitated changes in agriculture so that it did not drag too far behind holding back development generally.

The Pattern of Socio-Economic Relations after 1947

As far as the first source of change was concerned Britain's exit brought in its train a significant, but by no means fundamental shift in the balance of socio-economic relations. In the remnants of the pre-capitalist mode of production the new order witnessed certain changes in the Hierarchy of power but these were insufficient to really constitute an agrarian revolution. With India's rulers on the way out the period immediately prior to, and after, Independence was one of incipient revolt in the countryside.

'Indeed things seemed to be heading towards a show down. For a time it appeared as though nothing would stop a bloody and violent conflict in the countryside. In the months preceding India's Independence on August 15, 1947, and in the period following it, the entire countryside in India witnessed ceaseless agrarian conflicts.'[1]

The peasantry were moving behind the nationalist movement bringing forward their own demands for the seizure of the land. But due to the right wing policies of the Communist party—under orders from Moscow—the Congress succeeded in taking the leadership of the peasant movement and containing the incipient revolt. On paper Congress' attitude to the Agrarian

Question was extremely radical—in order to keep the allegiance of the peasantry a programme of thoroughgoing changes in the structure of land relations was embodied in the Karachi Congress Resolution and the Faizpur Congress Agrarian Programme. These radical proposals were elaborated and reaffirmed by the Congress Agrarian Reform Committee in the first years after Independence. The C.A.R.C. recommended that all land should belong to the tiller. Intermediaries should be abolished and the subletting of land prohibited except by widows, minors and disabled persons. 6 years continuous cultivation should lead automatically to full occupancy rights. Tenants should have the right to purchase land at reasonable prices and special emphasis was to be put on preventing evictions, rack renting and illegal exactions. Measures were also suggested to deal with rural indebtedness.[2]

Agrarian reforms came—not with a bang but with a whimper. The incipient revolt was bought off by making concessions to the top layers of the peasantry at the expense of the biggest landlords and the remnants of the aristocratic classes. These latter had been loyal props to British rule but now the British had left their economic, social and political power was curtailed. The first land reform measures abolished Zamindari, Jagirdari, Malguzari and similar intermediary tenures covering about 172 million acres of land, constituting about 45 per cent of the total cultivated area.[3] At the same time measures were taken to reduce the powers of the Princes and to integrate their states into the Indian Union. Undoubtedly this curtailed the power of the upper crust of the old order but it did not amount, by any means to a complete expropriation. The princes still retained an aggregate income of Rs. 5 crores a year free of income tax as privy purses as well as other perquisites and privileges. They retained substantial landed property, palatial buildings and other items of great value.[4] The intermediaries were compensated to the tune of about Rs. 660 crores—a sum financed by their erstwhile tenants who were required to pay to the State Governments the same amount in rent as they were paying to the zamindars.[5] Liberal provisions for exemptions also reduced the overall impact of the legislation. Thus the divested intermediaries were permitted to retain land that was under their 'personal cultivation' (known as sir, khundkasht, gharkhed or khas land). Only in Assam, Kashmir, Himachal Pradesh, Bengal and Saurashtra were limits put on this land area that could be retained for 'personal cultivation'.[6] Moreover, personal cultivation was generally defined in such a way that persons could 'cultivate', as the Thorners put it, without getting off their divans.[7] The following figures from the U.P. show how little changed prior to and after Zamindari Abolition.[8]

% Distribution of Cultivated Households and Cultivated Area According to Size of Holdings before and after Z.A. in Sample Village in U.P.

	Before Z.A.		*After Z.A.*	
Size group	*% households*	*% area*	*% households*	*% area*
less than 5 acres	51.33	16.95	51.89	18.25
5–15 acres	37.27	40.17	37.39	43.55
15 acres +	11.20	42.88	10.72	38.20

To the extent that the abolition of intermediaries did take place the main beneficiaries were the upper tenants—'occupancy tenants' or 'tenants-in-chief'. Most of these were high caste peasants—and quite a few were not actually tillers of the soil. In the period of upheaval this intermediate group of rural society 'made a joint front with the rural poor to oppose the feudal burden imposed by the landlord class. But it then made common cause with the landlords in order to oppose any interpretation of land reform which might mean redistribution of land in favour of the rural poor.'[9] It is for this reason that we find that the lower down in rural society one goes—and the closer to the actual tillers of the soil—the less changed beneficially in the existing order. The abolition of intermediaries did not much help tenants of occupancy tenants, share croppers or agricultural labourers. The poor peasants in ryotwari areas remained unaffected by this legislation.[10] To be sure some legislation was passed—supposedly to benefit the lower levels of rural society. This legislation, drawn up by the various State Assemblies, provided for security of tenure, the regulation and reduction of rents and the distribution of land to the poor and landless. Erstwhile tenants were to be converted into full owners upon payment of compensation in certain areas and land owned by big landlords above certain specified area ceilings was to be taken and redistributed.[11] But it was the landlords and kulaks who dominated the State Assemblies that are, in the Indian constitution, responsible for land reform legislation. Accordingly, since there is no historical precedent for a social class willingly expropriating itself, we find that land reform legislation was passed grudgingly, was riddled with loopholes and was indifferently implemented.

There are innumerable studies of the failure of land reform legislation so it is only necessary to mention the main findings. As far as the conversion of tenants into owners is concerned a mere 3 million tenants had, by the mid 1960's acquired ownership of just over 7 million acres of land—this is only about 2 per cent of the cultivated area in the country.[12] Land ceiling legislation has also failed—landowners have split their holdings up among family members to get under the ceiling and only 1.1 million acres of land in excess of ceilings had been distributed by 1970.[13] Regulated rents were often allowed to remain at high levels—in certain areas in Andhra, Jammu and Kashmir, Madras, Punjab and West Bengal the rent share as fixed by law was as high as one third–one half of the gross produce. Rents in other states were statutorily fixed at a quarter of the crop or less but there is widespread evasion of these regulations.[14] There is evasion, too, of the provisions in land reform legislation about security of tenure. Ejectments go on through the device of 'voluntary transfers' enforced by landlords who are too strong economically, socially and politically for the poor peasants to resist.[15] Thus in the Punjab the number of tenancies fell from 583,400 in 1955 to 80,520 in 1960.[16] The widespread prevalence of oral leases, the absence of records of land rights, and widespread ignorance of illiteracy among the peasantry all facilitate evasion.

'During my visits to villages I met quite a number of people from among different groups, owners, tenants, and landless. Few of them are aware of the provisions of the Land Reforms Act. Even some of the lower revenue officers were not aware of the basic provisions of the law. This is rather sad. It is little wonder then, in the absence of any awareness of the basic provisions of the law that there has been little enforcement. Whenever I made enquiries the customary rents are half the gross produce. The lands still continue to change hands from tenant to tenant or from tenants to owners. I understand that translation of the Act in local language was under print and would be made available to staff shortly. Much more needs to be done in this direction.'[17]

According to National Sample Survey (NSS) data the area leased in as a percentage of operated area fell from 20.34 per cent in 1953/4 to 10.7 per cent in 1960—but a substantial amount of tenancy is concealed.[18] A study in Eastern U.P. found that 28.8 per cent of the net land area was cultivated under illegal informal tenancy. In Western U.P. about 13.2 per cent of the net cultivated area was sublet informally.[19] K. N. Raj guesses that, taking all revealed and disguised tenancy arrangements together probably as much as 35–40 per cent of the total cultivated area is under some form of tenancy.[20] Certainly it may be taken as being indicative of a large amount of concealed tenancy that between 1953/4 and 1960/1 the number of permanent farm servants per acre rose by about 65 per cent. 'This may indicate that an increasing number of actual tenants (particularly share croppers) have been reported as permanent farm servants.'[21]

Sharecropping has remained prevalent and sharecroppers have received little protection in the land reform legislation. Thus in U.P. while the law prohibits leasing it permits partnership in cultivation (sajhedari). 'In practice, leasing on crop sharing is increasing. The sharecroppers usually pay half the produce as rent . . . sharecroppers are unable to claim any rights under the law.'[22] In West Bengal the State Government estimates that 34 per cent of the rice area is under barga (sharecropping)—the landowner taking half the gross produce. These sharecroppers are not recognised as tenants under the law.[23]

Likewise the agricultural labourers have gained little. As has been said only 1.1 million acres has been distributed from land in excess of ceilings. The proportion of completely landless rural households as a proportion of rural households has fallen from 23.09 per cent in 1953/4 to 11.68 per cent in 1960/61 but the proportion of households possessing less than 0.5 acres is not much different 41.10 per cent in 1953/4 and 37.9 per cent in

1960/61.' This means that any settlement of landless people has been on extremely tiny plots.'[24]

Overall the pattern of land ownership has remained highly unequal. The following table shows the distribution of land ownership in 1953.[25]

Size range of family holding (acres)	*% Rural Households*	*% Area*
no land	23.09	0.00
0.01–0.99	24.17	1.37
1.00–2.49	13.98	4.86
2.50–4.99	13.49	10.09
5.00–9.99	12.50	18.40
10.00–24.99	9.17	29.11
25.00–49.99	2.66	18.65
50.00 and above	0.94	17.54

As far as rural indebtedness was concerned the Congress Agrarian Reforms Committee recommended compulsory scaling down of rural indebtedness on the basis of the paying capacity of farmers. For agricultural labourers it was suggested that debts be completely wiped out. As a means of providing alternative credit the large scale use of the multi-purpose co-operative was suggested. Here again we find a slight, but not a great change.[26] The moneylender-trader still holds an important grip in village life. The following table shows the shift in the sources of credit over the fifties.

Cash Loans borrowed according to credit Agency
(All rural households)

Credit Agency	*Rural credit – % 1951–52*	*Rural credit – % 1961–62*
Government	3.3	2.3
Co-operatives	3.1	13.8
Commercial banks	0.9	0.7
Landlord	1.5	0.7
Agricultural Moneylender	24.9	33.9
Professional Moneylender	44.8	12.7
Trader	5.5	10.1
Relatives	14.2	8.8
Others	1.8	17.0

All India Rural Credit Survey, Vol. II General Report p. 167
All India Rural Debt and Investment Survey 1961–62, RBIB Sept. 1965.

As can be seen co-operative credit has increased but is by no means the dominant source of funds. A far more significant shift has taken place away from the non-agricultural professional moneylender to the agricultural moneylenders (top peasants and large landholders) and there is also a not insignificant shift towards traders.

Even the increase in co-operative credit has to be treated with great caution. Thorner's researches in the field have revealed that co-operative credit is not always an alternative source to the existing village sources of credit. This is because it is precisely the 'big people' in the villages that take over the co-operative credit societies where they are set up. 'One cannot help but be impressed by the position occupied in the co-operatives by one or another person who lends money. The cultivator who also does some moneylending figures prominently in co-operatives in Baroda, Saurashtra, Hyderabad and Rajasthan. The trader-cum-moneylender is found in societies in Saurashtra, Mysore, the Nilgris, Nellore and Kashmir. The formidable combination of the cultivating moneylender-cum-trader dominates the scene in Mysore and Coastal Andhra.'[27]

The situation, then, has probably not changed a great deal from what it was in the early 1950's when the Rural Credit Survey of the Reserve Bank of India revealed that 63 per cent of all rural families were in debt.[28] At this time there were substantial variations in interest rates among the regions.[29]

Frequency of loans at specified interest rates India 1952

	% loans
Less than 10	18
10 –12.5	25
12.5–18	9
18 –25	29
25 –35	9
Over 35	6
Not specified	4
Total	100

Similarly, little has changed with regard to exploitation of poor peasants by the traders—who are often also moneylenders and sometimes landlords as well. The situation is all right for the more substantial peasants who can take their produce to market where there is substantial competition among traders, or whose purchase of inputs and sale of produce is sufficiently large to attract merchants—however, 'the literature of protest describing exploitation of economically weak elements by the trading class is based on fact . . . there is little competition for the business of the farmer who has smaller quantities to market.'[30]

As with its credit policy the government has sought to deal with this problem of marketing with co-operatives—i.e. marketing and distribution societies. These are less numerous than the credit co-operatives—but they are certainly significant in some states —for example Bombay, Madras, Andhra, Punjab and Bihar. More than 75 per cent of chemical fertilisers are distributed by the co-operatives and they are also important in the distribution of seeds. In some States they have a legal monopoly of sugarcane marketing and sometimes take part in agricultural processing industries. As far as the weaker peasants are concerned, however, the problem is the same as with credit co-ops—in other words once they are set up it is the richer peasants that benefit most and the village traders may take them over for their own purposes.[31]

Apart from the development of co-operatives the government developed, in the 1960's, a public distribution network including 'fair price shops' so as to make food-grains available to the weaker sections of the community. But the public distribution system has not displaced the private traders by any means.

'Consider the Food Corporation of India, the State Trading Corporation, the Cotton Corporation et al; consider their modus operandi. In many instances they are public bodies only notionally, leaving aside the general social philosophy of the functionaries adorning these organisations, even in operational terms they can scarcely be regarded as supplanting private traders. The latter continue to flourish in practically all the so-called 'canalised' sectors, as commission agents of the public bodies. Private intermediaries have not been weeded out, they are now the percentage merchants who have acquired a vested interest in state trading . . .'[32]

The Relations of Production and Productive Forces in Indian Agriculture

The picture that emerges from all this is a fairly clear one. While there were some changes at the top of rural society the economically weak elements were, by and large, passed by in the changes brought about by the upheavals of Independence and its aftermath. But these economically weak elements are precisely the majority of rural society. To repeat, in 1953 61.24 per cent of rural households owned less than 2.5 acres each and 23.09 per cent owned no land at all. It is this situation which, in the last analysis, blocks the development of the productive forces. The economically weak put in most of the work and effort into the tilling of the soil—but they do so in conditions which are extremely unfavourable and which deny them the resources and inputs to unlock their energy and enthusiasm. The economically strong have the resources to plough back into the development of production but the nature of the agrarian structure checks this. On the one hand substantial incomes can be earned without any great agricultural investment—on the other hand returns in usury, trade and leasing land are often very favourable as alternative channels for funds as compared with productive investment.

To the extent that they put in the work and effort in the form of tenants their weakness makes them subject to a high level of rents and to insecurity of tenure. We have already seen that even the Land Reform Laws often allow rents up to one third to a half of the gross produce. The Land Reform Implementation Committee of 1966 cites the rents that it found in various states. In Andhra the prevailing rent was a half, going up to two thirds of the gross produce in fertile areas. In Bihar the tenants usually paid one half the gross produce, going up, in some cases to 65 per cent. In Madras the prevailing rent share was found to be 50 per cent of the gross produce. In Orissa the rents paid by the bhagchasis amounted 'in many cases' to half the gross product. In the Punjab rents 'exceeding the level of the law and going up to half the gross produce are quite common'. In Rajasthan though the law fixes the rent at not more than one sixth of the gross produce the prevailing rent share is generally a quarter of the gross produce. In Uttar Pradesh the crop sharers usually pay half the produce as rent.[33] In West Bengal also, the crop sharers pay half the gross produce.[34] With such high rents, and insecurity of tenure (the details of which have already been mentioned) tenants-at-will and sharecroppers are stripped of the resources, and divorced from any incentive, to increase production.

To the extent that labour is performed under hire to the maliks the extreme weakness of the rural poor pushes wages down to the very brink of starvation. Thus in 1956/57 when 25 per cent of all rural households were agricultural labour households 57 per cent of these lived below a consumption level of Rs. 150 per capita per annum.[35] Given the prevalence of unemployment agricultural wage rates have remained stagnant. For example in the Punjab between 1956–57 and 1964–65 the average daily male wage rate rose by about 17 per cent—but the general retail consumer price index rose by 34 per cent in the same period indicating a fall in real wages. Over this same time span agricultural production in the Punjab rose by 42 per cent.[36] Wages may be pushed lower still where unfree labour continues. Unfree labour may take a number of forms but its general characteristic, formulated by Thorner, is that the labourer cannot refuse to work for a given employer—particularly at the height of the season—and is tied by one of a variety of possible attachments—debt, traditional ties to a family or an estate, the allotment of a plot of land or tenancy. As Thorner notes 'Unfree labour almost invariably entails wages at lower than the market rates. It often involves longer hours, irregular payment, the performance of household as well as agricultural tasks, or a claim by the employer for the time of the labourer's wife and family.'[37]

Low wages, whatever may be their cause, make possible high profits. Utsa Patnaik has surveyed the sources of income of big farmers in a 1969 study of 66 big farmers (i.e. those having more than 20 acres) scattered over ten districts in five states. For her sample she finds the average rate of surplus value on the use of hired labour to be as high as 307.28 per cent.[38]

(Here the rate of surplus value is defined as $\frac{S}{V}$ where s = gross value of output minus depreciation on fixed capital plus all productive outlays in cash and kind, and v = cash + kind wages.)

The point that needs to be stressed is that these kind of high profits stem from the weakness of the rural poor and utter dependence on the landowning maliks, while this weakness persists the maliks can continue to extract social surplus from the direct producers without any great entrepreneurial effort or investment. Indeed entrepreneurial decision making can often be left to some person on the spot—the receiver of profits being a pure parasite little different from a rent receiver. So in Saurashtra we find that Girasdars possessing large holdings of 75 to 200 acres have the land cultivated 'by hired labourers under the supervision and guidance of the trusted and senior labourer who is paid somewhat higher than other labourers. The same type of bullocks and wooden ploughs were employed as were used by the tenants. Girasdars do not employ large scale production techniques or investment as the capitalists did in their factories or contribute their labour as the ordinary cultivators do.

'Girasdars do not perform either the functions of entrepreneurs in the true sense or employ their own labour power but only live on unearned income. (This) . . . is rendered easy on account of ample availability of cheap landless labour.'[39]

The unequal distribution of landownership and economic power makes it possible and profitable for the landowner to combine various modes of exploitation of the rural poor. The weak are in constant need of general and household credit which the landowner has the resources to provide. Because the landowner is either landlord and/or employer he can ensure repayment of principal and interest by suitable adjustments of rent or wages. The landowner can also act as the main agency for agricultural marketing. On the one hand his own lands produce in surplus to the needs of himself and his family, on the other hand his position as landlord and moneylender ensure access to the produce of the poor in rents, interest and repayment of principal on loans. Each of these modes of exploitation overlap and mutually reinforce each other.

A survey of 26 villages in West Bengal[40] shows how the intensity of exploitation can be screwed up by the combination of landlordism with the usury and trade. In this survey 40–50 per cent of the cultivators in the sample were kishans—a category covering cultivators having little or no land or capital of their own and having no security of tenure for more than one production cycle. As a result of indebtedness among the peasants 'while the legal share of the kishan is about 40 per cent of the harvest . . . his actual available balance of paddy after repayment of interest and principal was normally around 16 per cent. This is an average for 26 villages.' This particular system is particularly pernicious to the development of the productive forces. The landlord, since he depends for an important part of his income through usurious exploitation needs to keep the kishan indebted to him to continue this. Thus technological improvements raising the productivity level of the peasant 'become undesirable to the landowner to the extent that they increase the kishan's available balance of paddy in relation to his consumption level so as to reduce his requirements for consumption loans. For it weakens the system of semi-feudalism where economic and political power of the landlord is largely based on his being able to keep the kishan constantly indebted to him.'[41]

The moneylender-trader has powerful mechanisms to extract profits from the poor peasants. Because these poor peasants lack access to the commodity market they are unable to take advantage of price fluctuations in selling their products but rather become the victims of those price fluctuations. The kishan typically has to borrow just before the harvest at a time when prices are at a peak—they have to pay back after the harvest when current market prices are at their lowest. Bhaduri found examples where the price of a manund of rice could fluctuate from Rs. 20 to Rs. 60 in 3 months. Peasants having to borrow through the moneylender/trader found themselves borrowing at the higher price and then paying back 3 times over in terms of maunds of rice—in other words effectively paying an interest rate of 200 per cent.[42]

At the bottom end of this agrarian structure the rural masses are doomed to work under conditions of low labour productivity, underemployment and unemployment. While these masses do most of the work their super-exploitation denies them the inputs needed to increase their productivity. This is not due simply to lack of physical assets—but also for example, inadequate nutrition and education.

In education the pressure of the upper landed interest and of the urban middle classes has led to the creation of more and more places at the middle and higher educational levels while primary education has suffered neglect financially which has left it weak in its staffing, programmes and general effectiveness. The schools offer little of use to the poor whose children drop out early on. In 1968 only about 57 per cent of children aged 6 to 11 were attending school on a full time basis. In higher education, by way of contrast, courses are free, entry requirements easy and there is an oversupply of university graduates. Development directed at the needs of the rural (and urban) poor for education would give a much higher return than the existing set up.[43]

In terms of nutrition there is more evidence that economic development putting work and incomes at the disposal of the poor would pay off handsome dividends through increased labour productivity—quite apart from the reduction in human misery. The average Indian male aged 25–29 weighs 109 lbs and the average for landless labourers must be considerably less. This is less than two thirds the size of people in the prosperous Western Countries or in Latin America.[44] In an article in the RBI Bulletin Ojha found that in 1960/61 6.3 per cent of the rural population were deficient to an extent of 49 per cent of a minimum adequate foodgrain intake of 518 grammes per capita per day. 52 per cent of the rural population were deficient to the extent of at least 10 per cent. By 1967/68 the 52 per cent had risen to 70 per cent. Given the low nutritional intake the return on an improved diet would seem to be quite high.[45] It has been estimated, for example, that a 40 per cent rise in builders' wages would have improved nutrition enough to have raised productivity by 50 per cent in the construction of the Bhakra Nangal dam.[46]

On their own dwarf plots the rural poor utilise to the maximum their abundant labour power and scarce land resources. For this reason there is a far higher output per acre on small operational holdings.[47]

Output and Costs per Acre and per Man day by size of Farm, Punjab, India

Size of farm acres	*Cost of inputs per acre (Rs.)*	*Value of output per acre (Rs.)*	*Value of output per man day (Rs.)*	*Net labour return per man day (Rs.)*
0–5	240	200	3.77	0.69
5–10	203	186	4.15	1.04
10–20	180	173	4.67	1.33
20–50	154	154	5.32	1.66
50 and above	127	143	6.98	2.68
All farms	165	163	5.02	1.53

Cost of inputs include imputed values for family labour and family owned land and capital. Net labour return per man day is equal to total value of output minus all costs other than labour divided by man days of family and hired labour.

The theoretical explanation for this table is simple enough. There is large scale unemployment and underemployment of rural labour for reasons examined in earlier chapters. An estimate for the mid 50s suggests that, on average, an agricultural labourer could not find work for 60 days each year though willing to sell his labour power. The utilisation of labour that would otherwise be unemployed has zero opportunity costs and, as a result, family labour on small farms is employed to that point where the marginal product of labour is zero. On large farms, however, labour-power has to be hired to work the land and a wage, albeit a low one, has to be paid. Consequently labour use is less intensive and gross value of output per acre is lower on larger farms. This can be represented diagrammatically as on the opposite page.

On the larger holdings constituting the bulk of the land area cultivation by hired labour is restricted to the point where the wage rate OW is equal to the marginal product of labour. This gives output OT_1. On the smaller family cultivated farms, by contrast, the labour input is utilised to the point where the Marginal product equals the 'real' social opportunity cost—i.e. OL_2 where $MP = O$. This gives total output OT_2. But this higher output per acre is produced on the smaller proportion of land area. It is, then, only too evident that the existing relations of production prevent the development of the productive forces in agriculture. What is needed is for the power of the maliks,

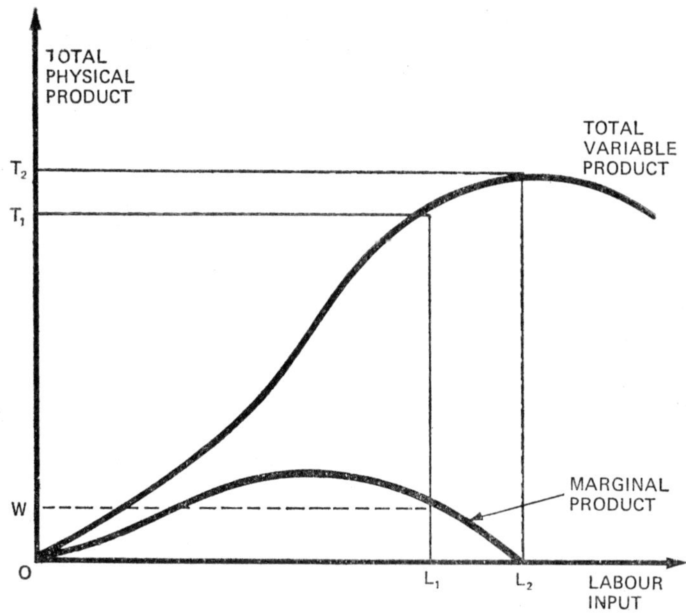

the moneylenders and traders to be broken, for the land to be redistributed to the actual tillers of the soil and for new modes of agrarian organisation to be developed to mobilise and utilise the energy and enthusiasm of a better fed and better educated rural labour force.

Apart from tilling larger plots expropriated from the land-owning groups the more egalitarian structure of rural society will make possible the widespread utilisation of otherwise unemployed labour-power in rural public works for general rural uplift. To some extent this may be done on a voluntary or on exposte payments system—but above all this effort must be obtained from the peasants willingly 'any attempt to transform this mobilisation into a system of forced labour would quickly lead to a fall in output and would be felt on a large scale as a waste of resources, from the standpoint of economic growth.'[49] The disastrous experience of forced collectivisation in the Soviet Union is a telling testimony to the dangers of coercion of the peasantry.[50] What seems to be necessary is the 'carrying out first of all of works which make possible an immediate raising of the standard of living of the rural communities themselves, for example, the building of peasants' houses, of schools, infirmaries and hospitals etc. An extensive, though often fragmentary, body of experience, is beginning to be accumulated in this sphere, in China, in ex-French Guinea and especially in Cuba.'[51]

All of this is quite incompatible with the present structure of rural society—voluntary labour would not benefit those who put in the work but the maliks. This accounts for the failure of the Indian government's Community Development schemes of the 1950s. These were designed to achieve rural uplift by multi-purpose programmes of self help activities. But in 1957, 5 years after the programme had been initiated, the Balwantrai Mehta Committee Report explained what was wrong. 'The upper castes will not soil their hands with labour or risk physical contact with untouchables, and the latter have little incentive to provide free labour on schemes which are most likely to benefit upper castes.'[52]

There is a marked contrast between Indian and Chinese experience in the utilisation of underemployed rural labour-power. After the failure of India's Community Development Programme it was recognised that people employed on India's rural public works would have to be paid wages and more serious thought was given to the operational and organisational problems of such public works. But in the Third Plan only Rs. 19 crores was made available and in the last year of the Third Plan expenditure stood at ammere Rs. 8 crores. This represented employment opportunities for a mere 0.1 million man years.[53] The situation in the Chinese Communes is otherwise—the Communes have been able to apply both systems of deferred wages and of unpaid collective labour and have thereby 'converted human labour directly into physical assets on a spectacular scale despite mistakes and excesses.'[54]

Lewis argues that unemployed rural labour power could be employed in a wide variety of productive activities—in land improvement, irrigation, draining, reforestation and to combat soil erosion.[55] As we shall argue later a considerable increase in the area under irrigation has, at first glance at least, much to argue for it as a strategy for Indian agriculture. For one thing in the irrigated areas—the peasants are kept busy for 280 days in the year, on average, as against only 114–118 days in the non-irrigated areas.[56] What must be stressed once again, though, is that a strategy to mobilise the rural masses can only be successful if these masses feel tangible and fairly immediate advantages to themselves and so participate willingly.

Finally it has to be asked how such an agrarian revolution could come about. History is made by the actions of social classes acting in conformity to their material needs. The existing power over land legislation is held in the State Assemblies that are dominated, by and large, by the maliks, traders and money-lenders themselves. History shows that where the landowners are pressurised by the threat of revolution or by pressure from outside to themselves transform the pattern of agrarian relations they do so only in a 'niggardly and thieving fashion.'[57] This is the experience of Russia described in the introduction to the thesis. This is also the experience of land reform legislation in India. Social classes do not expropriate themselves (if they did so history and society would be very difficult to analyse!). Maddison in his work on Class Structure and Economic Growth in India calls for a major redistribution to the landless and sharecroppers. Discussing a land reform which would fix an upper ceiling of 5 acres on a family holding he argues that 'A land reform on this scale would revolutionise the structure of village society and break the economic basis of the caste system. It would also rouse political opposition, and would result in widespread violence in rural areas because it would undoubtably contain a substantial element of confiscation. However, these costs of transition will probably have to be paid sooner or later, because there is no alternative to land reform if the bottom half of the rural population are to get any benefit at all from economic growth.'[58] But Maddison does not say which social class will implement the land reform.

Clearly it is the interests of the rural masses themselves to revolutionise the structure of village society and they will be the main force for the agrarian revolutionary upheaval. However:

'We know from our own experience—and we see confirmation of it in the development of all revolutions, if we take the modern epoch, a hundred and fifty years, say, all over the world—that the result has been the same everywhere: every attempt on the part of the petty bourgeoisie in general, and of the peasants in particular, to realise their strength, to direct economic and politics in their own way, has failed. Either under the leadership of the proletariat, or under the leaderships of the capitalists —there is no middle course.'[59]

Will the Indian bourgeoisie play a leading role in the liberation of the peasantry? The answer to this is unquestionably no. The central theme of this book is that, despite its successes in the advanced capitalist countries capitalism in the Third World does not have the same dynamic revolutionary character. Its representative, the bourgeoisie, is like the other bourgeoisie's described in the introduction—'slothful and craven'. Its prosperity is already dependent upon its links with the old order. The bourgeoisie itself participates in the exploitation of the countryside—it is dependent upon the maliks and landowners as the best customers for its products. Besides this the bourgeoisie fears that any revolt against landlord property would rebound against capitalist private property. A gigantic agrarian revolutionary upheaval on the scale that Maddison describes would undoubtedly have repercussions on the class struggle that is already at a high level in the towns. For all these reasons the bourgeoisie prefers to maintain the integration of the capitalist mode of production with what is left of the pre-capitalist mode of production—i.e. rural society and the agricultural sector of the economy—and to continue to share power in a coalition.

Since the bourgeoisie cannot liberate the peasantry then the leadership of the peasant masses falls to the proletariat. As Trotsky put it—only describing the Russian bourgeoisie in an analogous situation :

'The . . . bourgeoisie has bequeathed all revolutionary positions to the proletariat. It will have to abandon to it revolutionary hegemony over the peasantry as well.'[60]

This is the pre-condition of the realisation of Maddison's call for such a radical agrarian reform.

The Bourgeoisie's Strategy for Agriculture

When it became clear that agriculture's expansion was crucial to industrial expansion more stress came to be laid in this field. This was especially true in the 1960s and, in particular, after the disastrous harvests of 1965–66 and 1966–67. But instead of a strategy to unlock the energy and enthusiasm of the oppressed rural masses agrarian development has been directed towards and through the rural elite. The importance of agriculture and the growth of the marketable surplus for industry is clear. The figures given in a previous chapter indicate that this means concentration on the maliks who are the key to the rural market. It is in any case obvious that the big people in the countryside are able to collar the benefits of government development programmes. They can easily take over organisations set up by the government to channel resources into agriculture.

'Institutions established by the government like co-operatives, Vikas Mandals, Gram Panchayats and Nyaya Panchayats are . . . assisting in practice only the richer sections of the rural population and are further controlled by them.'[61]

The tendency of the government's village level workers and other agricultural extension services is to go to the 'natural leaders' of the village and concentrate their energies there.[62] The pretence of an egalitarian thrust in the land reforms of the 50s and the Community Development schemes became more and more shallow as this became clear. In the 1960s the pretence was dropped altogether and the agrarian strategy became much more openly concentrated on the maliks—and also on India's already developed areas. The Intensive Areas Development Programme was started in 1961 pioneered by the Ford Foundation in 15 of India's districts. The IADP emphasised the necessity of providing the cultivator with a complete 'package of practices' in order to increase yields—including credit, modern inputs, price incentives, marketing facilities and technical advice. In 1965 the policy was extended to 114 districts of the Intensive Area Agricultural Programme covering 20–25 per cent of India's land area with assured water supplies.[63] The use of new higher yielding varieties of seeds, in particular of wheat, was crucial to the programme. After two years of disastrous drought in 1965–66 and 1966–67 the Green Revolution got under way in earnest.

The Green Revolution is not a home grown flower. On the contrary its story 'is woven into the fabric of American foreign policy and is an integral part of the postwar effort to contain social revolution and make the world safe for profits.'[64] The Rockefeller and then Ford Foundations had already been active in agrarian research and development programmes throughout Asia and the Third World long before the IADP was initiated. Ford had moved money and people into the Indian Community Development Programme and the Rockefeller Foundation had begun work in India by sending agricultural experts to work on corn and sorghum.[65] In 1959 the Ford Foundation sponsored a team of experts who produced a 'Report on India's Food Crisis and Steps to Meet it' with the backing of the Indian government. The die was set and the IADP at birth was largely a child of the Ford Foundation.[66]

The 'New Strategy' for agriculture in many ways typifies India's economic development record after 'independence' from British imperialism. Devised and introduced from outside it is based on the agro-economic ideas of Theodore Schultz in his book *Transforming Traditional Agriculture*. Since the strategy involves a massive infusion of modern inputs—new seeds, fertilisers, pesticides and, increasingly, agricultural machinery—it is good pickings for international agribusiness.

'When India embarked on its agricultural programme, the U.S. Official agencies and private companies came forward with assistance for, or investments in, fertiliser plants (i.e. Coromandel, Madras, Bombay) and U.S. Companies such as International Harvester and Caterpillar are helping produce the agricultural equipment needed to modernise farming.'[67]

The American government has been on the ball making sure that American corporations get their share of the gravy.

'For a long time India insisted that it handle all the distribution of fertiliser produced in that country by U.S. companies and that it also set the price. Standard of Indiana understandably refused to accept these conditions. AID put food shipments to India on a month by month basis until the Indian government let Standard of Indiana market its fertilisers at its own prices.'[68]

Apart from collaring a significant share in the market for internally produced fertilisers substantial funds provided by USAID have financed the import of fertilisers.[69] All in all, because the production processes used are not complemented by internal production, roughly 60 per cent of the cost of production of wheat as produced in the new strategy finds its way into imports, according to the estimates of Ranajit Sau.[70]

Evidently the Green Revolution strategy is the most appropriate one for the profitability of the international corporations and there was, apparently, no consideration given to any other alternative strategies. This cannot be because it was the only possible one—on the contrary some economists have raised serious doubts as to whether it was the most appropriate. Sau, for example, has calculated the cost per extra tonne of wheat by two strategies. One involves changing production from traditional to the modern 'package' methods.[71] This, of course, has to be on lands that already have assured water supply. The other is a strategy based on simply irrigating areas using traditional methods of production. His results are as follows.[72]

Cost per tonne of wheat (Rs.)

Strategy	*Including direct labour cost*	*Excluding direct labour cost*
1 From traditional non-irrigated to traditional irrigated.	337·96	262·39
2 From traditional irrigated to non-traditional 'New Strategy'	349·04	336·45

The result is not conclusive but is at least suggestive of the alternative possibilities. Sau's alternative strategy would have had the added advantages of involving a much greater utilisation of the unemployed and underemployed rural labour power. By contrast, as will be explained below the Green Revolution may well actually have a net effect of displacing rural labour-power and increasing the level of unemployment. Simply expanding the irrigation area would not, moreover, have necessitated the import of foreign inputs or foreign capital and know-how.

Lipton has also thrown doubts on whether the Green Revolution is the most appropriate approach. He argues that risk distorts the production patterns of dry farmers with security being put before maximum output and with each farmer's tried and tested 'survival algorithm' coming before his desire to maximise profits. In such conditions as these a policy both to reduce risk and also efforts to improve traditional practices through education and demonstration might have been better.[73]

Much has been written about the development of capitalism in agriculture and the Green Revolution. In essence, while agriculture may stimulate industry in years of good harvests, it is putting the brakes on industrial expansion in the secular sense. This has been offset by large scale importing of agricultural products especially under P.L. 480 aid. In addition, however, agriculture has been pulled along by the stimulus of more rapid industrial growth—this is both a product of the operation of market forces and government efforts. There are signs that, in particular in the already more advanced areas in the country like Punjab, and Western U.P., the better off peasants and landowners are approaching agriculture in a more business-like manner. They are beginning to productively accumulate a larger volume of the social surplus.[74]

Here and there field researchers have discovered urban funds invested in agriculture by 'gentlemen farmers'. These urban entrants are capitalists in the 'pure' form. For them agriculture is a field of investment on a par with any other which is chosen when it seems to offer the best rate of return on invested funds—though it does have the special advantage of the absence of taxation and prying officialdom. Agriculture is an ideal haven for the investment of black money. These urban entrants are only a small element in the process of capitalist development but they 'exercise a demonstration effect out of proportion to their numbers.'[75]

Among the other landowners the move towards capitalist farming is more patchy but is definitely present. There are a number of aspects to this process and capitalist development appears, inevitably, in an impure form carrying strong traces of pre-capitalist attributes. Referring to her sample of 66 big landowners scattered over various districts in India Utsa Patnaik argues that 'To expect a former landlord or peasant to display all the characteristics of the pure-capitalist would be to abstract from his class background.'[76] Landlords and dominant landholders in her sample usually tied destitute labourers with loans, combined productive capital investment with moneylending and combined intensive capitalist production on a part of their land with leasing at high rents on other parts of their land.

But the trends are definitely there. New relationships of exploitation are replacing tenancy or the customary relationships of obligation between cultivators and the service castes. In the Punjab, for example, it is estimated that the number of tenants decreased from 538,000 in 1955 to 80,000 in 1964.[77] In the same state new relationships between employers and agricultural labourers are in evidence. The greater demand for labour at the harvests led to rising wages.[78] The landowners, resentful of this, have started to deny labourers traditional rights of taking fodder from the fields for their animals or have refused to continue to advance interest free loans. More seriously in a period of rising prices the landowners have determined to convert kind payments into cash. 'They have already succeeded in substituting cash for the traditional payment in kind given for winnowing operations and they clearly intend to press this pattern for harvesting operations as well.'[79] A higher proportion of agricultural output is now being marketed to non-agriculture. While in 1951/52 the agricultural sector was marketing 39 per cent of its output—by 1965/66 this percentage rose to 44.[80]

Employment by wage labour and the marketing of an increased volume of output are features of a tendency towards capitalist production but, as we have seen, wage labour and commodity production were already common features in the Indian countryside prior to Independence. They do not, in themselves alone, add up to capitalist production. The really important and significant change is the new entrepreneurial interest in farming and the increased productive accumulation of the social surplus. Even before the beginning of the IADP productive accumulation by agriculture was picking up from its very low level. Between 1951/52 and 1960/61 there was a 39 per cent increase in the purchase of intermediate goods from non-agriculture—notably fertilisers, pesticides, electricity, diesel oil and machinery.[81] This was not spectacular, to be sure, but it did represent a more rapid growth than prior to Independence. Thereafter the IADP and IAAP have facilitated the speed up of this process of investment. The change is most rapid after the mid sixties as is shown by the following figures from Etienne.[82]

	1965/66	1970/71
Number of private tube wells	114,000	500,000 (estimate)
Number of pumping sets	1,000,000	2,430,000

Consumption of chemical fertilisers (in terms of nutrients NPK)

1960/61	288,000 t
1965/66	766,000 t
1970/71	2,490,000 t

Area Under Higher Yielding Varieties

1966/67	1.8 million
1968/69	9.1 million
1970/71	13.6 million (wheat 6 million, paddy 5.5 million)

All this has produced an important upturn of foodgrain production especially after the drought years of 1965/66 and 1966/67 when IAAP really got into swing. The growth in wheat output has been the most spectacular—with a 14 per cent p.a. rate of increase between 1964/65 and 1971/72.[83] But over enthusiasm about the Green Revolution is not warranted. Progress has been slower in rice where the technological developments have not been so impressive. This is an important disparity because wheat accounts for about 15 per cent of the total acreage under foodgrains as compared with over 30 per cent for rice.[84] In other crops progress has been slower still or there has been a deterioration in the situation.

Expenditure elasticities of demand for cash crops are around unity or above—hence a rate of growth of per capita expenditure of about 3 per cent per annum and a population growth of about 2.5 per cent per annum would necessitate a rate of growth of cash crop production of about 5.5 per cent per annum. In fact, in the late sixties, the growth of cash crop production dropped back to 0.5 per cent p.a. (for 1964/65 to 1970/71) which is only one eleventh of the required growth.[85] This drop is due to the loss of acreage to the more profitable foodgrains production and it has produced a veritable crisis in the cotton textiles industry.[86] Additionally the pull of cereals has hit the acreage and production of pulses—the protein source of the poor.[87]

Production of Foodgrains in million tonnes

	1965/66	1966/67	1967/68	1968/69	1969/70
Cereals	62.4	65.9	85.0	83.6	87.8
Pulses	9.9	8.3	12.1	10.4	11.7

The significance of the increase in cereal production at the expense of pulses becomes clearer if we translate the growth of foodgrain output in terms of proteins. This 'is significantly lower at 2.97 per cent p.a. for the period 1949/50 to 1970/71 than it is at 3.33 per cent for the period 1949/50 to 1964/65.[88]

The spectacular increase in wheat output is not simply a result of high yields resulting from the infusion of new inputs, it is also partly due to high prices supported by the procurement policies of the government. The subsidy is substantial. The Agricultural Prices Commission estimated that procurement of wheat at high prices by the Food Corporation of India would involve a subsidy of Rs. 132 crores in the financial year 1972/73.[89] When assessing the net result of the Green Revolution one has to take this into account. Along with increased prosperity has gone increased power for India's farm lobby and this lobby has been able to prevent grain prices from falling despite the continued recommendations of the Agricultural Prices Commission.[90] Since, presumably, one of the main purposes of the exercise was to bring down farm prices the result is ironic, to say the least. The high support prices for wheat is an important factor pulling acreage away from cash crops and pulses and, in turn, dragging up their prices.

Whether even the breakthrough in wheat production is more than a flash in the pan is a question worth asking. Ashok Rudra works out a constant trend rate of growth for agricultural production for the 20 years since the beginning of the First Plan at 3.05 per cent. 'If one takes into account the marked cycles which characterise the time series of foodgrain production, the rise in the series during the last years could well be interpreted as the upswing part of the cycle with no change in the trend indicated.'[91]

It is difficult to see how growth can be sustained in the IAAP districts once most of the big farmers have adopted the new varieties of seeds and their complementary inputs. In fact the rate of growth in the more advanced areas seems to be falling off.[92] Simultaneously a turn in the weather has badly hit the dry farming states that were neglected by the Green Revolutionaries. In Maharashtra, for example, there have been at least three famines since independence the latest in 1973 after three years of drought. Only 7½ per cent of the sown area in the state is irrigated. 'In the plan period the government has spent just Rs. 821.7 millions on irrigation. But in the last two years alone the State has had to spend more than Rs. 1,000 million on famine relief.' State expenditure on famine relief has been insufficient to prevent a number of deaths. Reliable sources in May 1973 cite one thousand people dead through smallpox and 300 from starvation.[93]

In the areas of the Green Revolution itself by no means everyone has gained. Surveys have shown that in the initial years of the IAAP the authorities selected large and progressive farmers. Subsequently smaller cultivators started participating also—though not to the same degree. Francine Frankel's main conclusions are that the overwhelming majority of cultivators having uneconomic holdings of 2–3 acres have managed to increase per acre yields from the application of small doses of fertilisers but the aggregate gains in output have been insufficient an increase to create capital surpluses for investment in land development.[94] In the Punjab, for example, most classes have made 'some gains' yet large farmers get much higher profits.[95]

For tenants the situation is not so good. Figures for a high level of resumption of tenancies in the Punjab have already been given. Where land is retained by tenants it is at a higher level of rents with land values soaring. In the Punjab Frankel reports cash rents rising in 6 years from Rs. 300–Rs. 350 to Rs. 600 per acre.[96] In West Godavary Andhra Pradesh rentals under the fixed share system have increased by about one bag of paddy per acre annually to 11 bags per acre in 1968–69.[97]

The situation for agricultural labourers is also complex. At the outset the High Yielding Varieties need rapid seed bed preparation involving ploughing, planking, levelling, the application of farmyard manure, bunding and water-course levelling. All these required increased labour. The increased output has increased demand for labour-power for threshing and for harvesting. This has resulted in increased employment at certain seasons and also increased wages. Wages have risen in Punjab leading to deteriorating relations between landowners and labourers. In West Godavary, Andhra Pradesh 'Compared to very small farmers and tenant cultivators, it appears that agricultural labourers have experienced some greater, albeit modest improvements, over the last few years.'[98] Unfortunately for the agricultural labourers these look like being only short term gains. The response of the landowners has been a widespread move towards mechanisation. For the landowners, despite the labour surplus, this is the logical thing given the highly peaked demand for labour and the possibility of organisation among rural labourers at peak periods of labour demand. 'A further count in favour of mechanisation is that it may be land saving and this, in a land scarce situation is desirable.' Machines can be land saving both by replacing work animals and hence the land on which fodder is grown for these animals is released for other uses. Also machines allow the land to be used more intensively.[99]

In Punjab-Haryana in 1970 there were 25,000 tractors as compared with 8,000 in 1961. In the same year 24 per cent of the irrigated area was serviced by tube wells and pump sets, 50 per cent of the total wheat crop was mechanically threshed with 100,000 mechanical threshers in use as compared with 5,000 in 1964.[100] The implications for employment are obvious. A tractor takes about 20 per cent the number of man-hours as bullock drawn implements. A pump set requires 25 per cent of the man-hours of a persian wheel irrigation system. A mechanical wheat thresher cuts down to 25 per cent the number of man-hours as compared with indigenous methods.[101]

So even in the Green Revolution areas themselves some have not gained and many stand to lose in absolute terms. Finally, hanging as a big question mark over the entire Green Revolution are the longer term ecological effects. In a previous 'Green Revolution' described in an earlier chapter the British efforts to expand canal irrigation proved to be a mixed blessing with large areas turned desolate by salinity or swamping. The low kill specificity of pesticides—dictated by reasons of higher profitability—have poisoned fish ponds and their protein supply when rice fields have been sprayed. 'The run-offs from the heavy inorganic fertiliser applications called for by the new technology will also add to the process of protein destruction since they result in massive eutrophication of lakes, streams, and rivers.'[102] Not all the implications are yet known—they could be disastrous.

NOTES

1 Malayiva in Desai, *Rural Sociology in India*, p. 396.
2 R. Das Gupta p. 118. P. C. Joshi in Desai, *op. cit.*, pp. 453–454.
3 M. L. Dantwala 'Financial Implications of Land Reforms: Zamindari Abolition' *Indian Journal of Agricultural Economics*, Vol. XVIII, October/December 1962, No. 4, p. 1.
Also 'Implementation of Land Reforms', Planning Commission. G.O.I. New Delhi 1966, p. 277.
4 Das Gupta, *op. cit.*, p. 114.
5 Dantwala, *op. cit.*, Table 1, p. 2.
6 Desai, *op. cit.*, pp. 294–296.
7 Daniel and Alice Thorner, *Land and Labour in India*, Asia Publishing House, Bombay 1962, p. 7.
8 Quoted in Desai, *op. cit.*, p. 298.
9 P. C. Joshi 'Land Reforms in India and Pakistan'. *E. and P.W. Review of Agriculture*, December 1970, p. A148.
10 Desai, *op. cit.*, pp. 449–475.
11 Das Gupta, *op. cit.*, pp. 117–118.
12 Maddison, *op. cit.*, p. 103.
13 'Implementation . . .' p. 16.
14 *Ibid* p. 16.
15 *Ibid* pp. 8, 11, 16.
16 *Ibid* p. 11.
17 A. N. Seth, Director of Land Reforms for the Planning Commission, commenting upon observations in the field in Mysore, quoted in *Ibid*, p. 107.
18 Pranab Bardha 'Trends in Land Relations. A Note', *E. and P.W.* Annual Number 1970, p. 263.
19 Ruddar Datt 'Myth and Reality about the Green Revolution', *Economic Affairs*, Vol. 15, Nos. 6–8, August 1970, p. 359.
20 Cited in Das Gupta, *op. cit.*, pp. 136–137.
21 Bardhan, *op. cit.*, p. 263.
22 'Implementation . . .' p. 12.
23 *Ibid* p. 13.
24 Bardhan, *op. cit.*, p. 263.
25 In Maddison, *op. cit.*, p. 106.
26 Das Gupta, *op. cit.*, p. 118.

27 Daniel Thorner, *Agricultural Co-operatives in India. A Field Report*, Asia Publishing House, London 1964, p. 8.
28 J. G. Crawford, 'India' in *Agricultural Development in Asia*, R. T. Shand (Ed.), London 1969, p. 81.
29 Table computed by Mellor from RBI data in Mellor (Ed.), *Developing Rural India: Plan and Practice*, Cornell University Press, Ithaca, N.Y. 1968, p. 64.
30 *Ibid* p. 67.
31 Bettelheim, *op. cit.*, pp. 197–198.
32 *E. and P.W.* Special Number, August 1972, p. 1452.
33 'Implementation . . .' pp. 2–12.
34 *Ibid* p. 149.
35 V. M. Danekar and N. Rath, 'Poverty in India: Dimensions and Trends' Part I. *E. and P.W.* Jan. 2nd 1971, p. 33.
36 P. Bardhan, 'The Green Revolution and Agricultural Labourers', *E. and P.W.*, July 1970, p. 1240.
37 Daniel and Alice Thorner, *Land and Labour in India*, p. 38.
38 Utsa Patnaik, 'Capitalist Development in Agriculture', *E. and P.W.*, Sept. 25th 1971, Review of Agriculture, pp. A127–A128.
39 P. S. Sanghvi in Desai, *Rural Sociology in India*, p. 431.
40 A. Bhaduri, 'Agricultural Backwardness under Semi-Feudalism', *Economic Journal*, March 1973, p. 123.
41 *Ibid* p. 135. See also: Lasse and Lisa Berg, *Face to Face. Fascism and Revolution in India*, pp. 46–47.
42 Bhaduri, p. 123.
43 Maddison, *op. cit.*, pp. 134–135.
44 *Ibid* p. 104.
45 P. D. Ojha, 'A Configuration of Indian Poverty: Inequality and Levels of Living', *RBIB*, January 1970, pp. 23–24.
46 Cited in Michael Lipton, 'Strategy for Agriculture: Urban Bias and Rural Planning' in *The Crisis of Indian Planning. Economic Planning in the 1960s*, Paul Streeter and M. Lipton (Eds.), p. 129.
47 Table from Don Kanel, 'Size of Farm and Economic Development', *Indian Journal of Agricultural Economics*, April/ June 1967, p. 35.
48 See B. Mukhoti 'Agrarian Structure in Relation to Farm Investment. Decisions and Productivity in a Low Income Country—the Indian Case', *Journal of Farm Economics*, December 1966, pp. 1210–1215. The graph is as on p. 1213.
49 Ernest Mandel, *Marxist Economic Theory*, p. 620.
50 *Ibid* p. 553–4.
51 *Ibid* p. 621.
52 Maddison, *op. cit.*, p. 108.
53 Dandekar and Rath 'Poverty in India' Part II, *E. and P.W.*, January 9th. 1971 p. 133.
54 E. L. Wheelwright and Bruce McFarlane, *The Chinese Road to Socialism*, Monthly Review Press, London 1970, p. 52.
55 John P. Lewis, 'Wanted in India: A Relevant Production', p. 1221.
56 Mandel, *op. cit.*, p. 620.
57 See Chapter I—remarks on Russia's development by Trotsky.
58 Maddison, *op. cit.*, pp. 104–106.
59 V. I. Lenin 'Speech at Transport Workers Congress' in *Collected Works* Vol. 32, Moscow 1965, pp. 277–278.

60 L. D. Trotsky, *Results and Prospects*, p. 205.

61 Desai, *Rural Sociology in India*, p. 775.

62 W. F. Wertheim, *East-West Parallels: Sociological Approaches to Modern Asia*, Chicago 1965, pp. 255–277.

63 Francine Frankel, *India's Green Revolution: Economic Gains and Political Costs*, Princeton 1971, pp. 5–6.

64 Harry M. Cleaver, Jr. 'The Contradictions of the Green Revolution' in *Monthly Review* Vol. 24, No. 2, June 1972, p. 81.

65 *Ibid* pp. 84–85.

66 R. K. Sau, 'Resource Allocation in Indian Agriculture' *E. and P.W.*, September 1971, p. A106.

67 James S. Raj, 'Co-operation in private enterprise', *Commerce*, November 30th, 1968, p. 38.

68 Forbes Magazine quoted in Magdoff, *op. cit.*, p. 128.

69 S. Kumar Dev, 'Collaboration in Fertiliser Development', *Commerce*, November 20th, 1968, p. 80.

70 Sau, 'The New Economics', p. 1575.

71 Sau, 'Resource Allocation in Indian Agriculture', p. A109.

72 *Ibid* p. A115.

73 Lipton, *op. cit.*, pp. 111–117.

74 Utsa Patnaik, 'Development of Capitalism in Agriculture—II' *Social Scientist*, October 1972, pp. 3–19.

75 *Ibid* pp. 15–17.

76 *Ibid* p. 5.

77 'Implementation . . .' p. 11.

78 Francine Frankel, *op. cit.*, p. 38.

79 *Ibid* p. 38.

80 R. Thamarajakshi, *op. cit.*, p. A98.

81 *Ibid*, Table 9, p. A96.

82 Gilbert Etienne, 'The Green Revolution in India—Its Economic and Socio-Political Implications.' Paper to the 3rd European Conference of Modern South Asian Studies. Mimeo 1972, Appendix p. 1–2.

83 Dharm Narain, 'Growth and Imbalances in Indian Agriculture', *E. and P.W.*, March 25th 1972. Review of Agriculture p. A4.

84 Wolf Ladejinsky 'Ironies of India's Green Revolution' *Foreign Affairs*, July 1970, p. 760.

85 Narain, *op. cit.*, p. A4.

86 *Economic Survey* 1970/71 p. 15.

87 *Ibid* Table II p. 4.

88 Narain, *op. cit.*, p. A4.

89 *E. and P.W.*, April 1st, 1972.

90 T. J. Brynes, 'The Dialectic of India's Green Revolution', *South Asian Review*, January 1972, p. 110.

91 A. Rudra, 'The Green and Greedy Revolution', *South Asian Review*, July 1971, p. 299.

92 Editorial, Review of Agriculture, *E. and P.W.*, March 25th, 1972.

93 Kalyan Chaudhuri, 'Hunger Stalks Maharashtra—Anger Too', *Frontier*, May 19, 1973, pp. 4–5.

94 In Ruddar Datt, *op. cit.*, pp. 352–353.

95 Francine Frankel, *op. cit.*, p. 39.

96 *Ibid* p. 34.

97 *Ibid* p. 62: also p. 192.
98 *Ibid* p. 72.
99 Byrnes, *op. cit.*, p. 106.
100 *Ibid* p. 106.
101 *Ibid* p. 109.
102 Cleaver, *op. cit.*, p. 99.

CHAPTER VIII

General Conclusion

Between 1948/49 and 1967/68 India's per capita net national product grew by 29.5 per cent.[1] This growth is not impressive and there is no evidence that it will speed up substantially. The implications of the Green Revolution for long term agricultural growth do not look as bright as was at first thought. Industrial production has stagnated with the stagnation of public investment. The national income rose by 5.5 per cent in 1969/70, less than 5 per cent in 1970/71 and 4 per cent in 1971/72.[2] As important as the growth that has taken place is its nature and its distribution. Much of the 'growth' has been accounted for by a rising trend in the tertiary sector of trade, (transport, communications and other services) which grew at the expense of the primary sector (agriculture, forestry and fisheries) and even of the secondary sector (mining, manufacturing and small enterprises). Between 1948/49 and 1968/69 the share of the tertiary sector in total net domestic product increased from 34.2 per cent to as much as 44.5 per cent whereas that of the secondary sector fell from 17.1 per cent to 16.7 per cent.[3] This probably partially reflects a number of unhealthy trends—the tendency of surplus capital to flow back into financial pursuits and trade, the growth of a parasitic bureaucracy in the government service, the growth of disguised unemployment in the form of 'services'. Another notable feature of this growth of national income is that it does not include any clear upward trend in per capita availability of foodgrains.[4]

The lack of a clear trend upwards in these statistics throws suspicion over other statistics suggesting a small increase in the standard of living of the population These suspicions will be confirmed later by examining the distribution of the gains from development.

Net availability of Cereals and Pulses Per capita net availability per day in ounces

Year	*Cereals*	*Pulses*
1951	11.78	2.14
1952	11.47	2.09
1953	12.38	2.22
1954	13.68	2.46
1955	13.14	2.53
1956	12.70	2.49
1957	13.23	2.54
1958	12.35	2.07
1959	13.88	2.65
1960	13.50	2.31
1961	14.06	2.44
1962	14.13	2.20
1963	13.49	2.10
1964	14.05	1.79
1965	14.63	2.16
1966	12.55	1.69
1967x	12.59	1.38
1968x	14.00	1.95
1969x	13.79	1.64
1970x	13.91	1.80

Net availability = net production + net imports + change in government stocks.

Since Independence the rate of population growth has accelerated and continues to accelerate. The death rate has fallen further but the birth rate remains at a relatively high level. Malaria, tuberculosis, cholera and other killers are now firmly under control.[5] As a result the population rose by 21.46 per cent in the 1950s from 361 millions in 1951 to 439 millions in 1961. It rose a further 24.57 per cent in the 1960s to 547 millions in 1971. The government is trying hard to bring down the birth rate but for reasons already explained it will fail in the absence of a thoroughgoing change in the lives of the broad masses involving education, the guarantee of care and attention in old age and general economic and social development.[6]

Corresponding to the population growth the size of the labour force constantly expands. Low rates of growth in industry and agriculture and the low labour intensity of production cannot absorb this growth. There are conceptual problems in measuring unemployment in a country like India where much of it remains disguised and seasonal in nature—but the figures of the Indian Institute of Public Opinion can be taken as indicating the broad orders of magnitude. The backlog of unemployment was 5.3 millions in 1950, 7 millions in 1961 and 9–10 millions in 1966. One estimate of unemployment in 1971 is 8 per cent of the labour force. The number of workers in 1971 was 184 millions according to the Census of that year. This would make unemployment 15 millions. The I.I.P.O. estimates an addition to the labour force of 48 millions in the 1970s. Adding the presently unemployed 15 millions and subtracting 3 million people for death and retirement there would be 60 million people for whom jobs would have to be found.[7] If the manufacturing sector were to grow at the same rate as in the 1950s and 60s—i.e. at 8 per cent p.a. with a 3.9 per cent p.a. growth in productivity—then it would provide a mere 5 million more jobs between 1972 and 1982.[8]

Apart from open unemployment and seasonal underemployment in the countryside there is widespread disguised unemployment. A primary example of this is in the lower echelons of the Civil Service. The Central Government Civil Service Class IV consists of more than a million menials 'functionally redundant guards and bearers (chaprasis) who carry tea and files and salute their officers. Most of their time is spent loitering in corridors. One calculation suggests that, on average, they are usefully employed for twelve minutes a day.'[9]

Widespread unemployment keeps wages low and stagnant.[10]

Average Real Monthly Earnings of Factory Workers Earning less than Rs. 200 per month. Index 1951 = 100

Year	Index
1939	108.4
1945	81.2
1950	97.7
1951	100.0
1955	123.7
1960	113.8
1965	105.6
1969	102.2

While wages remain stagnant the average product per worker is increasing so the share of labour in total value added is falling—the benefits of increasing production accruing to the employing class and a small gain to salaried employees.

% *Shares in value added in Manufacturing Industry*[11]

Year	*Wages* (1)	*Salaries* (2)	*Benefits* (3)	(1) + (2) + (3)
1949	58.3	10.6	1.1	70.0
1952	51.6	10.7	1.3	63.6
1955	41.8	10.6	2.7	55.1
1958	39.8	11.6	3.3	54.7
1960	39.6	11.4	4.7	55.7
1961	39.2	10.6	4.5	54.3
1962	39.6	11.9	4.7	56.2
1963	37.6	11.9	4.7	54.2
1964	36.5	13.7	5.1	55.3

Our study of the Green Revolution found indications that incomes were also tending to polarise in the countryside.

In both industry and agriculture it is the already well-off who have got the pickings from the government 'development programmes'. The rich peasants and landowners getting access to supported co-operative finance and the IAAP 'packages'. The industrialists also have had access to cheap loans, tax concessions, underpriced inputs from government companies. While high industrial incomes bear income tax widespread evasion reduces this burden. The development programmes have been born by the poor in high indirect taxation and deficit financing.

The overall trend is clearly one to increasing inequality. The mere fact of rising per capita national income does not prove significant rises in the standard of living of the broad masses. Various estimates have been made into the extent of poverty and its broad trends. Dandekar and Rath take as their criteria for poverty a level of consumption expenditure which secures an adequate diet of 2,250 calories per day. This comes to Rs. 170 per capita p.a. in rural areas and Rs. 271 in urban areas in 1960/61 prices. 'With these minima it seems that in 1960/61 about 40 per cent of the rural population and about 50 per cent of the urban population lived below the desired minimum.'[12] The rural poor consists predominantly of agricultural labourers (57 per cent were below the minimum in 1960/61) and small landholders with less than 5 and particularly less than 2.5 acres. The urban poor is fundamentally an extension of the rural poor concentrated geographically round the cities in the unfulfilled hope that work can be found there.[13] Between 1960/61 and 1968/69 the incomes of the bottom 20 per cent of the rural population increased by less than 2 per cent in the period. Conditions definitely deteriorated for the bottom 20 per cent of the urban population as a result of the continuous migration of the rural poor into urban areas. The next highest 20 per cent in urban areas faced a more or less stagnant position. Overall per capita consumer expenditure rose by about 4.8 per cent between 1960/61 and 1968/69.[14]

From all the trends indicated above—of rising unemployment, stagnant wage earnings in industry, increased polarisation of incomes in agriculture the future trends are no brighter. Even taking optimistic assumptions about future growth the perspective for the poor is not bright. The 4th Plan document estimates that per capita consumption of the second poorest tenth of the population will reach Rs. 15 per month (in 1960/61 prices) in 1980/81. This is 'appreciably below Rs. 20 per capita per month, which was deemed a minimum desirable consumption standard.'[15] If one corrects the Planning Commissions' estimates for over optimism then the prospects are a lot more bleak. Dandekar and Rath project the trends of the 1960s of a 3.75 per cent p.a. growth of national income and a 1.75 per cent growth of population and assume that the pattern of inequality of consumption as in 1968/69. On this basis it will not be till the year 2005/6 that the second poor decile of the population reach the minimum desirable consumption standards of Rs. 20 per capita per month in 1960/61 prices.[16] But this is also an optimistic estimate because it assumes the existing patterns of inequality and inequality is increasing. Dandekar and Rath do not project the declining standard of living of the poorest 20 per cent in urban areas for obvious reasons.

But it will be all right for some. A good indication of increasing prosperity is the growing consumption of consumer durables. The I.I.P.O. has constructed an index of aggregate consumption of eight selected durables (bicycles, electric fires, sewing machines, radio receivers, air conditioners, refrigerators, motor cycles and scooters, motor cars). While per capita income rose from 100.00 to 113.29 from 1960 to 1970 at 1960/61 prices the index for expenditure on consumer durables rose from 100.00 to 217.00. The I.I.P.O. projects that 'the seventies are likely to witness an explosive growth in the aggregate consumption of these 8 durables. By 1980–81, the index will reach 856 points.' (The I.I.P.O.'s projected per capita income in 1980–81 is 172.9 on a 100.00 base in 1960.)[17]

Examination of past trends and their projection into the future are useful starting points for an analysis but they are insufficient by themselves because trends beget their own negation.

If the growth rate were to continue at the level of the past and incomes were to continue polarising the resultant 'pseudo-industrialisation' would be a strain on the foreign exchange reserves because of the import requirements of luxury good production. As it happens imports have been substantially reduced in the last few years from Rs. 1,908 crores in 1968/69 to 1,625 crores in 1970/71. This is partly due to the success of the Green Revolution with foodgrain imports falling from Rs. 333.6 crores to Rs. 213 crores over the same period.[18] But the harvests failures of 1972/73 are pushing up foodgrain imports again. A key reason for the decline in imports is that the growth rate has not been maintained but, as indicated by figures at the beginning of this chapter, has slid downwards. This has led to declines in certain imports—e.g. machinery. The recession and underutilised capacity are also responsible for the high level of exports in certain industries—pipes and tubes, railway coaches and wagons, power cables and wires, machine tools etc.[19] If growth were to pick up again it would probably run up against the foreign exchange constraint again. If the present trend in the rising share and influence of foreign private capital were to continue this would also continually increase the foreign exchange drain.

But the sustenance to continue the present growth rate is being exhausted. The mid-term Appraisal of the Fourth Five Year Plan finds a decline in the investment level of 11 per cent of National Income from the 14 per cent level at the end of the Third Plan. A revival of public investment is needed to boost the growth rate: 'The revival of investment demand by the public sector is necessary both for the fuller utilisation of the existing capacity and for the creation of fresh capacity which can ensure steady growth of national income in the coming years.'[20] But where are the resources to come from to sustain another boost to public investment? Industrialisation or foreign credit is not on any longer. Gross aid declined from Rs. 1,196 crores in 1967/68 to Rs. 778 crores (estimated) in 1971/72 and net aid from Rs. 863 crores to Rs. 328 crores.[21] Even if foreign capitalist powers were prepared to give, the volume of repayments and debt servicing would progressively eat away the effects of further aid. Stronger and stronger doses of medicine would be necessary to keep the patient alive. Moreover the room for squeezing out domestic resources is becoming progressively narrower. If the propertied classes cannot be made to pay the poor cannot be squeezed indefinitely—as has been shown not only is there no income tax on the increases in agricultural incomes but the Green Revolution has been bought partly by public subsidy—here is a clear case where increased production does not give rise to increased resources for development. If anything the reverse has been the case. If the poor are squeezed too hard then they either starve or they rebel. If they rebel then more resources have to be laid out to defend the propertied classes. The rapid growth of 'defence' expenditures is not solely a product of fear of external enemies—the government's central reserve police force now have experience of putting down rebellion inside India itself. India's intervention in Bangla Desh was as much for its own internal reasons as anything else. A Red Bengal would have been an uncomfortable example to the rest of the Indian sub-continent and a base for further revolutionary activity.

Even if growth is maintained at its level of the past twenty years—which seems unlikely given the falling investment rate—then India's impoverished masses will still be flung into rebellion. We have seen that the projection of current trends leads to massive unemployment and poverty and holds out no hope to these masses. The Indian ruling class realise their impasse. Indira Ghandi's election victory in 1971 was based on the slogan 'Garibi hatao' (Down with poverty) and there has been much talk of rural public works and land ceilings on the holdings of large landowners. In 1971 crash schemes for rural employment totalling Rs. 500 millions a year were announced—but in reply to the large number of applications from the districts only Rs. 50 millions could be spent during three quarters of the financial year 1971–72.[22] It is the same with land ceilings. As the Economic and Political Weekly comments 'none of the circumstances which have thwarted the implementation of the existing laws have really changed.'[23] There is no reason to assume that administrative efficiency has increased and there has been no change in the pattern of economic and political power in the countryside. If anything the maliks have been strengthened in the past years and their power and influence in the structures of the state have grown.[24]

The Evidence of the Rising Social Crisis is easy to find.[25]

Incidence of Industrial Conflict, Crime, and Riots

	Industrial Conflict Index No. of man days lost Base 1950	Total cognisable crime. Index No. of cases reported 1950 = 100	Total riot cases. Index No. 1953 = 100
1950	100.0	100.0	–
1951	92.8	102.2	–
1952	91.8	96.3	–
1953	96.8	94.7	100.0
1954	102.3	87.6	111.0
1955	147.3	84.2	115.0
1956	163.2	92.0	120.3
1957	150.0	96.6	115.7
1958	182.0	96.6	121.5
1959	132.2	99.1	131.5
1960	152.6	95.4	131.0
1961	114.8	98.4	132.5
1962	142.9	106.9	141.7
1963	76.3	103.7	136.9
1964	180.3	119.4	159.3
1965	144.1	118.3	160.5
1966	323.3	125.1	169.0

The rising rebellion against the social system slows down the rate of economic growth yet, paradoxically, it is this rebellion that provides the key to the development of the productive forces. The reason is that it is this rebellion of the toiling masses that can destroy precisely that pattern of relations of production that is inhibiting the development of the productive forces.

It is quite understandable that the bourgeois economists—who can see no further than their own noses—should believe that economic development necessitates a concentration of wealth in the hands of those who are already wealthy and its denial to those who are most needy. If you proceed from the fact of the existing pattern of property relations without questioning those relations then it is quite natural that you will not question—perhaps not even notice—that economic development means necessarily the 'development' of those who *own* the economy. To whom else should resources be channelled but to the industrialists that do the investing? On whom else should agricultural development be concentrated but on the maliks—why, after all, give seed, fertilisers and tractors to the rural poor who own no land?

Proceeding from the 'simple facts' the unbiased bourgeois economists end up the accomplices in the exploitation and impoverishment of the masses. This is because it is precisely in the facts that the bourgeois economists do not question—the existing pattern of property relations—that the problem rests. Fortunately the working masses do not proceed from the ideology of unbiased bourgeois economists but from the standpoint of their pressing and urgent material needs. We have seen that the masses want food and education—and that better nutrition and education for the masses would considerably increase their productivity. We have seen that the masses want employment—and that the utilisation of the vast reserves of rural labour-power is the key to a rational development of Indian rural society. While there are thousands of graduates in engineering and the sciences out of work and wanting employment India needs their employment in the development of a technology adapted to its own conditions. The Indian masses want necessities—not the import-intensive luxury knick-knacks that increase the size of the foreign exchange gap. It is thus in a society subordinate to the needs of the masses that the productive forces can best be unleashed. But such a society cannot, of course, come about without the suppression and expropriation of the exploiters.

Economic analysis thus necessarily carries over into political analysis and practice. To solve the problems of what the bourgeois economists call 'underdevelopment' it is necessary to pose a revolutionary strategy for the Indian masses.

Just as surely as the development of the economic crisis generates a social crisis and a polarisation of exploiting and exploited classes so too, it must generate a vanguard in the mass movement—a social layer that is characterised by its attempt to find a way forward for the masses in their struggle, by its higher and more dedicated attention to the task of finding the adequate tools for struggle to unify the masses and enable them to defeat and suppress the possessing classes. The winning of this vanguard, in the course of the struggle, to the theory and practice of an adequate strategy represents the task of building an Indian revolutionary party.

It would be improper and dishonest for the present author to lay out fully such a strategy given that his knowledge of the Indian class struggle is limited and gleaned solely from pamphlets and books and not from practical experience. However, given that there is a relative autonomy of theory from practice it is possible to make some general remarks about such a strategy.

Firstly, the strategy for the South Asian revolution—as for any revolution—must take as its starting point the actual fight for material needs of the masses themselves. A revolution can be made on no other basis but through the fight of the masses for their material needs—a fight which necessarily runs up against the logic of the existing social order as a whole. The task of the communists in this fight is to continually search for the way forward for the mass struggle—to anticipate its dynamic, and to prepare the mass movement for the tasks that it will have to face and deal with on the road to revolutionary victory. Because they approach the struggles of the toiling masses from a scientific standpoint the communists are the most effective fighters for the needs of the masses and the revolutionary party can only be formed through proving itself in the struggle. It is in this process that the party increases its prestige—first of all in the vanguard of the masses and later, at a higher point in the development of the struggle, among the masses as a whole. As Marx and Engels put it in the *Communist Manifesto* the communists have no separate interests from the proletariat as a whole. However, the communists are 'on the the one hand, practically, the most advanced and resolute section of the working class parties of every country, that section which pushes forward all others; on the other hand theoretically, they have over the mass of proletarians the advantage of clearly understanding the line of march, the conditions and the ultimate general results of the proletarian movement.'

What then is the 'line of march, the conditions and the general results' of the Indian revolution? Many on the Indian left, in particular the two Communist Parties, believe that the struggle for liberation will pass through two stages. In the first stage they believe that it is necessary and possible to detach a 'progressive' section of the 'national' capitalist class away from the rest of the possessing classes into an anti-feudal and anti-imperialist alliance under the leadership of the working class. This is a profound misconception which can only have harmful consequences for the movement of the masses. The rise of the struggles of the working class and the poor peasants inevitably pushes *all* sections of the exploiters into the camp of the counter-revolution. This is for the simple reason that the rise of the mass struggle cannot but put into question the very continued existence of the bourgeoisie. Thus an 'alliance' can be maintained with the bourgeoisie only by tail-ending the left sounding demagogy of the bourgeois parties and through restraining the struggle of the masses. Since no section of the bourgeoisie accepts the leadership of the working class the supposed working class parties end up accepting the leadership of the bourgeoisie.

It is necessary to cut the gordian knot in this argument. The struggle to expropriate the bourgeoisie is not a task for some later stage in the process of liberation. It cannot be separated off from the 'anti-feudal' and 'anti-imperialist' struggle. On the contrary as Trotsky argued in the case of China:

> Really to arouse the workers and peasants against imperialism, is possible only by connecting their basic and most profound life interests with the cause of the country's liberation. A workers' strike—small or large—an agrarian rebellion, an uprising of the oppressed sections in city and country against the usurer, against the bureaucracy, against the local military satraps, all that arouses the multitudes, that welds them together, that educates, steels, is a real step forward on the road to the revolutionary and social liberation of the Chinese people . . . Everything that brings the oppressed and exploited masses of the toilers to their feet, inevitably pushes the national bourgeoisie into an

> open bloc with the imperialists. The class struggle between the bourgeoisie and the masses of workers and peasants is not weakened, but, on the contrary, it is sharpened by imperialist oppression, to the point of bloody civil war at every serious conflict.[26]

In the analysis developed in this book we have shown that pre-capitalist, 'national capitalist' and imperialist relations of exploitation overlap and intertwine with one another and this is an inevitable feature of uneven and combined development. There are, to be sure contradictions and antagonisms between different sections of the exploiting classes. However, these do not have the irreconcilable character of those contradictions between the exploiters and the toiling masses. Indeed, while the development of the economy is widening the gulf between the exploiters and the exploited, it is, if anything, tending to a greater integration between the maliks, the national capitalists and the imperialists (trend towards foreign collaborations, Green Revolution etc.). The implication of this overlap in the relations of exploitation is an inevitable overlap in the processes of the class struggle—and hence also in the tasks of the revolution.

The organisation of the masses in their revolt thus provides the key to the liberation of South Asia—not illusory alliances with sections of the ruling classes. The masses are thrown into struggle by the very logic of the economic situation but their struggle is a fragmented one. It is thus possible for different sections of the masses to be isolated and defeated.

Over the last few years there have been numerous examples of this throughout the South Asian sub-continent. The defeats suffered by the heroic militants of the JVP in Ceylon in 1971; the smashing of the strike wave in Karachi in West Pakistan in 1972–73 and the brutal and vicious manner in which the Indian ruling class crushed the railway workers' strike of May 1974, not to mention numerous other examples, illustrate this point amply. And while the depth and gravity of the crisis of social relations in South Asia will continue to generate spontaneous upsurges of militancy by the rural and urban masses, we should nonetheless understand that if the mass movement continues to suffer defeats the cumulative impact of this on class consciousness could be rather disastrous. Thus the task of revolutionaries is to overcome this fragmentation and to seek to unify all the struggles of the oppressed masses. Various struggles generated by the economic and social crisis have to be brought together and focused on the establishment of a raj of the workers and peasants—these are the struggles of the industrial working class, of the rural poor (agricultural labourers and poor peasants) and the oppressed nationalities and linguistic groups (e.g. the Tamils).

As far as the struggle of the national groups is concerned this has provided a continual source of tension within India's federal political structure. Where jobs, foreign exchange, taxation resources and lucrative government contracts are all in short supply one area or region can get more if another area gets less. The revolutionaries cannot ignore the conflicts that are generated in this way. Such conflicts have been used for example by bourgeois nationalists to deflect the revolt of the masses into linguistic or nationalistic channels. They seek to prevent the class struggle within a spurious unity in the national, cultural or linguistic group. The revolutionaries have to practically oppose the national and linguistic oppression of the workers and poor peasants—in the same way that they will oppose all the oppressions of these masses—at the same time they must win the struggle of these masses both theoretically and practically to the general revolutionary and anti-capitalist perspective, seeking thereby to break these masses from movements bound by the limits of bourgeois nationalism.

We have said that it is not possible to win any section of the exploiters into an alliance with the oppressed masses. This does not mean, however, that it is impossible to win over sections of the professional and middle classes who are impoverised by the economic crisis. However, in order to do this it is not sufficient to put forward a programme of demands for this sector corresponding to its needs—protection against inflation etc.—it is also necessary to prove that the working masses are really capable of being able to implement such a programme. The middle classes cannot be won over by vacillations and concessions to their prejudices. Only by being resolute, and by proving that they mean business, will the workers and peasants win over this layer. Otherwise the middle classes will turn to the fascist groups like Shiv Sena that are currently proliferating.

How is the struggle of the masses to be organised? The answer to this question must be through the emergence of soviets—councils of the rural and urban proletariat and poor peasantry. The function of the soviet is the democratic self-organisation of the masses in the face of the class enemy. The establishment of the councils is a necessary stage on the line of march of the mass struggle as it unfolds. As the mass movement develops many problems are posed that the masses must be organised to answer. The ruling class will sabotage the economy and they will certainly organise represssion. At the same time the revolt of the masses itself throws chaos into the normal functioning of the economy. Bodies representing the power and authority of the masses are necessary to answer the questions such as these that are raised. Thus it is the council's job to organise the seizure of those sectors of the economy sabotaged by the class enemy, the councils ensure supplies and transport for the masses themselves but not for the class enemy and so on. Federated on a regional, and eventually on a national, basis such bodies represent the embryo of the new state power of the masses.

The struggle will not be short or an easy one. The Indian masses do not lack the spirit of rebellion. On the contrary the very desperation of their position drives them to rebel. However, their revolt is fragmented, ill-organised and ill-defended. On the other hand the repressive forces are highly organised, trained and powerful. Given the degree of social instability and the explosive state of class relations violent repressive actions are resorted to by the ruling classes as soon as the struggle begins to be organised. The ruling classes hope, thereby, to nip in the bud any development of a mass movement that cannot be controlled. There have been many examples of such brutal harassment of the masses. One such was in Kilvenmani in East Thanjavur in 1968 where landlords dragged the families of agricultural labourers into a hut which they set on fire—killing 44 people. Again there is the brutal and indiscriminate attack on the Dalit Panthers by the police in Bombay in January 1964, the murders of militants in West Bengal, the mass arrests and use of troops in the railway strike and so on.

What flows from all these examples, and the many more that can be given, is the key necessity to prepare the masses to resist repression—to arm the masses with the desire to arm Since, moreover armed struggle is an art which h acquired—especially where it is being used against highly repressive forces—the vanguard will have to develop th in the skirmishes in the class struggle, in between, and l up to the generalised confrontations. It is particularly im tant to note, in this regard, that the armed struggle must alw be co-ordinated with the mass struggle—used where it is logical and necessary extension of that struggle and so where can be understood and actively supported by the masses them selves. In such skirmishes both the vanguard and the masses learn and the struggle is impelled forward with the confidence born of success to the next general upsurge and confrontation. At this point the armed vanguard has to fuse itself into the mobilisations, giving general military leadership to the workers and peasant militias—these militias being the armed extensions of the soviets of worker-peasant power.

Such then, put very sketchily, are some of the necessary elements of a strategy for the South Asian revolution. It is necessary to stress and reiterate the method by which this strategy is arrived at, namely, it flows from an analysis of the dynamics of the struggle and the necessities that that struggle will face as it unfolds. Thus there is a necessity for unity of all the oppressed masses against their oppressors—hence for united programmes to be fought for in the mass struggle. The mass struggle poses the question of who runs the country—thus this question must be answered by the establishment of councils of the workers and poor peasants. The upsurge will be met by repression—so the actions of the vanguard have to prepare and push ahead the self-defence of the mass struggle.

Success in this struggle will put India on the way to solving its fundamental problems. It would, however, be illusory to imagine that the post-revolutionary society would not have problems of its own. The experience of Russia, China and Cuba teach us that many dangers lie ahead. In an inherited situation of backwardness, where there are not enough goods for all and where the toiling masses have been deprived of access to cultured life, there is a tendency for the post-revolutionary society to be plagued with bureaucratisation. Thus an elite strata is formed which secures for itself privileges out of the limited national fund and moves towards protecting those privileges with an apparatus of repression. The alliance between the workers and peasants will not be totally non-antagonistic. Continued private property in the land makes for a regeneration of the differentiation of the peasantry. But the experiences of the other workers' states allows us to define how such tendencies should be fought. There is a need for workers' control of production; the development of industry adapted to suit the consumption and productive needs of the peasantry; to need to begin the processes of co-operation and collectivisation by inducements rather than by force—offering the peasants a better life on the collectives which would be established only when they could offer superior access to agricultural technologies and equipment, superior modes of organising rural labour-power to the rapid and immediate benefit of the rural masses. Above all there would be the need to spread the revolution to other countries—including the imperialist countries. Through fraternal economic assistance they could then begin to repay for centuries of oppression and exploitation.

NOTES

1 *Economic Survey 1970/71*, G.O.I., New Delhi 1971, p. 80.
2 *E. and P.W.*, March 18th 1972.
3 *Economic Survey 1970/71*, p. 79.
4 *Ibid* Table 1.9, p. 88.
5 B. Das Gupta 'Popuation Policy: The Crucial Factor', p. 334.
6 *Ibid* pp. 337–342.
7 I.I.P.O., *Monthly Commentary*, Annual No. 1971, p. 87.
8 *Ibid* p. 93.
9 Maddison, *op. cit.*, p. 95.
10 Table from Ranjit Sau 'Indian Economic Growth. Constraints and Prospects', p. 367.
11 Table from 'Report of the National Commission on Labour', in Sau, p. 369.
12 Dandekar and Rath, Part I, p. 31.
13 *Ibid* p. 33.
14 *Ibid* p. 40.
15 *Ibid* p. 43.

16 *Ibid* pp. 43–44.
17 *I.I.P.O. Q.E.R.*, December 1971/January 1972, 'Changing Indian Standards of Living and Comfort—A New Analysis of Shifts in Durables Consumption 1950–1980.' pp. 28–29.
18 *E. and P.W.*, March 18th 1972.
19 RBIB, *Exports of Engineering Goods: Problems and Prospects*, October 1970, p. 1718.
20 *E. and P.W.*, March 18th 1972.
21 *Ibid.*
22 Etienne, *op. cit.*, p. 36.
23 *E. and P.W.*, April 8th 1972.
24 Byrnes, *op. cit.*, p. 110. Lewis, *op. cit.*, pp. 1213–1215.
25 The table is from B. R. Nayer, *The Modernisation Imperative and Indian Planning*, Table 20, p. 220.
26 Trotsky, 'The Chinese Revolution and the Theses of Comrade Stalin' (May 17 1927) in *Problems of the Chinese Revolution*, University of Michigan Press, p. 22.

Appendix

The following table shows the high degree of excess capacity.

% Utilisation of Estimated Productive Capacity India 1969

Sector	Average number of shifts	Capacity Utilisation On 1 shift basis	On 2 shift basis
Automobiles (all types)	2	115	57
Diesel Engines	1.68	97	48
Power Driven Pumps	1.31	100	50
Air compressors	2.03	59	30
Transformers	1	150	75
Electric motors	1	94	47
Electric fans	2	71	36
Storage batteries	2	118	59
Dry batteries	2	95	47
Railway wagons	2	–	66
Cranes and hoists	1	59	30
Structural fabrication	1	52	26
Pulp and paper making plants	1.56	31	16
Building and construction machinery	1.33	28	14
Bicycles complete	1.1	84	42
Sewing machines	1.38	43	22

Little, Scitovsky and Scott. Table 3.5 p. 94.

Bibliography

Government and Official Publications etc.

Pre-Independence

Report on the Census of British India 1821, Volume I. H.M.S.O., London 1885.

Report of Indian Famine Commission 1901, G.O.I., Nainital 1901.

Report of the Indian Irrigation Commission 1901–03 G.O.I., Calcutta 1903.

Census of India 1911, Volume 1, Part 1. Report by E. A. Gait G.O.I., Calcutta 1913.

Report of the Indian Industrial Commission 1916–18 G.O.I., Calcutta 1918.

Royal Commission on Agriculture in India 1928 H.M.S.O., Cmnd 3123.

Indian Central Banking Enquiry Committee, Part 1, Majority Report G.O.I., 1931.

Census of 1931, Volume 1, Part 1, by J. H. Hutton G.O.I., Delhi 1933.

Famine Inquiry Commission, Final Report G.O.I., Madras 1945.

Post-Independence

Indian Tax Reform. Report of a Survey by Nicholas Kaldor, Department of Economic Affairs, Ministry of Finance. G.O.I., 1956.

Report of the Direct Taxes Administration Enquiry Committee 1958–59. G.O.I., 1960.

Report of the Committee on Distribution of Income and Levels of Living (Mahalanobis Committee) Part 1, Distribution of Income and Wealth and Concentration of Economic Power. Planning Commission, G.O.I., 1964.

Report of the Monopolies Inquiry Commission, Volume 1, 1965, Implementation of Land Reforms. Land Reforms Implementation Committee of the National Development Committee, Planning Commission, G.O.I., August 1966.

Economic Survey 1970/71. Ministry of Finance, G.O.I., 1971.

Books and Articles

Ahmad, J., 'Import Substitution and Structural Change in Indian Manufacturing Industry', *Journal of Development Studies*, April 1968.

Bagchi, A. K., 'Long Term Constraints on India's Industrial Development 1951–1968' in *Economic Development in South Asia*, Kidron and Robinson (Eds.), IEA. 1970.

——, 'Aid Models and Inflows of Foreign Aid', *Economic and Political Weekly* (E. and P.W.) Vol. 5, Nos. 3, 4 and 5, Annual No. 1970.

——, *Private Investment in India 1900–1939*, Cambridge University Press 1972.

——, 'Some International Foundations of Capitalist Growth and Underdevelopment', *E. and P.W.*, Special No. 1972, Vol. VII Nos. 31–33.

Bailey, F. C., *Caste and the Economic Frontier*, Manchester University Press 1957.

Bailly, J. and Florian, P., 'L'exacerbation des contradictions dans les economies semi-industrialisées', *Critiques de l'Economie Politique*, No. 3, April/June 1971.

Bain, Joe S., *International Differences in Industrial Structure: 8 Nations in the 1950s*, Yale University Press 1966.

Baran, P., *The Political Economy of Growth*, Monthly Review Press, 1957.

Bardhan, P., 'Trends in Land Relations. A Note', *E. and P.W.*, Annual No. 1970.

——, 'The Green Revolution and Agricultural Labourers', *E. and P.W.*, Special No. July 1970.

Berg, Lasse and Lisa, *Face to Face. Fascism and Revolution in India*, Ramparts Press, Berkely, 1970.

Bettelheim, C. *India Independent*, Monthly Review Press, New York, 1968.

Bhaduri, A., 'Agricultural Backwardness under Semi-Feudalism', *Economic Journal*, March 1973, Volume 83, No. 329.

Bhagwati, J. N. and Desai, P., *India. Planning for Industrialisa-*

tion. Industrialisation and Trade Policies since 1951, Oxford University Press, 1970.

Brown, M. Barratt, *After Imperialism*, Heinemann, London 1963.

Buchanan, D. H., *The Development of Capitalistic Enterprise in India*, New York, 1934.

Byrnes, T. J., 'The Dialectic of India's Green Revolution', *South Asian Review*, Volume 5, No. 2. January 1972.

Calvert, H., *The Wealth and Welfare of the Punjab*, Lahore, 2nd Edition 1936.

Chandra, Bipan, 'Reinterpretation of Nineteenth Century Indian Economic History', *Indian Economic and Social History Review* (*IESHR*), March 1968.

Chandra, N. K., 'Western Imperialism and India Today', Mimeo 1972.

Chattopadhyay, Paresh, 'Mode of Production in Indian Agriculture—An Anti-Kritik', *E. and P.W.*, December 30th, 1972, Review of Agriculture.

Chaudhuri, K. N. (Ed.), *The Economic Development of India under the East India Company 1814–1858. A Selection of Contemporary Writings*, Cambridge University Press, 1971.

Chaudhuri, Kalyan, 'Hunger Stalks Maharashtra—Anger Too', *Frontier*, Volume 6, No. 6, May 19th, 1973.

Chelliah, R. J., 'Tax Potential and Economic Growth in the Countries of the E.C.A.F.E. Region', United Nations' *Economic Bulletin for Asia and Far East*, Volume XVII, No. 2, September 1966.

Cleaver, Harry M., 'The Contradictions of the Green Revolution', *Monthly Review*, Volume 24, No. 2, June 1972.

Crawford, J. G., 'India' in *Agricultural Development in Asia*, R. T. Shand (Ed.), London, 1969.

Dandekar, V. M. and Rath, N., 'Poverty in India : Dimensions and Trends' Part I, *E. and P.W.*, Volume VI, No. 1, January 2nd 1971.

Part II, *E. and P.W.*, Volume VI, No. 2, January 9th 1971.

Dantwala, M. L., 'Financial Implications of Land Reforms: Zamindari Abolition', *Indian Journal of Agricultural Economics*, Volume XVIII, No. 4, October/December 1962.

Das Gupta, A., 'Trade and Politics in Eighteenth Century India', in *Islam and the Trade of Asia. A Colloquium*, D. S. Richards (Ed.), Oxford, 1970.

Dasgupta, Biplab, 'Population Policy: The Crucial Factor', *South Asian Review*, Volume 3, No. 4, July 1970.
——, *The Oil Industry in India*, Cass, London 1971.
Das Gupta, Ranjit, *Problems of Economic Transition. Indian Case Study*, National Publishers, Calcutta 1970.
Datt, Rudder, 'Myth and Reality About the Green Revolution', *Economic Affairs*, Volume 15, Nos. 6–8, August 1970.
Dastur, M. N., 'Implications' in *Seminar*, No. 131, July 1970.
Davis, K., *The Population of India and Pakistan*, Princeton University Press, 1951.
Deane, P. and Cole W. A., *British Economic Growth 1688–1959. Trends and Structure*, Cambridge University Press 1964.
Desai, A. R., *Social Background of Indian Nationalism*, Popular Book Depot, Bombay 3rd Edition, 1959.
——, *Recent Trends in Indian Nationalism*, Bombay, Popular Prakashan 1960.
——, *Rural Sociology in India*, Bombay Popular Prakashan, 4th Edition 1969.
Desai, V. V., 'Pursuit of Industrial Self Sufficiency. A Critique of the First Three Plans' *E. and P.W.*, May 1st, 1971.
Dev, S. Kumar, 'Collaboration in Fertiliser Development', *Commerce*, Volume 117, No. 3004, Bombay November 30th, 1968.
Dobb, M., 'Transition from Feudalism to Capitalism' in *Papers on Capitalism, Development and Planning*, London 1967.
Doodha, Kersi, 'Capital Formation in the U Sector', *Economic Weekly*, October 29th, 1960.
Dutt, R.C., *The Economic History of India Under Early British Rule*, Routledge and Kegan Paul, London 1956.
——, *The Economic History of India in the Victorial Age*, Routledge and Kegan Paul, London (Reprint of 1906 Edition).
Dutt, R. P., *India Today*, Left Book Club, Gollancz, London 1940.
Etienne, Gilbert, 'The Green Revolution in India—Its Economic and Socio-Political Implications' Paper to the Third European Conference of Modern South Asian Studies, Mimeo 1972.
Frankel, Francine R., *India's Green Revolution: Economic Gains and Political Costs*, Princeton University Press 1971.
Fukazawa, Hiroshi, 'Rural Servants in Eighteenth Century Maharashtrian Village—Demiurgic or Jajmani System?'

Hitotsubashi *Journal of Economics*, Volume 12, No. 2, February 1972.

Gervasi, Sean, 'Arrested Development and Multi-National Corporations' Paper to Seminar on Theories of Imperialism, Oxford, Mimeo 1970.

Ghose, Aurobindo, 'Monopoly in Indian Industry. An Approach', *E. and P.W.*, Annual No. 1972.

Ghosh, Ajoy, 'The Impact of Commercial Growth on Agricultural Tenure Systems in India', *Manchester School*, Volume 23, May 1955.

Gowda, K. V., 'U.S. Aid: A Critical Evaluation', *Commerce*, November 30th, 1968, Bombay.

Gokhale, B. G., 'Capital Accumulation in XVII Century Western India', *Journal of Asiatic Society of Bombay*, Volumes 39/40, 1964–65.

——, 'Ahmadabad in the 17th Century', *Journal of the Economic and Social History of the Orient*, Volume XII, Part 11, April 1969.

Habib, Irfin, *The Agrarian System of Mughal India 1556–1707*, Asia Publishing House, Bombay 1963.

——, 'Problems of Marxist Historical Analysis', *Enquiry, N.S.*, Vol. III, No. 2, Monsoon 1968.

——, 'Potentialities of Capitalistic Development in the Economy of Mughal India', *Journal of Economic History, Volume XXIX*, No. 1, March 1969.

Hanson, A. H., *The Process of Planning. A Study of India's Five Year Plans 1950–1969*, Oxford 1966.

Hazari, Bharat R., 'Import Intensity of Consumption in India', *Indian Economic Review*, n.s. II, 2. 1967.

Hazari, R. K., *The Structure of the Corporate Private Sector. A Study of Concentration, Ownership and Control*, Asia Publishing House, London 1966.

Hunter, W. W., *The Indian Empire. Its History, People and Products*, London 1882.

India Institute of Public Opinion, 'A Blueprint for Indian Employment 1901–1971', *Monthly Commentary on Indian Economic Conditions*, Volume XIII, No. 5. 149 Annual No. December 1971.

——, 'Blue Supplement on Taxation Policy and the Wanchoo Report', *Monthly Commentary on Indian Economic Conditions*, Volume XIII, No. 9, April 1972.

——, 'The Changing Structure of Growth of India's Industries

1960–1970', *Quarterly Economic Report*, Volume XVIII, No. 1, September/October 1971.

——, 'Changing Indian Standards of Living and Comfort—A New Analysis of Shifts in Durables Consumption 1950–1980', *Quarterly Economic Report*, Volume XVIII, No. 2, December 1971/January 1972.

Jenks, L. H., *The Migration of British Capital to 1875*, Knopf, London 1927.

Joshi, P. C., 'The Decline in Indigenous Handicrafts in Uttar Pradesh', *IESHR*, Volume 1, No. 1, July/September 1963.

——, 'Land Reforms in India and Pakistan', *E. and P.W.*, Review of Agriculture, December 1970.

Kanel, Don., 'Size of Farm and Economic Development', *Indian Journal of Agricultural Economics*, April/June 1967.

Kelkar, P. K., 'U.S. Assistance to Technical Education', *Commerce*, Bombay, November 30th 1968.

Kemp, T., *Industrialisation in Nineteenth Century Europe*, Longmans, 1969.

Kidron, Michael, *Foreign Investments in India*, Oxford University Press, London 1965.

——, 'Excess Imports of Capital and Technology' in *Foreign Collaboration*, R. K. Hazari (Ed.), Bombay 1967.

——, *Western Capitalism Since the War*, Weidenfeld and Nicolson, London 1968.

Kochanek, Stanley A., 'The Federation of Indian Chambers of Commerce and Industry and Indian Politics', *Asian Survey*, Volume XI, No. 9, September 1971.

Kumar, Dharma, *Land and Caste in South India. Agricultural Labour in the Madras Presidency during the Nineteenth Century*, Cambridge University Press 1965.

Kumar, Ravindar, 'The Rise of Rich Peasants in Western India', in *Soundings in South Asian History*, D. A. Low (Ed.), Weidenfeld and Nicolson, London 1968.

Ladejinsky, Wolf, 'Ironies of India's Green Revolution', *Foreign Affairs*, Volume 48, No. 4, July 1970.

Lamb, Helen B., 'The "State" and Economic Development in India', in *Economic Growth: Brazil, India, Japan*, Kuznets, Moore and Spengler (Eds.), Durham, N.C., 1955.

Lenin, V. I., *Collected Works*, Moscow, 1962.

Lewis, J. P., 'Wanted in India: A Relevant Radicalism', *E. and P.W.*, Volume V, Nos. 29–31, Special Number 1970.

Lipton, Michael, 'Strategy for Agriculture: Urban Bias and

Rural Planning' in *The Crisis of Indian Planning. Economic Planning in the 1960s*, Paul Streeten and Michael Lipton (Eds.), Royal Institute of International Affairs, Oxford University Press 1968.

Little, Scitovsky, T., Scott, M., *Industry and Trade in Some Developing Countries. A Comparative Study*, OECD, Oxford University Press, London, 1970.

Maddison, Angus, 'Historical Origins of Indian Poverty', Banca Nazionale Del Lavoro, *Quarterly Review*, March 1970.

——, *Class Structure and Economic Growth, India and Pakistan Since the Mughals*, London, 1971.

Magdoff, Harry, *The Age of Imperialism: The Economics of U.S. Foreign Policy*, Monthly Review Press, London 1969.

Mandel, Ernest, *Marxist Economic Theory*, Merlin, London 1968.

——, *The Inconsistencies of State Capitalism*, I.M.G. Publications (undated).

——, 'Laws of Motion of Capitalism and History of Capitalism', Paper to the Tilburg Conference on Capitalism in the Seventies, Mimeo 1971.

Marx, Karl, *Capital* Volume I, Kerr, Chicago, 1919.

——, *Karl Marx on Colonialism and Modernisation*, Shlomo Avineri (Ed.), Anchor Books, Garden City, N.Y. 1969.

Marx, K. and Engels, F., *Selected Works*, Volumes I and II, Progress Publishers, Moscow 1962.

McLane, John R., 'Peasants, Moneylenders and Nationalists at the End of the Nineteenth Century', *I.E.S.H.R.*, Volume I, No. 1, July/September 1963.

Mellor, Ed., *Developing Rural India: Plan and Practice*, Cornell University Press, Ithaca, N.Y. 1968.

Merhav, M., *Technological Dependence, Monopoly and Growth*, Oxford 1969.

Misra, B. B., *The Indian Middle Classes. Their Growth in Modern Times*, Oxford University Press, 1961.

Morris, Morris D., 'Towards a Reinterpretation of Nineteenth Century Indian Economic History', *Journal of Economic History*, Volume XXIII, No. 4, 1963.

——, 'Trends and Tendencies in Indian Economic History' *I.E.S.H.R.*, Volume V, No. 4, December 1968.

Mukhoti, B., 'Agrarian Structure in Relation to Farm Investment. Decisions and Agricultural Productivity in a Low

Income Country—The Indian Case', *Journal of Farm Economics*, Volume 48, No. 5, December 1966.

Muller-Plantenberg, Urs, 'Technologie et Dependance' in *Critiques de l'Economie Politique*, No. 3, April/June 1971.

Murti, B. V. Krishna, 'The Plan and the U Sector', *Economic Weekly*, September 24th, 1960.

Namboodripad, E. M. S., *The National Question in Kerala*, Peoples Publishing House, Bombay 1952.

Narain Dharm, 'Growth and Imbalances in Indian Agriculture', *E. and P.W. Review of Agriculture*, March 25th, 1972.

Nayar, B. R., 'Business Attitudes Towards Economic Planning in India', *Asian Survey*, September 1971.

——, *The Modernisation Imperative and Indian Planning*, Vikas Publications, New Delhi, 1972.

Nayar, Kuldip, *Between the Lines*, New Delhi 1969.

Neale, Walter C., *Economic Change in Rural India—Land Tenure and Reform in the Uttar Pradesh 1800–1955*, Yale University Press, 1962.

Ojha, P. D., 'A Configuration of Indian Poverty: Inequality and Levels of Living', *Reserve Bank of India Bulletin*, January 1970.

Pant, Nandita, 'Leaking Foreign Exchange Tap', *E. and P.W.*, July 22nd, 1972.

Patnaik, Prabhat, 'Imperialism and the Growth of Indian Capitalism', in *Studies in the Theory of Imperialism*, Sutcliffe and Owen (Eds.), Longman, London 1972.

——, 'The Political Economy of Underdevelopment', in *Bulletin of the Conference of Socialist Economists*, Spring 1972.

Patnaik, Utsa, 'Capitalist Development in Agriculture—A Note', *E. and P.W.*, Volume VI, No. 39, September 25th, 1971.

——, 'Development of Capitalism in Agriculture', Part I. *Social Scientist*, Volume I, No. 2, September 1972.
Part II. *Social Scientist*, Volume I, No. 3, October 1972.

——, 'On the Mode of Production in Indian Agriculture', *E. and P.W. Review of Agriculture*, September 1972.

Prasad, Brahmanad, 'The Problems', *Seminar*, No. 131, July 1970.

Raj, James S., 'Co-operation in Private Enterprise', *Commerce*, November 30th, 1968.

Raychaudhari, Tapan, 'The Agrarian System of Mughal India', *Enquiry N.S.*, Volume II, No. 1, Spring 1965.

——, 'A Re-interpretation of Nineteenth Century Economic History', *I.E.S.H.R.*, Volume V, 1968.

Reeves, P. D., 'Landlords and Party Politics in the United Provinces 1934–1937', in *Soundings in South Asian History*, D A. Low (Ed.), London 1968.

Reserve Bank of India, *Annual Report on Trend and Progress of Banking in India for the Year Ended June 30, 1971.*

——, *Exports of Engineering Goods: Problems and Prospects;* October 1970.

——, *Problems and Prospects for Indian Tea Exports During the Fourth Plan,* March 1971.

——, *Trends in Employment Growth in the Factory Sector in India 1951–1958*, July 1971.

Rothman, H., *Murderous Providence: A Study of Pollution in Industrial Societies*, London 1972.

Rudra, Ashok, 'The Green and Greedy Revolution', *South Asian Review*, Volume 4, No. 4, July 1971.

Rungta, R. S., *The Rise of Business Corporations in India 1851–1900*, Cambridge University Press, 1970.

Sau, Ranjit, 'Resource Allocation in Indian Agriculture', *E. and P.W. Review of Agriculture*, September 1971.

——, 'Indian Economic Growth—Constraints and Prospects' *E. and P.W.*, Volume VII, Nos. 5–7, Annual No. 1972.

——, 'The New Economics', *E. and P.W.*, Special No., 1972. Volume VII, Nos. 31–33.

Sen, A. K., 'The Commodity Pattern of British Enterprise in Early Indian Industrialisation 1854–1914', in *Second International Conference of Economic History, 1962*, Mouton and Co., Paris, 1965.

Sen, Bhowani, *Evolution of Agrarian Relations in India*, Peoples Publishing House, New Delhi, 1962.

Social Scientist Research Section, 'Inflationary Rise in Prices', *Social Scientist*, Volume 5, No. 4, November 1972.

Singh, M., *India's Export Trends*, Oxford 1964.

Subramanian, K. K., 'Indiscriminate Import', *Seminar*, No. 131, July 1970.

Suri, M. M., 'Deliberate Choice', *Seminar*, No. 131, July 1970.

Swamy, Subramanian, 'Structural Changes and the Distribution of Income by Size. The Case of India', *Review of Income and Wealth*, Series 13, No. 2, June 1967.

Takahashi, H. K., 'Transition from Feudalism to Capitalism' in *The Transition from Feudalism to Capitalism: A Symposium*, Science and Society (undated pamphlet).

——, 'Quelques Remarques Sur La Formation des Classes

Ouvrières Industrielles au Japon', in *Third International Conference of Economic History, 1965*, Paris, 1968.

Thamarajakshi, R., 'Intersectoral Terms of Trade and Marketed Surplus of Agricultural Produce 1951–52 to 1965–66', *E. and P.W. Review of Agriculture*, June 1969.

Thorburn, S. S., *Musalmans and Moneylenders in the Punjab*, William Blackwood, London 1886.

Thorner, D., 'Long Term Trends in Output in India', in *Economic Growth: Brazil, India, Japan*, Kuznets, Moore and Spengler, (Eds.), Durham, N.C., 1955.

——, *Agricultural Co-operatives in India. A Field Report*, Asia Publishing House, London 1964.

Thorner, Daniel and Alice, *Land and Labour in India*, Asia Publishing House, Bombay 1962.

Trotsky, Leon, *History of the Russian Revolution*, Gollancz, London 1934.

——, *Permanent Revolution* and *Results and Prospects*, Pathfinder Press, New York, 1970.

United Nations, 'The Role of Foreign Private Investment in Economic Development and Co-operation in the ECAFE Region'. *Economic Survey of Asia and the Far East*, Bangkok, 1970.

Varma, C. R. T., *Taxation in Developing Countries*, Eastern Economist, February 18th, 1972.

Velajudham, T. K., 'Financing Public Sector Investment with Special Reference to the Role of Domestic Borrowing and Small Savings: Case Study of India', *U.N. Economic Bulletin for Asia and the Far East*, Volume XIX, No. 2, September 1968.

Wertheim, W. F., *East–West Parallels: Sociological Approaches to Modern Asia*, Chicago, Quadrangle Books, 1965.

Wheelwright, E. L. and McFarlane, B., *The Chinese Road to Socialism*, Monthly Review, London 1970.

Whitcombe, Elizabeth, *Agrarian Conditions in Northern India. Volume I. The U.P. under British Rule 1860–1900*, University of California Press, 1972.

Wright, H. R. C., *The East India Company and the Native Economy in India. The Madras Investment 1795–1800*, International Conference of Economic History, 1965, Paris 1968.

Books and Articles devoted to questions of political strategy in South Asia more generally.

Ali, Tariq, The Class Struggles in Pakistan, *New Left Review* No. 64, Nov–Dec. 1970.

——, *Pakistan: Military Rule or People's Power,* Jonathan Cape, 1970.

——, Bangla Desh—Results and Prospects, *NLR* No. 68, July–August 1971.

Appa, Gautam, The Naxalites, *NLR* No. 61, May–June 1970.

Cooray, Upali, 'Perspectives for the Socialist Revolution in the Indian Sub Continent', *South Asian Marxist Review* (London), No. 1 Feb 1974.

Desai, Meghnad, 'Vortex in India', *NLR* No. 61, May–June 1970.

Deutscher, Tamara, 'Letter from Ceylon', *NLR* No. 64.

Gough, Kathleen, 'The South Asian Revolutionary Potential' *Bulletin of Concerned Asian Scholars* IV : 1, Spring 1972.

—— and Sharma, Hari *Imperialism and Revolution in South Asia*, Monthly Review Press 1973.

Halliday, Fred, 'Towards a Red Pakistan', *NLR* No. 65, Jan--Feb 1971.

—— 'The Ceylonese Insurrection', *NLR* No. 69, Sept–Oct 1971.

Nations, Richard, 'The Economic Structure of Pakistan : Class and Colony', *NLR* No. 68, July–August 1971.

Sappal, Prit. 'A Marxist Critique of Indian Stalinism', *South Asian Marxist Review*. No. 1, February 1974.

Wijeweera, Rohan, 'Speech before the Ceylon Criminal Justice Commission', NLR No. 84.

Index